ARAGON
ISSUES IN
PHILOSOPHY

PARAGON ISSUES IN PHILOSOPHY

THE PARAGON ISSUES
IN PHILOSOPHY SERIES

At colleges and universities, interest in the traditional areas of philosophy remains strong. Many new currents flow within them, too, but some of these—the rise of cognitive science, for example, or feminist philosophy—went largely unnoticed in undergraduate philosophy courses until the end of the 1980s. The Paragon Issues in Philosophy Series responds to both perennial and newly influential concerns by bringing together a team of able philosophers to address the fundamental issues in philosophy today and to outline the state of contemporary discussion about them.

More than twenty volumes are scheduled; they are organized into three major categories. The first covers the standard topics—metaphysics, theory of knowledge, ethics, and political philosophy—stressing innovative developments in those disciplines. The second focuses on more specialized but still vital concerns in the philosophies of science, religion, history, sport, and other areas. The third category explores new work that relates philosophy and fields such as feminist criticism, medicine, economics, technology, and literature.

The level of writing is aimed at undergraduate students who have little previous experience studying philosophy. The books provide brief but accurate introductions that appraise the state of the art in their fields and show how the history of thought about their topics developed. Each volume is complete in itself but also complements others in the series.

Traumatic change characterizes these last years of the twentieth century: all of it involves philosophical issues. The editorial staff at Paragon house has worked with us to develop this series. We hope it will encourage the understanding needed in our times, which are as complicated and problematic as they are promising.

John K. Roth   Frederick Sontag
Claremont McKenna College   Pomona College

THE
PHILOSOPHY
OF SEX
AND LOVE

Also by Alan Soble

*Pornography: Marxism, Feminism and the
  Future of Sexuality*
The Structure of Love
Sexual Investigations
The Philosophy of Sex (editor)
Eros, Agape, and Philia (editor)
Sex, Love, and Friendship (editor)

ALAN SOBLE

THE
PHILOSOPHY
OF
SEX AND LOVE
AN INTRODUCTION

PARAGON
ISSUES IN
PHILOSOPHY

PARAGON HOUSE ✦ ST. PAUL

FIRST EDITION, 1998

PUBLISHED IN THE UNITED STATES BY
PARAGON HOUSE
2700 UNIVERSITY AVENUE WEST
ST. PAUL, MINNESOTA 55114

LIBRARY OF CONGRESS CATALOGING-IN-PUBLICATION DATA

Soble, Alan.
    The philosophy of sex and love: an introduction / Alan Soble.
            p. cm. — (Paragon issues in philosophy)
      ISBN 1-55778-716-6 (alk. paper)
      1. Love. 2. Sex. 3. Sexual Ethics. I. Title. II. Series.
    BD436.S585 1997
    128'.46—dc21   97-13965
                                                                CIP

MANUFACTURED IN THE UNITED STATES OF AMERICA

For my lovely, bright, and tenacious sisters,
Janet and Phyllis

CONTENTS

LIST OF ILLUSTRATIONS

PREFACE

I taught an entire course devoted to the philosophy of sex and love for the first time in the summer of 1979 at Southern Methodist University. During that summer session, I was also preparing for publication the first edition of my anthology *The Philosophy of Sex: Contemporary Readings*. That course, as a result, focused on "reductionist" and "expansionist" accounts of sex, the series of papers by Thomas Nagel, Robert Solomon, Janice Moulton, and Robert Gray that had appeared in the *Journal of Philosophy* in the late 1960s and 1970s, and various Freudo-Marxist and feminist themes in ethical, social, and political philosophy. Since leaving my one-year replacement position at SMU, I have taught the philosophy of sex and love on a regular basis. At the University of New Orleans, I have done several dozen sections of this course. Over the years, the content of these courses has naturally changed. For one thing, they have become more analytic, largely in response to the fact that conceptual questions about sex and love were increasingly being discussed by professional philosophers. For another thing, the social and political issues addressed have become more sophisticated and intricate, owing in good measure to the development of various different (and not altogether consistent) feminist lines of thought. Both these trends, the analytic and the normative, are fully taken into account in this book. Indeed, in keeping to what an introductory textbook should be, I have spent in these pages equal space laying out the analytic and normative views of all persuasions—the conservative, the religious, the liberal, and the feminist. You will find, then, discussions of both Aquinas and Adrienne Rich, and of Roger Scruton and the feminist sadomasochists. If there was one central goal that I had while composing this introductory text-book, it was to make it as thematically and argumentatively rich as possible.

I want to thank a number of people: Suzanne Goldberg and the Lambda Legal Defense and Education Fund in New York, for information about sodomy laws; Nick Street, former editor at Paragon House, who in 1994 encouraged me to draw up a proposal for this book; Sára Szabó Soble, my ex-wife, for all the small but cumulatively important things she did that helped my research; Roger Lamb, a philosopher at the University of Queensland, for his comments on my discussion of the union view of love; Ruth Mills, editor at John Wiley, for a German version of the Brezhnev-Honecker kiss; Amy Bordelon, a student in my summer 1996 philosophy of sex and love course, whose questions and remarks contributed to the final rewriting of the manuscript; and the staff at *The New Yorker*, who made it possible for me to get in touch with Joseph Farris. The entire book was written during a period of release time from teaching made possible by funding from the University of New Orleans Research Council and the College of Liberal Arts. Special thanks go to these people, from each of whom I learned something about love and sex: W. Holztman, P. Brinkman, V. Quesada, D. Schulman, V. Balsero, L. Spurlock, S. Taylor, N. Sanchez, A. Jetter, L. Favaza, J. Sumner, V. Sabludowski, K. Tar, and J. O'Hana.

ACKNOWLEDGMENTS

Some material from the following publications of mine has been reworked and incorporated into this book: "Sexuality and Sexual Ethics," in Lawrence Becker and Charlotte Becker, eds., *Encyclopedia of Ethics*, 1st ed. (New York: Garland Press, 1992), 1127-33; "A Szexualitás Filozófiájáról," *Magyar Filozófiai Szemle* 36:5-6 (1992): 1046-68, trans. Módos Magdolna; "La Morale Sexuelle," in Monique Canto-Sperber, ed., *Dictionnaire de philosophie morale* (Paris: Presses Universitaires de France, 1996); "Sexuality, Philosophy of," in Edward Craig, ed., *Routledge Encyclopedia of Philosophy* (Cambridge, Eng.: Routledge, 1998); "Pornography and the Social Sciences," *Social Epistemology* 2:2 (1988): 135-44; "Union, Autonomy, and Concern," in Roger Lamb, ed., *Analyzing Love* (Boulder, Colo.: Westview, 1997), 65-92; "Egyesülés és Jóakarat," *Athenaeum* 2:2 (1994): 55-89, trans. Módos Magdolna; "Union and Concern," *Existentia* 3-4:1-4 (1993-94): 299-323; several of the essays I contributed to my anthology *Sex, Love, and Friendship* (Amsterdam: Editions Rodopi, 1997); "Analyzing Love," essay review of Robert Brown, *Analyzing Love* (New York: Cambridge University Press, 1987), in *Philosophy of the Social Sciences* 19:4 (1989): 493-500; review of Mark Fisher, *Personal Love* (London: Duckworth, 1990), in *Canadian Philosophical Reviews* 12:1 (1992): 24-5; review of Irving Singer, *The Nature of Love*, vol. 3: *The Modern World* (Chicago: University of Chicago Press, 1987), in *Canadian Philosophical Reviews* 8:2 (1988): 74-6; and review of Thomas Laqueur, *Making Sex: Body and Gender From the Greeks to Freud* (Cambridge, Mass.: Harvard University Press, 1990), in *Teaching Philosophy* 14:3 (1991): 339-42.

CREDITS

"Two People in a Restaurant": photograph by Kristin K. Mott (New Orleans, May 1996).

René Magritte (Belgium, 1898-1967), *La trahison des images* (Ceci n'est pas une pipe): (c) 1997 C. Herscovici, Brussels / Artists Rights Society (ARS), New York; Los Angeles County Museum of Art, purchased with funds provided by the Mr. and Mrs. William Preston Harrison Collection.

"Please Choose" (*Fidesz* poster): photograph by Alan Soble (Szentendre, Hungary, June 1990).

"Failure": cartoon by Joseph Farris.

Cover: "Adam and Eve," by Lucas Cranach the Elder, reproduced by permission of the Národní Galerie V Praze, the Czech Post, and the engraver J. Herčík.

The writer who deals with a sexual theme is always in danger of being accused...of an undue obsession with his subject.

—Bertrand Russell, *Marriage and Morals*

By the time I got to college, I had been thinking about sex for *years*.

—Camille Paglia, "The M.I.T. Lecture," *Sex, Art, and American Culture*

INTRODUCTION

TWO PROJECTS

The philosophy of love and sexuality, like the philosophy of the sciences, the arts, law, or religion, is the study of the concepts and propositions surrounding their central protagonists; in this case, the core notions are "love" and "sex." It is useful to divide the philosophy of sex and love into two major areas.

Conceptual analysis. The conceptual philosophy of love tries to define "love," to distinguish the various types of love, and to make significant and illuminating claims about both the concept and the phenomenon. Many students are acquainted with Leo Buscaglia's *Love* or M. Scott Peck's *The Road Less Traveled.* These popular books can be uplifting; whether intentionally or not, they serve primarily the purpose of providing practical advice. The conceptual philosophy of sex attempts to go beyond such achievements, to add logical rigor to the discussion of love. Among the questions that a comprehensive analytic philosophy of love must address are these: (1) *Why* is it that a person loves whomever or whatever it happens to be that he or she loves? What is the "basis" or "ground" of a person's love? Does love involve explanatory reasons or is it ultimately inexplicable? (2) What role does free choice or a decision play in loving and in selecting a beloved? Does the constancy of love, when it exists, depend on continuing satisfaction or on a promise? (3) Does a lover necessarily desire that the beloved reciprocate the love? How does the desire to benefit the beloved fit into love? What other desires might be a part of love? (4) What is the role of the lover's evaluations of the beloved in the formation (and termination) of the lover's love for the beloved? What does it mean—elusive notion—to love someone "for himself or herself"? And

(5) how is love to be distinguished from other emotions or affective states?

The conceptual philosophy of sex analyzes, primarily, the notions of sexual desire, sexual activity, and sexual pleasure (Chapter One). For example, what makes a feeling a sexual sensation? Manipulation of and feelings in the genitals are not necessary, since other body parts yield sexual pleasure. What makes an act sexual? A touch on the arm might be a friendly pat, an assault, or sex; physical properties alone seem not to distinguish them. Other conceptual questions have to do not with what makes an act sexual, but with what makes it the category of sexual act it is. What is "rape"? Is there any conceptual difference between obtaining sex through physical force and obtaining it by offering money? (See Chapter Four.)

Normative analysis. The philosophy of love and sex also explores the perennial questions of sexual and marital ethics (Chapters Two and Three). The central questions have long been: In what circumstances is it morally permissible to engage in sex or experience sexual pleasure? With whom or what? To achieve what goal? And with which body parts? The historically important answers come from the Natural Law ethics of St. Thomas Aquinas (1225?–1274), the deontological ethics of the German philosopher Immanuel Kant (1724–1804), and from the British Utilitarians, most notably Jeremy Bentham (1748–1832) and John Stuart Mill (1806–1873). Normative philosophy of sex and love also addresses legal, social, and political issues (Chapter Four). Should society steer people in the direction of heterosexual love, marriage, and family? May the law regulate sexual conduct by prohibiting prostitution, pornography, and homosexuality?

The broad scope of the philosophy of sex and love is shown by the variety of topics it investigates: abortion, contraception, acquaintance rape, pornography, sexual harassment, objectification, and the relationships among sex, love, and marriage. The philosophy of sex and love begins with a picture of a privileged pattern of relationship, in which two adult heterosexuals love each other, are faithful to each other within a formal marriage, and look forward to procreation and family. The philosophy of sex, as the Socratic scrutiny of our sex-love practices, beliefs, and concepts, intellectually challenges this privileged pattern by exploring not only the vices but also the virtues of casual sex, adultery, prostitution, sadomasochism, group sex, and intergenerational sex and love.

The boundary between conceptual and normative questions is hardly firm. Consider adultery (see Chapter Seven). It can be defined as a sexual act that occurs between two persons, at least one of whom is married but not to the other. But we cannot fully understand or apply the derivative sexual concept "adultery" until we have defined "sexual act." If two people, x and y, send to each other sexually arousing messages through the internet, have they engaged in a sexual act ("cybersex," "netsex")?[1] Or suppose that they share a few kisses, then go their separate ways. There are really three questions we can ask. (1) Has there been enough contact, quantitatively, for (some) sex to have occurred, or enough of the qualitatively right kind of contact? (2) Has enough or the right kind of sex occurred to amount to adultery or unfaithfulness, if either person involved is married? And (3) has enough or the right kind of adultery or unfaithfulness occurred to amount to a moral wrong, or to a serious moral wrong? Here we can see the intertwining of conceptual and moral matters. A lack of clarity about "sexual act" and the derivative concept "adultery" allows the moral exoneration of suspicious behavior by a convenient redescription of what occurs between two people—it was only "fooling around," not "real" sex. For example, Ann Manning reported about her sexual activity with the married Newt Gingrich: "We had oral sex.... He prefers that modus operandi because then he can say, 'I never slept with her.'"[2]

Here is another example. The feminist writer Robin Morgan defines "rape" in such a way (see Chapter Four) that if a woman, under pressure from her husband (for example, his pleading with her), agrees to have sex with him even though she prefers to watch television, she has been raped.[3] This definition of "rape" makes it relatively easy to confirm Morgan's thesis that the exposure of men to pornography causally contributes to rape. Morgan's view, as unusual as it is, has the virtue of alerting us to the fact that all social science investigations into the connection between pornography and rape are unavoidably value-laden. Suppose we define "rape" as it is commonly defined: one person x has raped another person y if x has had sexual contact with y in the absence of y's consent. Then, whether we should classify an act as rape depends on how we understand "consent." That, however, is not a matter solely of empirical fact, but of values. Both confirmation *and* refutation of the thesis that exposure to pornography contributes to rape presuppose that we can define "rape" (and "pornography," too), and doing that presupposes, in turn, that we have made a value judgment (perhaps even merely an arbitrary one) as to when consent is and is not genuine.

THE SIGNIFICANCE OF SEX

What is the meaning or significance of love and sex—for the individual person, for the entire species, for the cosmos? What are sex and love all about, anyway? That love and sexual desire are, on the one hand, hormone-driven instincts implanted by nature acting in the service of the species and, on the other hand, that they have a profound spiritual or interpersonal dimension, are two (not necessarily incompatible) possibilities. Perhaps the significance of sexuality is little different from the significance of eating, breathing, sleeping, and defecating—they are all instigated by the needs and drives of the natural biopsychological body. Or maybe, as the theologian J. C. B. Gosling claims, "sexual intercourse has to be understood as primarily an expression of the relation between the partners.... Ideally, it is the expression of Christian love, and an act of gratitude to God."[4]

In any event, in love and sex relationships, unlike sharing table at Burger King, we are *vulnerable* to another's seductive words and touches. We can be dominated both by our own desires and the other's physical strength, power, or beauty. The detailed scrutiny of our bodies, minds, and personalities by the other and, stimulated by this, by ourselves is risky. In seeking the pleasure of the body and the comfort of intimacy, we become susceptible to embarrassment and betrayal. The psychological complexity of sex and love provides, therefore, plenty of reason for taking these things seriously. The possible consequences of sex and love relationships, including the transmission of disease and the existence of a new human being, also provide reason for thinking carefully about sex and love. Sexual procreation may be a couple's contribution to God's ongoing work of creation, their way of adding to the fullness of God's universe. Or, in a more secular vein, sexual personality might be fundamental to, or a fundamental sign of, moral personality; how we perceive and behave toward sexual partners both influences and is a mirror image of how we perceive and interact with people more generally.[5] If so, the training of sexuality may well impinge on a person's developing character: failing to learn to control the pursuit of sexual pleasure, like failing to control the pursuit of other pleasures, could undermine the achievement of moral virtue.

Given these solemn reflections on the significance of sex, perhaps we can understand the rationale for the hostility of the world's religions to sex, including Christianity. St. Augustine (354–430), Bishop of Hippo, provides a sharp example of what has been called "sex-negativity":

> A man turns to good use the evil of concupiscence... when he bridles and restrains its rage...and never relaxes his hold upon it except when intent on offspring, and then controls and applies it to the carnal generation of children... not to the subjection of the spirit to the flesh in a sordid servitude.[6]

On this view, sex is a sin when anyone engages in it not for procreation but simply for the joy and pleasure of it (this is true even of a married couple using contraception). The view that sexuality must be aggressively constrained by an act of will, by the rational faculty of the soul—Augustine apparently means that men, in particular, must control themselves—is not unique to, and did not begin with, Augustine. A similar view about the need to restrain a wild sexuality (symbolized by an ignoble, ugly horse of poor breeding) can be found in *Phaedrus* (246b), one of the dialogues written by the ancient Greek philosopher Plato (c. 427–348 B.C.).

Nor did Judeo-Christian sex-negativity begin with Augustine. Parts of the earlier Leviticus in the Old Testament are positively frightening when it comes to sex. Here is what the Lord told Moses to tell the Israelites:

> 20:10 If a man commits adultery with another man's wife... both the adulterer and the adulteress must be put to death.
> 20:13 If a man lies with a man as one lies with a woman, both of them have done what is detestable. They must be put to death; their blood will be on their own heads.

The Old Testament God, Yahweh, who here commands the killing of those who engage in homosexual acts or commit adultery, is a strict father, indeed.[7]

In 1780, Immanuel Kant, famous for his metaphysics and theory of ethics, had equally unkind words for sex: "Sexual love makes of the loved person an Object of appetite.... Taken by itself it is a degradation of human nature."[8] Sexual urges, because they are so powerful, engender deception and manipulation. My sexual desire for another objectifies the other person; it pushes me to seek pleasure without regard for my partner's subjectivity or her own ends and to treat her as an edible object—like a pound of crawfish, to be seasoned, cooked, and consumed, the shell and head tossed away. For Kant (see Chapter Three), only one special circumstance—a contractual marriage—makes acting on sexual desire permissible.

These gloomy characterizations of human sexuality have been disseminated largely by fundamentalist, conservative, and religious thinkers; but in the United States today, they have also been advanced by some feminists.[9] The prohibitive sexual morality that flows from such a pious view of sexuality is rejected by liberals who deny that sexual desire is necessarily selfish and the quest for sexual pleasure automatically suspicious. The sexual urge is, by its own nature or in ordinary situations, linked to affection and gratitude; sexual desire and pleasure constitute a wholesome, natural bonding mechanism. At its best, sexual activity involves pleasing the self and the other at the same time, without deceit or manipulation that can be avoided by candid communication between the partners. Sexual pleasure is also a valuable thing in its own right, even when achieved in relationships devoid of love;[10] it represents a cardinal affirmation of the goodness of bodily existence. Hence, that love and sex are often psychologically and physically risky does not necessarily lead to a negative assessment of them.

Love and sex can be enormously important. Yet some writers seem to get carried away with this theme. The theologian Gilbert Meilaender, for example, thinks that heterosexual coitus is "the act in which human beings are present most fully and give themselves most completely to another"[11] (as if in homosexual sex the partners do not give themselves totally to each other).[12] The contemporary American secular philosopher Robert Nozick opines that sex is "metaphysical exploration, knowing the body and person of another as a map or microcosm of the very deepest reality, a clue to its nature and purpose"[13] (as if investigating the pimples of your partner's bottom provides a reflection of cosmic order). The psychologist Rollo May thinks that the key "moment" in sex is the precise instant of the penetration of the erect penis of the man into the vagina of the woman"[14] (as if that brief event never eventuated in a premature ejaculation depressing to both partners). Timothy Murphy claims that sex—whether straight or gay—"is a rich and fertile language for discovering and articulating the meanings of human life"[15] (as if English or Hungarian weren't good enough for that purpose). Finally, the philosopher Janice Moulton has written that "sexual behavior differs from other behavior by virtue of its unique feelings and emotions and its unique ability to create shared intimacy"[16] (as if a platoon of soldiers, buddies one and all, fired upon in battle, didn't experience profound shared intimacy).

Sexuality may be important, but does its importance derive from its purported uniqueness? "The most intense way we relate to another person is sexually," says Nozick, thereby suggesting one way sexuality might be unique.[17] But sexuality is not special in the depth of the relation between persons it elicits; think about the intensity of reciprocal bursts of anger or hatred, or a body-enveloping fear in response to the impending attack of the mugger. Nor is there much intensity in the dull coitus routinely performed by a long-married couple. (Would Nozick here remind us that, on his view, sexual activity is a metaphysical exploration, examining the minutiae of the other's body? Is that all there is to do together when passion is gone? See Chapter Seven.)

Perhaps the uniqueness of sexuality lies in its capacity to submerge reason by emotion, to destroy logic with passion: "Eros surpassing every immortal in beauty,... a loosener of limbs, brings all immortals and mortals under his power and makes them unable to think as they should."[18] But wine does as well, if not better, to loosen the limbs (and tongue) and damage the mind. Or, in Kantian fashion, "it is in the experience of sexual desire that we are most vividly conscious of the distinction between virtuous and vicious impulses."[19] But we experience the conflict between our being pulled by an angel on one shoulder and a devil on the other just as often, and sometimes more strongly, in matters of money, career, and political power. Further, nothing about sexual activity, be it straight or gay, seems to be so special as to allow it to function continuously and reliably as a premier expression of love or approval (see Chapter Seven). Nor is sexuality unique in its ability to bring a human being extreme, joy, grief or bewilderment. There's also the World Series.

In none of these respects is sexuality convincingly unique. We might try, however, an approach that can be understood either theologically or biologically (or both): sexuality is unique in its capacity to generate new life. Until we can construct human babies *de novo*, in a test tube filled with a mixture of organic chemicals, this might be the only way sexuality is unique. Again we have a way to understand why the Judeo-Christian tradition has always been suspicious of and opposed to sexuality divorced from marriage and family.

THE DEEPER PICTURE

Plato, in his dialogue *Symposium*, issued a warning: what we think we are seeking in our sex and love relationships is not really what we want or need; our *eros*, our yearning, erotic desires, for good-looking bodies and excellent minds is really *eros* for the ideal Beauty and Goodness that is barely represented by and in the objects of our attachment (211a). We think, at first and for a while, that our happiness will be attained by forming a blissful relationship with a person who "knocks our socks off." But we eventually discover dissatisfaction there, and hunt for Goodness and Beauty elsewhere. Augustine similarly thought that the search for God was hidden beneath the search for sensual pleasure in erotic love:

> I had not yet fallen in love, but I was in love with the idea of it.... I began to look around for some object for my [romantic] love.... Although my real need was for you, my God,... I was not aware of this hunger.... To love and to have my love returned was my heart's desire, and it would be sweeter if I could also enjoy the body of the one who loved me.[20]

In the naturalist vision of sex of the German philosopher Arthur Schopenhauer (1788–1860), the beauty of the object of sexual desire is nature's way of tricking us (he meant men in particular) into thinking that the satisfaction of erotic love for our beloveds is for our own individual good. To the contrary, for Schopenhauer, sexual love benefits only the species, for the good of which nature makes mere use of us, often causing us to give up fortune and freedom (note the irrationality brought about by sexual urges) to attain our erotic goals:

> Nature can attain her end only by implanting in the individual a certain *delusion*, and by virtue of this, that which in truth is merely a good thing for the species seems to him to be a good thing for himself, so that he serves the species, whereas he is under the delusion that he is serving himself....
>
> It is a voluptuous delusion which leads a man to believe that he will find a greater pleasure in the arms of a woman whose beauty appeals to him than in those of any other, or which, exclusively directed to a *particular* individual, firmly convinces him that her possession will afford boundless happiness. Accordingly, he imagines he is making efforts and sacrifices for his own enjoyment, whereas he is doing so merely for the maintenance of the regular and correct type of the species.[21]

The feminist philosopher Ti-Grace Atkinson also thinks that our sexuality is manipulated by a higher force in order to preserve the species, but in her view that force is not God or Nature. Instead, both heterosexual desire and the desire for the specific act of coitus are engineered by society. "Sexual intercourse is a political construct, reified into an institution."[22] Atkinson means that people have been engaging in sexual intercourse just because doing so serves a political purpose, not their own individual needs: sexual intercourse satisfies the social need to keep the species going by replenishing the population. Atkinson's view of sex is thus not far removed from Schopenhauer's, who also sees its purpose in the cosmic terms of the species and not in terms of the person, even though Schopenhauer is the arch-naturalist and Atkinson the arch anti-essentialist (see Chapter One). People have been groomed by society to perform the act of intercourse, their desire-pleasure system manipulated, indeed created or "constructed," to serve the social purpose of reproduction.[23] Hence, for Atkinson, when the development of reproductive technology eliminates the social function of coitus, individuals' "sexual 'drives' and 'needs' would disappear" as well.[24]

If Atkinson's view of our affective lives is right, Thomas Nagel's apparently reasonable picture of human sexuality turns out to be naive:

> Sex is the source of the most intense pleasure of which humans are capable, and one of the few sources of human ecstacy. It is also the realm of adult life in which the defining and inhibiting structures of civilization are permitted to dissolve, and our deepest presocial, animal, and infantile natures can be fully released and expressed, offering a form of physical and emotional completion that is not available elsewhere.[25]

To the contrary, it might be said by an anti-essentialist like Atkinson, our love relationships and sexual acts are permeated by culture and social meanings. Civilization, as the psychoanalyst Sigmund Freud (1856–1939) argued at great length,[26] occupies the bed with us; it does not sit outside the door like a neglected puppy. Atkinson brings to our attention that there are social and political questions to be pursued about sex and love: what influence does culture have on our styles of loving, on the nature of our loves? Might there be styles of loving that are better for the individuals themselves, if not also for their society? The analytic task of defining love and the concepts of sex is empty without an attempt to fill in the body of love with ethical, social, and political deliberation; and cultural critique is blind without the guidance supplied by rigorous conceptualization.

Note the twist that Schopenhauer puts on the Christian view of marital sex and parenthood as representing the human's contribution to God's creative project. For Schopenhauer, nature resorts to deceptive beauty to enlist the aid of otherwise reluctant humans in its creative scheme. And on Atkinson's view, our sex and love relationships have been manufactured by an oppressive regime. Why might we have to be tricked by God, nature, or society into having sex? On an Atkinsonian view, we are not born heterosexual but, as in Freud, polysexual.[27] Because our sexual natures lead us away from a narrow procreative sexuality, it must be groomed to be socially useful.

A different perspective is offered by two Christian theologians: "sex pleasure has been ordained by God as an inducement to perform an act which is both disgusting in itself and burdensome in its consequences."[28] With the last point, Schopenhauer would readily agree; sex is burdensome, since pursuing a mate requires resources and the act produces children we then have to care for. But how is sexual activity "disgusting in itself" (or "dirty"), especially when, as twentieth-century Christian morality has it, the act is performed with a loving spouse for the purpose of contributing to God's plan? Schopenhauer, in his own way, again agrees with these two theologians: the "sense of beauty... directs the sexual impulse, and [is that] without which this impulse sinks to the level of a disgusting need." It is the mere fact that sexuality involves desires or needs that makes it disgusting.[29]

The gnosticism of the contemporary art and culture critic Camille Paglia provides the beginning of another kind of answer:

> We must frankly face the mutilations and horrors in [Robert] Mapplethorpe's sexual world and stop trying to blandly argue them away as fun and frolics of "an alternative lifestyle." His grim sadomasochists are not lovable, boppy Venice Beach eccentrics on roller skates....

> Degradation is at the heart of his eroticism…. Such acts [urolagnia] have never been sanctioned in any culture. This is why they are now and will remain radical…. Sadomasochism is a sacred cult, a pagan religion that reveals the dark secrets of nature. The bondage of sadomasochism expresses our own bondage by the body, our subservience to its brute laws, concealed by our myths of romantic love…. It is nature, not society, that is our greatest oppressor.[30]

Sex, by its nature, does not merely instigate deception and manipulation, as in Kant; sex may be, even when it occurs under the sweet but illusionary umbrella of loving attachments, essentially and unavoidably an exercise in sadomasochism, an arena in which power is pitted against power or in which power and submission naturally complement each other.[31] If so, there is not much hope for John Stoltenberg's egalitarian (or "vanilla") sexual vision of "an authentic erotic potential between humans such that mutuality, reciprocity, fairness, deep communion and affection, total bodily integrity for both partners, and equal capacity for choice-making and decision-making are merged with robust physical pleasure, intense sensation, and brimming-over expressiveness."[32]

There are also the facts of the body itself to take into account, some of which those who live in the perpetually hot South never forget: the body's various parts often stink. Think about oral sex, either cunnilingus or fellatio. Putting your face in someone's crotch is easily seen as degrading and humiliating. It takes a humble sense of one's own smallness to do it, whether one's motive is to produce pleasure for the other person or it is done selfishly for the sensual joy that somehow overrides one's nausea. Your mouth touches an organ that even after bathing soon becomes caked with pungent excretions. The poet William Butler Yeats made the point this way: "Love has pitched his mansion in the place of excrement."[33] Perhaps this is why the early Christians, like Augustine, blessed only genital-genital intercourse and condemned oral-genital sex, not because oral sex was nonpro-creative but because the genitals can be repulsive. Their ban on oral sex was a Christian version of the Hebrew ban on eating the flesh of a pig.

SEXUAL PLURALISM

Suppose that sexual activity were unique in its procreative func-tion. Even so, that procreation is a function of sex, and that no other human activity can achieve that goal, does not mean that sexuality has no other function. Engaging in sex, beyond being intrinsically rewarding for its pleasure, has many uses: to express affection, make money, kill time, or avoid the task of studying for (or grading) exams. Consider Annie Sprinkle's list of the ben-efits of sex: "sex can cure a headache, relieve stress and tension, help digestion, strengthen the heart, relieve menstrual cramps, help you sleep, wake you up, clear the mind, open you up to feel-ings, improve concentration, create life, burn unwanted calories, and cure depression."[34] This wide variety in the uses humans have given to sexual activity applies as well to homosexuality, as Timo-thy Murphy points out:

> As much as heterosex, the expressions of homosex may…
> be an adventure in discovery, an act of vengeance, a cold
> manipulation, an experiment in pleasure, a flirtation, an
> act of cowardice, an expression of sympathy, an act of
> theater, a passing fancy, an act of trust, a thoughtless re-
> lief, a defiance, a bored obligation, a willful expression
> of difference, a cozy evening at home, a fiery crash in the
> night, a rescue, and a way of belonging.[35]

This important pluralist point will be made several more times in the chapters that follow. It is a warning that we should not try to force the power and deliciousness of love and sexuality into an all-encompassing philosophy.

The recognition of the value of pluralism in advanced Western countries seems to parallel the relative collapse of monistic, especially religious monistic, sexual philosophies. The theologian Ronald Green claims that "traditional sexual ethics and theologies of sexuality... have been killed by technological, social, and cultural changes in our era."[36] Among the features of biblical sexual philosophy that have been "challenged" by these developments, Green includes "the idea that sexual conduct, especially genital sexuality, is [in itself] morally and religiously significant," "the idea that human sexuality is properly expressed only in a context of an enduring, lifelong personal relationship," and "the idea that human sexuality is normatively heterosexual."[37] In what follows, we shall examine reasons for and against these pieces of traditional sexual philosophy.

PART ONE

SEX

CHAPTER ONE

SEXUAL CONCEPTS

Philosophy: "(x)(y)[x love y → (∃w) w is a representation such that........)))))]"

Love: ♥ How I do dote upon thee ....♥

—Arthur Danto, "Foreword," Robert Solomon and Kathleen Higgins, eds., *The Philosophy of (Erotic) Love*

ANALYTIC QUESTIONS

Conceptual philosophy of sex focuses on these central items: sexual desire, sexual pleasure, sexual sensation, sexual act, sexual perversion, sexual arousal, sexual intention, sexual body part, sexual touch, sexual look, and sexual satisfaction. The central task in each case is to come to an illuminating understanding of what sexual pleasure, sexual desire, sexual activity, and so forth, *are*. What is it that makes a pleasure—say, the pleasure of a caress—a sexual pleasure? The issue is interesting at least because some sexual pleasures are non-genital, and some genital pleasures are not sexual (for example, urinating). It follows that another part of the conceptual enterprise involves distinguishing analytically between a sexual touch and a nonsexual touch, and also between a sexual sensation and a nonsexual sensation. What is the difference between a sexual desire and a nonsexual desire? If I feel an urge to bite you before or during intercourse (or even apart from other contact), is that something sexual or, instead, an aggressive desire—or both? What features of sexual acts, then, can be relied on to distinguish sexual acts from nonsexual acts? Is there a valid criterion of the *sexual* that applies to all persons or cultures? A complete analysis of our sexual concepts would also disentangle the conceptual and causal connections among these various sexual things. Which of these concepts is logically prior to the others, in the sense that the analysis of the other concepts depends on its analysis? Shall we understand a sexual act in terms of the sexual desire that gives rise to it, or in terms of the sexual pleasure that the act is performed to provide?

One more part of the analytic task is to "unpack" the meaning of derivative sexual concepts, concepts whose definition in part refers to sexuality. Consider *adultery*, which is often defined as a sexual act engaged in by persons who are married but not to each other. We cannot ultimately understand adultery unless we understand the logically prior notion of sexual activity (see the Introduction). Further, there are questions about the role of sexual fantasies and desires in adultery, even if no physical activity (say, a touch) occurs. Can thoughts be adulterous? Another derivative concept is *pornography*, which can be defined as linguistic, pictorial, or photographic depictions of sexual acts. Again, without an understanding of what a sexual act is, it would be impossible to identify pornography so defined. If we were to take a functionalist approach, defining pornography, instead, as depictions that cause sexual arousal, or are intended to cause arousal (regardless of the content of the depictions), the identification of the pornographic depends on our understanding of a different sexual concept, in this case sexual arousal. *Prostitution* is also a derivative sexual concept; it can be defined as the selling of sexual services, i.e., exchanging sexual acts for money or other compensation. But, then, is a woman who has married for economic reasons a prostitute? And what about women who provide "phone sex"? Are they prostitutes? Other examples of derivative sexual concepts include sexual abuse, sexual harassment, and rape. Precise definitions of "sexual act" are also needed for social scientific studies of sexual behavior and orientation: How often do people engage in sex? Who engages in homosexual acts, and Does this correlate with genetics? Our interest in defining "sexual act" is not only philosophical but also practical.

Analytic philosophy is, when done well, known for its clarity, precision, and carefulness. Sometimes it is not done altogether as it should be. It will be helpful, in becoming acquainted with the methods of conceptual philosophy of sex, to examine an example of a well-meaning attempt at analysis that goes astray—committing the mortal philosophical sin of equivocation.

I once thought that the feminist philosopher Alison Jaggar was making, in the following passage, the simple point that the involvement, touching, or manipulation of the genitals is neither necessary nor sufficient for an act to be sexual (i.e., that an act can be sexual even if the genitals are not touched—hence, not necessary—and that touching the genitals does not necessarily mean the act is sexual—hence, not sufficient):

> A philosophical theory of sexuality… must help us draw
> the conceptual boundaries of sexual activity, enabling us
> to answer both how non-genital activity can still be sexual
> and even how genital activity may not be sexual. Given
> our ordinary ways of thinking, this latter suggestion may
> sound paradoxical….[1]

Note that Jaggar does not use the word "touch," but "activity" instead; this is the source of her difficulty, as we shall see. Non-genital "activity" can obviously be sexual, as Jaggar says: sucking the breast, massaging the toes. But why does Jaggar emphasize the possibility of genital nonsexual "activity" by using a word ("even") that puts us on alert for the unexpected and the "paradoxical"? Genital "activity" can *just as obviously* not be sexual: think about a normal gynecological examination. Jaggar proceeds to explain what she means by the claim that non-genital activity might not be sexual:

> Given our ordinary ways of thinking, this latter sugges-
> tion may sound paradoxical but it is becoming common-
> place for feminists to define rape as a form of physical
> assault rather than as a form of sexual expression.

Her suggestion is that coitus, heterosexual intercourse, might not be a sexual act. This *is* paradoxical, although not, on those grounds alone, to be judged wrong; nor, for that matter, to be judged right, merely because it is becoming "commonplace" among feminists. Now we realize why Jaggar did not appeal to the straightforward gynecological examination example to make her point, and felt she had to rely on the emphatic "even." In this passage, Jaggar is using "activity" in two different senses: in claiming that genital "activity" might not be sexual, she means *only* "intercourse," but when claiming that non-genital "activity" can be sexual, she means something much broader than that. This is the equivocation: failing to use a word in the same sense throughout an argument.

It does not take a paradoxical view of rape to refute the claim that the involvement of the genitals is sufficient for an activity to be sexual. Jaggar should be happy about this; for her "even" implies that were this paradoxical view wrong, Jaggar would lose the support she has chosen for her claim that a philosophical theory of sex should illuminate how nonsexual genital "activity" is possible. To restrict the word "activity" to coitus is an odd mistake for Jaggar to make, for it was feminism that most dramatically made the point that sexuality encompassed more than just the penis-into-vagina-penetration definition of sex that has long been popular in patriarchal cultures.[2] It is not even the most accurate way of putting things to say that rape can be "defined" not as a sexual but as a physical assault; that redefinition is proposed mostly in legal contexts. In a philosophical context—which is Jaggar's, who is speaking about developing a philosophical theory of sex—it seems better to say that rape in general might be *describable* as a physical assault, one carried out by sexual means rather than by nonsexual means (for example, a beating with the fists).

SEXUAL ACTIVITY

In carrying out our conceptual tasks, let's first take a look at attempts to analyze "sexual activity."[3]

(1) Sexual acts might be defined as those involving contact with a sexual body part, a hand rubbing someone's genitals, for example. In this analysis, the sexual parts of the body are first catalogued; acts are then judged to be sexual if and only if they involve contact with one of these parts. But flirting visually, talking over the phone, and sending e-mail messages can be sexy, and sexual, even though no contact is made with a sexual body part. It seems, then, that contact is not necessary. Further, massaging a breast is sexual when done by lovers, but not when done during a cancer exam; and we have already mentioned the gynecological exam and urination examples. So it also seems that contact with a sexual body part is not sufficient for an act to be sexual.

"Sexual act," on this view, is logically dependent on "sexual part." But do we clearly understand "sexual part"? Two people might shake hands briefly, without the act being sexual; but they could, alternatively, warmly press their hands together and feel a surge of sexual pleasure. Sometimes, then, the hands are used nonsexually and sometimes they are used sexually. Are the hands a sexual part? Whether the hands are a sexual part depends on the activity in which they are engaged. Hence, instead of an act's being sexual because it involves a sexual body part, a body part is sexual, at least sometimes, because of the sexual nature of the act in which it is used. So there is a case to be made that "sexual body part" is logically dependent on "sexual activity," not the other way around.

(2) The *morality* of sexuality has been understood by some philosophers and theologians in terms of its procreative function (see Chapter Two). Alternatively, the procreative nature of sexual activity might be employed analytically rather than normatively. Sexual acts, on such a view, can be analyzed as those having procreative potential in virtue of their biological structure. The principal case of such an act is, of course, heterosexual intercourse.

This analysis is too narrow, if taken as stating a necessary condition for an activity to be sexual, for there are many acts that we ordinarily call sexual that have no connection to the procreative act (e.g., kissing, anal intercourse, oral sex). Here, then, is a more plausible formulation of this analysis: sexual acts are (i) acts that are procreative in structure *and* (ii) any acts that are the physiological or psychological precursors or concomitants of acts that are sexual by (i). This version casts a wider net. But is it wide enough? Masturbation, when performed by a person sitting at home alone, is neither a procreative act nor a precursor of coitus. This seems to provide a decisive counterexample to the modified analysis. It still might be true, though, that satisfying condition (i) or (ii) is sufficient for an act to be sexual.

One more emendation suggests itself: (iii) acts that bear an acute physical resemblance to the acts judged sexual by (i) or (ii) are sexual as well. Masturbation, then, might be a sexual act by (iii): a penis (for example) wrapped by fingers is to be seen as sufficiently similar to a penis wrapped in a vagina. But this vague third condition does not really save the proposed analysis. Many of the sexual perversions (for example, fondling shoes) are sexual even though they bear no resemblance to coitus or its concomitants. Perhaps, then, these three conditions are better understood as an analysis of "normal" or "moral" sexuality rather than of sexuality *per se* (see Chapter Two). Further, this analysis implies that homosexual acts, none of which are procreative, are sexual *because* (or when) they sufficiently resemble, or mimic, heterosexual acts.[4] That seems to be the wrong reason for the right conclusion. Homosexual and heterosexual acts might both be considered sexual in virtue of the similarities in the pleasure or sensations they are able to produce.

(3) The problems with the first two attempts at analyzing "sexual act" make it reasonable to suppose that sexual acts are those that produce sexual pleasure: holding hands is sexual when sexual pleasure is produced; procreative (and nonprocreative) acts are sexual when they produce sexual pleasure. Indeed, the contemporary philosopher Robert Gray thinks that "we are forced to the conclusion" that producing sexual pleasure is both necessary and sufficient for acts to be sexual: "any activity might become a

sexual activity" if sexual pleasure is derived from it, and "no activity is a sexual activity unless sexual pleasure is derived from it."[5] In this analysis, "sexual act" is logically dependent on the notion of sexual pleasure.

It is no doubt true that sexual activity and the experience of sexual pleasure are strongly correlated, because sexual activity causally leads to that pleasure. But if pleasure is the mark of the sexual, pleasure cannot be the gauge of the quality of sex acts. That is, this analysis seems to confuse what it is for an act to be a *good* (pleasurable) sexual act with what it is for an act to be sexual *per se*, which might not, sadly, produce any pleasure. The long-married couple who have lost sexual interest in each other, and who engage in routine coitus from which they derive no pleasure, are still performing a sexual act. We are forbidden, by this analysis, from saying that these spouses engage in sex, but it is "bad sex" they are having. Rather, we would have to say that they tried to engage in sex, and failed. Further, because in this analysis "sexual act" is logically dependent on "sexual pleasure," we cannot say that sexual pleasure is just that type of pleasure produced by sexual acts. Then how might we distinguish sexual pleasures from others?

The philosophers Deborah Rosen and John Christman have proposed a similar analysis of sexual activity:

> Sexual *activity*... is that range of activity in which the sexual feeling... is the essential subjective element.... Sexual activity is one that essentially *involves* such feeling, an activity in which such feeling is the principal component.[6]

In contrast to Gray, Rosen and Christman define sexual activity in terms of the broader category of sexual *sensations* (or feelings) rather than in terms of sexual *pleasure*, because some people, they say, report that their sexual sensations are painful or intense or similar to tension and conflict. (If true, that fact would not rule out the presence of pleasure at the same time.) But there are plenty of acts that involve no sexual feelings of any kind, yet are still sexual. Consider, from a calloused prostitute's own perspective, the multiple acts of fellatio that she or he performs in an evening, experiencing no sexual pleasure or sensations from any of them; or the cunnilingus that a bored and unaroused man, who prefers to be watching basketball on television or even working, performs on his demanding wife or girlfriend. The point is that the kind of analysis proposed by Rosen and Christman conflates sexual activity with, we might say, "responsive" sexual activity; it confuses the question of the ontological category of the act (as sexual or not) with the question of its contingent causal consequences.

(4) We have already seen that physical motions and movements are "polysemous": two hands in contact might be performing a sexual embrace or might be engaging in a friendly handshake. Can we rely on the intentions or purpose behind the movements to disambiguate the sexual from the nonsexual and thereby to clarify "sexual act"? The philosopher Jerome Neu thinks so:

> A person who washes his hands fifteen times a day need not be obsessive-compulsive, he may be a surgeon. Similarly, a "golden shower" performed out of sexual interest has a very different significance... than one done as an emergency measure to treat a sea urchin wound.[7]

Thus, a handshake done with the intention of obtaining sexual pleasure, under the disguise of being only a conventional symbol of friendship, is likewise a sexual act—at least for the sneaky participant. The idea that sexual acts are to be analyzed in terms of a sexual intention occurs in the law; on one legal definition of "sexual contact," it is "any intentional touching of intimate parts of either the victim or the actor or the clothing covering them, if that intentional touching can 'reasonably be construed' as being for the purpose of sexual arousal or gratification."[8]

But an intention to produce or experience sexual pleasure seems not to be necessary for an act to be sexual. A couple engaging in coitus, both parties intending only that fertilization occur and neither concerned with sexual pleasure (taking the advice of Augustine), performs a sexual act. Some women operating treadle sewing machines discovered that they could masturbate while working.[9] There was some point at which the discovery was made by the women, accidentally, that treadling was arousing. For a brief period before this point, then, the women might have been unintentionally experiencing sexual pleasure and, hence, inadvertently masturbating—engaging in a sexual act. So the intention to experience sexual pleasure is not necessary for an act to be sexual.

Maybe the intention to experience sexual pleasure is not exactly the sexual intention involved in sexual activity. But the intention to procreate is not it, either: gays and lesbians experience desire and arousal and engage in sex without any procreative purpose. Many acts of heterosexual coitus are not accompanied by an intention to procreate; indeed, the use of contraception is meant to eliminate procreation and thereby involves an intention *not* to procreate (on the morality of such behavior, see Chapter Three). But the main point is that intentions are likely irrelevant in making sexual acts sexual. A rapist might force a victim into a sexual act to get sexual pleasure from it, or just to humiliate his victim, or assert his masculinity and dominance (say, in prison)—or, in some cases, all three. From the fact that in some rapes the rapist primarily intends to degrade his victim, to dominate and exert power over her or him, it does not follow that the act is not sexual. Indeed, the rapist might have chosen a sexual act on purpose as an exquisitely effective method to humiliate and degrade, believing that his victim will in a forced sexual act experience overwhelming shame. The plurality of purposes that give rise to or accompany the performance of sexual acts weighs heavily against our being able to understand sexual activity in terms of some "sexual intention."

SEXUAL DESIRE

Another attempt is to define sexual activity in terms of a logically prior notion of sexual desire. The philosopher Alan Goldman has approached the analytic task this way, offering the following definitions:

> Sexual desire is desire for contact with another person's body and for the pleasure which such contact produces; sexual activity is activity which tends to fulfill such desire of the agent.[10]

Three questions arise here. First, what are the pleasures of physical contact? Aren't there some pleasures of contact that are sexual, while others are not sexual? How these are to be distinguished is not always clear—recall the bite example. Since not all the pleasures of physical contact are sexual pleasures, Goldman's definition of sexual desire has to be modified: sexual desire is desire for contact that produces sexual pleasure. In this case, the analysis of both sexual desire and sexual activity depend on a logically prior distinction between contact that produces sexual pleasure and that which produces some other pleasure.

Second, is sexual desire accurately characterized as a desire for physical contact and its pleasures? For example, James Giles defines sexual desire as "the desire for mutual baring and caressing of bodies."[11] The last part, the desire to caress, is another way of stating Goldman's definition. But is either the desire for contact or the desire to caress necessary for sexual desire? Sometimes, at least, sexual desire is only the desire for the "baring" of bodies. And sometimes, as in the paraphilias, sexual desire manifests itself as neither of these things but, say, as a desire to fondle shoes or underwear.[12] Further, someone—a young person whose sexuality is just awakening—might experience sexual desire for another person yet have *no* idea what to do to or with that person as a result of having sexual desire, no idea that physical contact, what kind of physical contact, or even the baring of bodies, is the next, but hardly mandatory, step. Or we might experience an objectless sexual desire, as in horniness, and not know quite what to do about it. The difficulty of specifying any single event as the goal of desire, or any set of events, implies, as argued by the philosopher Jerome Shaffer, that sexual desire is not a desire *for* something or *that* some event occur at all.[13] What, then, are the features of a desire that make it sexual, if referring to its goal is not the answer? On Shaffer's view, sexual desire is distinguished by being accompanied by sexual excitement and arousal. That makes sense, since sexual desire, in appropriate contexts, leads to sexual arousal. But we must ask, in turn, what sexual excitement and arousal are, as opposed to other kinds of excitement and arousal. For Shaffer, sexual arousal is "sexual in that it involves the sexual parts, viz., the genital areas." If this is true, non-genital sexual activities (kissing, passive anal intercourse) could be sexual only if they induced genital arousal in addition to their own type of pleasure; but that that would happen seems not to be necessary in human sexuality.[14]

The third question is the most fundamental: even if we accept Goldman's analysis of sexual desire, is analyzing sexual activity in terms of sexual desire viable? Goldman agrees that not all physical touchings are sexual: if a parent's desire to cuddle (or caress) his or her baby is only a desire to show affection, and not the desire for the pleasure of physical contact itself, then the parent's act is not sexual.[15] On Goldman's definition of a sexual act, if the desire that causes or leads to the act is not a sexual desire, then neither is the act. But if this is right, a woman who performs fellatio on a man for the money she gets from doing so is not performing a sexual act. The act does not fulfill the sexual desire "of the agent," for, like the baby-cuddling parent, the woman has no sexual desire to begin with. Thus the prostitute's contribution to this act of fellatio must be called, instead, a "rent-paying" or "food-gathering" act, since it tends to fulfill her desires to have shelter and eat. If Goldman's analysis is right, we have a reason to take "anti-essentialism" or "social constructionism" (see below) seriously. Performing fellatio does not have any sexual meaning for the prostitute, even if it does for her client, and so the social context in which she performs the act prevents what we would ordinarily call a sexual act, on her part, from being one.

SOCIAL CONSTRUCTIONISM

What, then, are sexual acts? Maybe all the acts we think of as sexual have no common denominator, no essence, and the conceptual project is doomed from the start. There are good reasons for this view. Acts involving the same body part are sometimes sexual, sometimes not. Some touches and movements are deemed sexual in one culture but not in others. The fragrances, mannerisms, and costumes that are sexually arousing vary from place to place and from time to time. Thus, bodily movements acquire meaning—as sexual or as something else—by existing within a culture and social context that attach meaning to them. There are, if this is right, only variable social definitions of the sexual. The history of human sexuality is primarily the history of our customs and "discourse" about sex, as Michel Foucault might have put it.[16] We create social things by using words. There really is no such item as masturbatory insanity[17] or nymphomania—no medical condition, no psychological character trait, no underlying pathology. Well, there are such things, but only because we have picked out some behaviors and made up a word for them, not because masturbatory insanity and nymphomania have, like the moon, an existence independent of our language, our observations, and our evaluations of it. Social facts, such as the existence of "peasants," "witches," and "yuppies," have an odd nature.[18] Similar considerations might apply to "perversion," "philanderer," and "homosexuality."[19] Homosexuality did not exist before "homosexual" was coined by Károly Mária Benkert in 1869, as implied by the title of David Halperin's *One Hundred Years of Homosexuality*.[20]

Such is the view known as social constructionism (or anti-essentialism). As one proponent puts it, "the very meaning and content of sexual arousal" varies so much among genders, classes, and cultures that "there is *no* abstract and universal category of 'the erotic' or 'the sexual' applicable without change to *all* societies."[21] Nancy Hartsock has elaborated this claim:

> We should understand sexuality not as an essence or set of properties defining an individual, nor as a set of drives and needs (especially genital) of an individual. Rather, we should understand sexuality as culturally and historically defined and constructed. Anything can become eroticized.[22]

Hence, *pace* Ti-Grace Atkinson (see Introduction), even heterosexuality and its "main event," coitus, can *become* eroticized, or de-eroticized, as the social need may be. We cannot even count on the procreative act to be natural, or to be sexual. Sexual desire might be about or aimed at no specific goal or object; anything might become psychologically attached to the experience of sexual desire.

How many sexes are there? The answer that every child learns (by the age of three, if not sooner) is "two." The female has a vagina; the male has a penis. Of course, unclear cases exist: persons who are anatomically deficient or abundant, hence members of neither sex or of both.[23] Despite these congenital oddities, the biological categories "female" and "male" are solid, unlike "gender," "sexual identity," and "sexual orientation." And even though the intellectual similarities of the human male and female are greater than their differences, and the transvestite or transsexual can be confusing (see figure 1),[24] we have no trouble recognizing two distinguishable sexes, both among humans and lower animals, and even some plants.

Or so it seems. The very idea of how many sexes there are among human beings is open to a social constructionist analysis. In *Making Sex*, a history of the biomedical science of sex, the historian Thomas Laqueur tells a rich and more sophisticated story about human biological sex. Laqueur claims that there are two pictures of sex within biomedical science: a "one-sex" model that originated with the ancients (including the Greeks) and still survives, and a "two-sex" model, the contemporary distinction between the human female and male, which emerged in the eighteenth century. On the one-sex model, there is only one human sex, the male. Despite the clear evidence for the distinctiveness

Figure 1: Two People in a Restaurant

This photograph was taken in Lucky Cheng's restaurant in the French Quarter (New Orleans, Louisiana). Both persons are genetic males. The person on the left, a waitperson at the restaurant, looks female. Viewers of the photograph who do not know that the waitperson is a genetic male usually judge her to be attractively feminine and might even experience some sexual interest or arousal looking at her. It is not necessarily true, of course, that she is homosexual, either in behavior or orientation.

of females (pregnancy and birth), or perhaps because (through a convoluted psychological defense) of those facts, ancient scholars (men, by and large) saw the female as merely a modification of the male. For example, the vagina was perceived as a penis projecting inward, or as a penis turned inside out; and the uterus was thought of as an internal scrotum. The Greek word *kaulos* was used for both penis and vagina. The one-sex model persists in the English language: consider the pairs "male" and "female" and "man" and "woman," which imply that the latter is a mere modification of the former.

According to Laqueur, these two views of the number of human sexes were not derived from the observations of biological science. The ancients and their medieval successors who promulgated the one-sex model did so not for empirical reasons, and at times in the face of contradictory "factual" or observational evidence. We often see biological sex as an unchanging substrate, while gender is a cultural superstructure that assumes many forms. But biological sex was not always conceived of as an ultimate, natural material base that interacts with social, cultural, or ethnic factors to produce gender. For the Greeks, it was gender—the masculine and its social prerogatives, the feminine with its low status—that was both primary and natural.[25] The Greek cultural values of gender thereby played an important part in the ancient Greek biological notion that there was only one "canonical body," the male.[26] The emergence of the modern two-sex model did not coincide with, in fact preceded, and is therefore not explainable by, advances in the accuracy of anatomical dissection and medical illustration and in the experimental power of biomedical science.[27] Allegiance in the scientific community to the modern two-sex model came about well before sufficient empirical warrant was available (the way heliocentrism was ousting geocentrism—among scientists, even if not the clergy—well before empirical warrant for doing so existed).[28] Empirical evidence was called on retroactively to justify a model of sex, either the one-sex or the two-sex, that had already been accepted on other grounds. We might, then, conclude that sex is "made" (socially constructed) by cultural phenomena: the social, the political, the religious and metaphysical, and the philosophical.

One might object to Laqueur's view by pointing out that there are certain simple organisms, amoebae and such, that reproduce asexually, and exist in only one sex (if any); but humans are not like that. And humans do not (yet?) reproduce by parthenogenesis—if we did, males would be useless and humans would be, in this sense, a one-sexed species.[29] Hence, it is reasonable to think, contrary to Laqueur, that two sexes have always existed in humans, and it is only our notion of sex, not sex itself, that is socially constructed. Perhaps, though, Laqueur is right that there is "no scientific way to choose between" the one-sex and two-sex models when applied to human beings.[30] About humans, at least, there are no brute facts of the matter for science to discover; we are left to our own resources (including Machiavellian political manipulations) in constructing whatever we want. And if language—the act of naming, the introduction of neologisms—has the power of creation, if designating determines social reality, then it is futile to ask, "are humans *really* one-sexed or two-sexed?"

Despite the attractiveness of Laqueur's view about anatomical sex, the social constructionist position about sexuality is another story. Recall Hartsock's claim, "anything can become eroticized." If true—and it might well be true—this means that our preferred or desired sexual partners, positions, and activities are strongly under the control of cultural forces. The implication is that "anything" can be linked to sexual arousal and pleasure, which might also be true; after all, unusual items bring paraphiliacs sexual joy. If so, however, there is a common denominator to all sexuality after all, an essential even if narrow core: an unchanging, culturally invariable subjective experience of sexual arousal and sexual pleasure (or sensation). So there is a universal category of the sort that Hartsock denies. Even should it turn out that analyzing such a subjective thing as sexual arousal and pleasure is philosophically vain, that would not be much consolation for social constructionism. I see no prospect of successfully arguing that the experience of sexual pleasure itself radically varies from culture to culture or that it, too, has no essence.[31]

POLYSEMICITY

Consider a photograph of a nude woman sitting in a chair with her legs spread. She might be seen as prepared to be used for sex, a vulnerable object; or as demanding prolonged oral attention; or as simply watching television. Or consider a photograph of a woman licking an erect penis. She is in control, she is responsible for his pleasure, she can stop inconsiderately, or nibble the wrong way or cause distraction by coughing, she has the choice and the power to prolong or end his pleasure, and he is grateful. Or he is in control; he is taking all the pleasure he can get from her lips and tongue, he is using her mouth. Or the scenario is an experiment, she is curious about the taste and feel of a penis, he is curious about the warmth and wetness of a woman's mouth. For both photos, multiple interpretations are possible that are not fixed, internally, by their content. Nor is the meaning of the photographs fixed, externally, by the social context in which they were made and are viewed; the social construction of sexuality is not powerful enough to compel us to interpret these photographs, or the acts they depict, in just one way. The same is true for sexual activity itself:

> What if a woman says to a man, 'fuck me'? Is that begging, or is it demanding? Is she submitting, or is she in control?[32]

Our cultural milieux does push us into seeing some sexual acts in one dominant way; for example, a woman performing fellatio, or a photograph of her doing so, is often perceived as her being degraded by such a foul act. But, at the same time, we can come to the realization that this interpretation is infused with Augustinian sex-negativity, and that our reactions to the act (or the photograph) will differ to the extent that our home perspective is more sexually liberal. Both depictions of sexual acts and the sexual acts themselves are polysemous and resist being fixed by their social context. Indeed, the fluidity and pluralism of the social context is that which allows us to devise alternative meanings for sexual acts and to perceive them in various ways.

The cover of the June 1978 *Hustler* provides a good example of the polysemicity of representations. The cover depicts a pair of female legs and bottom sticking out from a meat grinder; the head and torso have already been ground into raw hamburger. Eva Kittay includes this cover in a list of pornographic items that she considers to be especially objectionable: depictions of a gun in a woman's mouth, whippings, handcuffs, rape, and bondage.[33] The cover of *Hustler*, on her view, straightforwardly endorses the brutalization of women for men's sexual pleasure. But this interpretation of the cover—which in its surrealism must mean more than this—is not very promising. At the least, we should go one step beyond this crude reading of an unusual and complex representation and suggest that *Hustler* was creatively admitting that, in displaying in its pages women's bodies for the masturbatory pleasure of men, it treats women as hunks of meat. No, not merely admitting but celebrating it, as if to reply "so what" to criticism of pornography. As soon as we see this political statement in the cover, other readings become possible. For example, the cover is sarcastic, mocking what sexual conservatives and some feminists claim about pornography.[34] "*You* say we treat women like meat," says the cover. "Well, *this* is what it is to treat women like meat; look inside, we *don't* do this." Or the cover "refers to a male desire to eliminate 'the female head'... and just be left with the sex," and so it "play[s] on men's *fear* of thinking women."[35] And do not overlook the phallic shape of the woman's body and the dreadful implication, dwelling in the deepest part of the male viewer's unconsciousness, that it is actually the head of his own penis, not a woman, being ground into hamburger. Finally, we need to acknowledge the printed announcement on the cover, below the depiction, and signed by Larry Flynt (*Hustler*'s publisher), which functions as a caption: "We will no longer hang women up like pieces of meat." Does this mean, "better, we shall grind them"? Or was it meant earnestly, to tell his audience that *Hustler* would henceforth be pure and clean? Or—to mention just one more possibility—is Flynt's remark more like René Magritte's playful caption to his painting *La trahison des images* (see figure 2), a caption that provokes us not to take the content of paintings—and even their captions—so seriously?

SEXUAL SENSATIONS

Another feature of Goldman's analysis deserves discussion: his assertion that in a sexual act we (tend to) fulfill the desire for contact with *another person's* body.[36] But why do we want to receive the touch of (or to touch) the other instead of our own touch? My touching my own arm and your touching it can be physically indistinguishable, can involve exactly the same bodily movement. The philosopher Robert Solomon has suggested that one person wants to touch and be touched by another person instead of himself or herself because sexuality is essentially communicative; sexual interaction is more about the expression of attitudes and emotions than it is about the experiencing of sexual pleasure.[37] In rejecting Solomon's answer, another philosopher, Russell Vannoy, replies to the question differently:

> I am aroused [by another] because I am being touched by someone I find to be quite sexually attractive and whose body I would like to touch in turn. Desire does not escalate and messages from body language mean nothing sexually unless I first find the flesh of the other to be the embodiment of sexual pleasure.[38]

Perhaps Vannoy is right that sexual interaction cannot serve as a vehicle for the expression of attitudes and emotions unless the interaction produces sexual pleasure. (Would that mean that sexual activity is communicative only when it is *good* sex?) But his alternative view sounds wrong, for that the other person is "sexually attractive" is neither necessary nor sufficient for the desire to touch him or her sexually to arise in us or for us to anticipate that the touch will lead to pleasure.

Figure 2: René Magritte, La trahison des images, 1929.

If this is not a pipe, then what is it? One answer is that it is a picture or a painting of a pipe. (But imagine a construction composed of a pipe glued to a canvas, also labeled "This is not a pipe." Then what is it? Perhaps a piece of wood. Perhaps a representation of Pipehood.) Another answer— if Magritte is illustrating the Freudian interpretation of dreams—is that it is a symbol of the penis. Were you to dream about a pipe, the analyst would say, "this is not a pipe in your dream, but something else more threatening to you that you are concealing, barely, from yourself." Or Magritte might be *mocking* Freudian analysis: this is obviously a pipe, but the analyst is screwy enough to deny it. Analogous things can be said about Larry Flynt's remark, attached to the depiction of a woman being ground into hamburger, that his magazine does not treat women like pieces of meat.

Recall Ti-Grace Atkinson's view that when artificial reproduction of the species—a much more efficient and less barbaric, animalistic method—replaces procreation by heterosexual intercourse, the social need for sexuality will be gone, and sexual activity and sexual desire will wither away (see Introduction). Atkinson means, more precisely, that sexuality as we know it today will no longer exist. But she does suppose that the sexual body might have a remainder, a sensuality of simple physical contact itself, patch of skin against patch of skin, that could be the individual's alone, apart from the social function of intercourse.[39] Atkinson wonders what this remainder would be like, once it finally existed in its pure state ungroomed by social needs. She immediately knocks up against our question: if the pleasure of the touch would remain, why would it have to be the touch of another person? Why wouldn't the touch of the self suffice?[40] The answer that I prefer is that paired or multiperson sex, be it gay, straight, or bisexual, provides certain sensual pleasures that can be achieved only through other bodies.

Atkinson resists this answer. She argues:

> Since what is being received [through the touch of the other] cannot be a technical or physical improvement on that same auto-experience, any positive external component must be a psychological component.... Since neither individual can *add* to the physical experience of the other, it must be that the contribution is a mental one.[41]

Atkinson's idea is similar to Solomon's: sexuality will become largely a communicative activity, undertaken or pursued not for reasons of bodily pleasure but to affirm the worth of the person. But the argument fails if the assumption, that the body of the other person provides *nothing* additional, is false. Notice where the argument ended up. Atkinson supposes that the mental or psychological component of paired sex, in which one person x receives the touch of another person y, is its reason for occurring.

The "positive" feeling of "approval" transmitted from toucher to touched is the rationale for our touching each other.[42] Once the reproductive function of sex is gone, sexual caresses take on the sole function of expressing caring and supportive emotions. Atkinson, for all her radical philosophy, cannot get beyond a pre-occupation that is surely traditional. But she does ask the right question about her proposal: "why would such feelings [of approval] have to be expressed by touching instead of verbally"— or even by nonsexual activity? Precisely. If these emotions or attitudes can be better expressed some other way than through the erotic body,[43] on her own account sex would serve no purpose and would be abandoned altogether.

The question is still interesting, however, why we might want to touch or be touched by the other instead of a self-touch. The answer that I mentioned above is that we have a desire for novel sensations. We seek other people for sexual interaction because of the sensations—odors, tastes, sounds, touches, and sights— they make possible. Why is it that I want the touch, odor, taste, or sound of the other instead of my own? I cannot smell, see, or taste myself or, if I can, the odor, taste, or sight is not sharp and lively; I am too familiar with my own odor, my own voice, and the taste of my own body. The power of the touch of the other, or the allure of touching the other, lies in its novelty. To feel the skin of another against my skin, to taste another's skin or to be tongued, is to sense something different and piercing.[44] Novelty plays an important role in sexual pleasure, just as human beings seek novelty and variety in a wide range of other activities: the books we read, games we play, and routes we take to work. But is emphasizing novelty and variety in sexual contexts a male bias, since familiarity—through, for example, long-term monogamy— is more important to women? (See Chapter Eight.)

Another question arises here. If there is a difference between x's touching himself or herself and x's touching y, what might the difference be between x's sexually touching y and x's sexually touching someone else z? Consider a thought experiment devised by Russell Vannoy. He asks us to imagine that we are in a room without any light, and we do not know whether we are having oral sex performed on us by a male, a female, or a mechanical device.[45] What effect might not knowing have on our pleasure and arousal? What would the effect be of later finding out which it was that brought us sexual pleasure? (Assume equal talent—the same touches—among the male, female, and mechanical device.) Here's a variation, from the Old Testament:

> Jacob served seven years [working for Laban] to get Rachel, but they seemed like only a few days to him because of his love for her. Then Jacob said to Laban, "Give me my wife. My time is completed, and I want to lie with her." So Laban brought together all the people of the place and gave a feast. But when evening came, he took his daughter Leah and gave her to Jacob, and Jacob lay with her.... When morning came, there was Leah! So Jacob said to Laban, "What is this you have done to me? I served you for Rachel, didn't I? Why have you deceived me?"[46]

Similar things actually happen: a woman charged a man with rape, because he snuck into her bed in the dark of night and she made love with him, believing, through his deception, that he was her boyfriend.[47] In all three cases, the effect of knowledge, social expectations, and norms on our sexual pleasure (or our retroactive judgments about what we experienced) implies that the cultural is an important influence on our sexuality. A change in our experience, from sexual joy to nauseating disgust, hints that the cultural plays a large role in shaping why a person x prefers to touch and be touched by another person y instead of yet another one z, when those touches are indistinguishable. Nevertheless, even if social constructionism is right about the variable sources of both pleasant and unpleasant sexual sensations, the fundamental, subjective, human experience of sexual arousal and pleasure seems immune to cultural manipulation.

CHAPTER TWO

SEXUAL PERVERSION

So long as we think of the world as divided into homosexuals and heterosexuals and regard the commission of a homosexual act, or even the entertaining of a homosexual desire, as an irrevocable step across a frontier which divides the normal, healthy, sane, natural and good from the abnormal, morbid, insane, unnatural and evil, we shall not get very far in understanding Greek attitudes to homosexuality.

—K. J. Dover, *Greek Homosexuality*

Nor shall we get very far in understanding our own sexuality, if we draw a sharp line between homosexuality and heterosexuality, such that even the faintest fantasy or briefest glance of a same-sex nature in an otherwise self-consciously straight person is regarded as a sign of the perverted. Human sexuality, both ours and that of the ancient Greeks, is much too complicated to be put into these neat boxes; and heterosex and homosex are too similar, producing similar physical pleasures and constituted by similar physical movements.

Roman Catholic ethicists have drawn the conceptual line between the sexually unnatural (or the perverted) and the sexually natural in such a way that homosexuality turns out to be unnatural—and for that reason morally wrong if manifested in behavior.[1] Indeed, as of late 1996, although thirty states and the District of Columbia had repealed their sodomy or "crimes against nature" laws, which made "deviate" or "unnatural" sexual acts, usually oral and anal sex, between two people of the same sex (and sometimes of different sexes) a crime, twenty states still had such laws on their books.[2] In *Bowers v. Hardwick*,[3] the United

States Supreme Court ruled that the state of Georgia did not violate any U. S. constitutional provision by prohibiting homosexual acts that occur between two consenting adults in their own bedroom. So the popular line of reasoning from an act's being sexually nonprocreative to its being sexually unnatural and perverted (and disgusting to contemplate), and from there to its being sexually immoral (or abhorrent), has been and may well continue to be part of the law in a country otherwise respected for its promotion of individual freedom. (See figure 3.)

ST. THOMAS AQUINAS

Although the idea that homosexual behavior is contrary to human nature and hence shameful and wrong can be found in the writings of the ancient Greek philosopher Plato (see *Laws* 636; but compare that with *Symposium*),[4] the great codifier of "Natural Law" ethics and its application to nonprocreative sexual activity was the medieval Catholic theologian Thomas Aquinas. Whereas Augustine (see Introduction) had condemned sex itself, or concupiscence, as one of the results of the Fall, Aquinas refused to do so: "It is impossible for carnal union to be evil in itself," he argued, on the grounds that heterosexual coitus results from a natural inclination implanted by God and in the act of coitus the sexual organs fulfill their natural purpose.[5] But these reasons for judging coitus unobjectionable gave Aquinas all the philosophical material he needed to condemn everything sexual, including masturbation and homosexuality, except that which is procreative. For Aquinas, the natural purpose of the emission of semen by the penis is procreation, and semen intentionally emitted otherwise is contrary to nature and hence morally wrong.

Sexual acts can be morally wrong, according to Aquinas, in two different ways.[6] First, "when the act of its nature is incompatible with the purpose of the sex-act [procreation]. In so far as generation is blocked, we have unnatural vice, which is any complete sex-act from which of its nature generation cannot follow."

Aquinas gives four examples of sexual acts that are unnatural vice because not procreative: "the sin of self-abuse," "intercourse with a thing of another species," acts "with a person of the same sex," and acts in which "the natural style of intercourse is not observed, as regards the proper organ or according to other rather beastly and monstrous techniques."[7] Second, sexual acts can be morally wrong even if natural, that is, procreative in form; in these cases, "conflict with right reason may arise from the nature of the act with respect to the other party," as in incest,[8] rape, seduction, and adultery. The unnatural sexual acts, in Aquinas's moral hierarchy, count as mortal sins, while the natural acts that are wrong in virtue of violating proper relations among human beings living in civilized society are only venial sins. (Note that a single sexual act might be wrong on several counts at once. Identify all the separate sins involved in a married man's anally raping his own seven-year-old son.)

Thus, for Aquinas, sexual sins in the first category are the worst: "unnatural vice flouts nature by transgressing its basic principles of sexuality, [so] it is in this matter the gravest of sins."[9] Aquinas is replying to the objection, which he states himself in his Socratic quest for truth, that unnatural vice is *not* the morally worst sex. "The more a sin is against charity," goes the objection, "the worse it is. Now adultery and seduction and rape harm . . . our neighbor, whereas unnatural lust injures nobody else, and accordingly is not the worst form of lust." Aquinas rejects this way of thinking. Seduction, rape, and adultery violate only "the developed plan of living according to reason" that derives from humans associating with each other in society, while "unnatural sins," which violate the plan of creation, are an "affront to God." If some sexual acts are unnatural, they are morally wrong, in Aquinas's sexual ethics, just for that reason, even if they do not cause harm to one's neighbors. It is worse, for Aquinas, to snub a nose at God than to snub a nose at other people.

Aquinas's sexual ethics, as regarding the first set of sexual sins, can be summarized by this argument:

Figure 3: Please Choose (Fidesz poster, 1989-90)

The top half of this Hungarian political campaign poster, the kiss between Leonid Brezhnev (left) of the Soviet Union and Erich Honecker (right) of the German Democratic Republic (East Germany) has been displayed by itself in Germany (I have seen it on a German postcard) and in the Soviet Union (as a mural). John Boswell reproduces the mural as Figure 2 in *Same-Sex Unions in Pre-Modern Europe* and comments on it: "Many areas... such as the former Soviet Union... find public displays of affection between men [the Brezhnev-Honecker kiss] ordinary and untroubling. Although such gestures may not be indicative of homosexual interest, in the United States or England or Germany they would be taken as such and would inspire horror or disgust or be considered immoral" (xxiv-xxv). Boswell continues in the caption to his Figure 2 (facing p. 192): "The Russians were... not shocked: a contemporary mural of Leonid Brezhnev... and Erich Honecker... greeting each other with a kiss. In the West, many observers would regard this picture as immoral." I do not doubt that many people would find this lips-to-lips kiss disgusting, but I am not sure that, once the kiss is properly understood, it would be judged in the U. S. as either immoral or "indicative" of homosexuality. Boswell thinks that this kiss is a display of "affection," but that is not quite right. It is customary in many (all?) European societies for people to greet each other with kisses, little pecks, on one or both cheeks (in Poland, three kisses are delivered, first to one cheek, next to the other, and finally back to the first). These kisses are typically mere formalities, like a business handshake, and are not taken as signs of affection (unless they occur between close kin or friends). Hence there is nothing to object to morally, nor any hint of perversion. Further, the fact that in the Brezhnev-Honecker kiss the lips land on each other is a fluke; one or both guys, in a hurry to perform the formality and get it over with, aimed at the wrong cheek, and this resulted in a lipsmacking kiss that was probably not intended. Knowledge of this might help those who see the picture as disgusting to overcome that reaction, and to laugh along with the rest of Europe at yet more bumbling or buffoonery by the Leaders of Important Countries. The Hungarian political party Fidesz (which at the time required a person to be under thirty-five years of age as a condition of membership) distributed this poster before the first democratic election in that country after the collapse of Communism. The text can be translated "Please choose," with a pun on "please elect." Choose or elect what? Select the young couple, as representative of the new free, democratic order in Hungary; replace the old guard with a breath of fresh air. The poster, then, is not a statement about or against homosexuality, as if displaying its disgusting nature in comparison with the sweetness of heterosex, but about the superiority of youth over corrupt and hilariously incompetent old age.

(1) Whatever is done intentionally that is (sexually) unnatural is morally wrong. It violates God's plan, design, or commands.
(2) What is sexually natural is a biological notion; its content is determined by the rational inspection of the world, including the subhuman animal world, as God created it.[10]
(3) Nonprocreative sex (homosexual intercourse, heterosexual oral sex) is unnatural in this biological sense.

Hence—the conclusion—the intentional commission of the sexual behaviors mentioned in (3), and any other behaviors that fall within the scope of (3), are morally wrong. It is useful to lay out the Natural Law position this way, with the logically independent claims kept separate, for doing so allows us to fashion several distinct criticisms of Aquinas's view.

PROBLEMS WITH NATURAL LAW

To begin with, we might not be able to make out, with enough accuracy, what is natural and unnatural in human sexual behavior. The difficulty is due not only to the resistance of nature to our experimental science, but also to the fuzziness of the concept of the natural. Perhaps biology, that which humans share with the lower animals, is not the place to go to investigate natural human sexuality; perversion might be better understood psychologically, instead of anatomically or physiologically, which would add to the difficulty of discovering human sexual nature. Further, even if we remain within the biomedical sciences, nonprocreative sexual desire and activity might be natural to human beings: not only because there may be a genetic foundation for homosexuality, but also because the plasticity of human desires and the variety of acts we enjoy performing result from the higher intelligence and consciousness made possible by our developed brains. And, finally, it is debatable whether acts that are unnatural are for that reason immoral.

There seems to be no easy equivalence between an act's being moral or immoral and its being natural or unnatural.[11] Of course, in advancing the objection by laying out counterexamples a lot rides on what we take to be natural and unnatural. Again we have a situation in which our ethical concerns intertwine with conceptual matters. The following examples will perhaps be enough to make the point, as long as it is remembered that we still need to address the question of what is genuinely natural.

Suppose it were true that, among humans, heterosexual rape, male promiscuity, and homosexuality were perfectly natural; it would seem contrary to our moral intuitions to deduce from their just being natural that they were immune from moral criticism. In principle, Aquinas agrees; his class of venial sexual sins includes sexually natural acts. It is unclear how these acts being natural makes much of a moral difference, since these behaviors, when and if they are right or wrong, would seem to be right or wrong on more sturdy grounds that have nothing to do with nature.

Nonsexual examples also come to mind: suppose, which is not implausible, that our natural self-interest, if not selfishness, commonly leads us to tell lies and to manipulate other people; it could still be a valid purpose of moral norms against cheating and deception to encourage us to avoid, as well as we can, these behaviors. Conversely, it seems to be unnatural, in the sense of interfering with the course of nature (or it is as much an interference with the course of nature as employing contraception during heterosexual coitus or engaging in nonprocreative sexual acts) to rely on laboratory-produced antibiotics to kill off infectious bacteria. One might argue that the use of these drugs, which *is* wrong to the extent that doing so is unnatural, is justified by other moral considerations; the wrongness is *overridden* by its good purpose. But that reasoning is unconvincing; the mere fact that the use of such artificial things may be unnatural seems not to have any moral weight at all. Perhaps medical intervention in the course of nature is altogether natural, insofar as it represents the human use of our natural rationality and intelligence; but, if so, we have abandoned a biological criterion of the natural for a psychological criterion—in which case an account of human sexual nature must be more subtle than Aquinas's.

A continuing problem with Aquinas's line of thought is the difficulty of formulating an intelligible account of the design of nature, an account that perceptively illuminates *human* nature. For Patricia Jung and Ralph Smith, for example—two theologians of a nontraditional yet self-proclaimed Christian bent—being gay is like being left-handed, "part of God's original blessing."[12] And consider Christine Gudorf's Christian defense of the pursuit and enjoyment of sexual pleasure for its own sake:

> If the placement of the clitoris in the female body reflects the divine will, then God wills that sex is not just oriented to procreation, but is at least as, if not more, oriented to pleasure.[13]

Gudorf's argument has exactly the same structure as Aquinas's. She has discerned, through a rational investigation of the design of biological nature, that the clitoris has no other purpose except the provision of sexual pleasure, and she concludes that nonprocreative sex is, for that reason, a perfectly acceptable activity for Christians to engage in. This kind of thinking frequently yields jokes (of which Aquinas has often been the brunt) rather than a serious point of the kind Gudorf wants to make. "If God had wanted us to be thin, he would have made glazed donuts logically impossible," or "God must like assholes, since he made so many of them." At the very least, however, Jung and Smith and Gudorf alert us to the difficulty of determining what God's plan is, the problems involved in interpreting the facts of the natural world as a sign of His intentions.

Nonetheless, the contemporary philosopher Michael Levin, in a well-known essay, has employed a version of Aquinas's Natural Law metaphysics in arguing that homosexual sexual "acts involve the use of the genitals for what they aren't for."[14] Such a view, however, depends on a myopic construal of what the genitals are *for*. The penis, given the cultural values that play a role in determining its functions beyond urinating and ejaculating, is for lots of things: not only for procreating and relieving the bladder, but also, most importantly, for experiencing pleasure, for waving to strangers at Mardi Gras, for playing with in times of distress— in short, for whatever human creativity decides to do with it. For Levin to claim that being inside another man's anus and rectum is not what a man's penis is "for" is not merely to deny that a discrete function of the penis (and rectum) is the provision of pleasure in its own right. It also leads to implausible conclusions, if followed out logically. Does masturbation also misuse the penis, or the hand? Does cunnilingus misuse the tongue? Does anilingus misuse *both* the tongue and anus?[15] Drawing a line between heterosexual oral sex (as natural) and homosexual oral sex (as unnatural) would seem to be futile.

Hence, even if "one normal function of sexual desire is to promote reproduction,"[16] human sexuality has other functions, including, but not restricted to, the provision of pleasure for the individual that makes a direct contribution to his or her welfare and, in turn, to its survival and longevity. Homosexuality, then, is not a perversion of the human system of sexual desire, arousal, and pleasure. On the sexual score, homosexuals, bisexuals, heterosexuals, and anyone else not engaged in reproductive activity by intention or default, do not, just because they are homosexual, bisexual, heterosexual, or sterile, suffer from a *sexual* defect, even if they do have a reproductive disadvantage. (But, of course, many gays and lesbians procreate.)

A resurgence of the application of the natural sciences to our understanding of human nature has contributed to the complexity of the problem of sorting out the natural and the cultural. If we are to believe recent sociobiology, promiscuity in men and women's inclination toward monogamy are genetically entrenched, the result of evolutionary mechanisms. Hence the notion that a married man "is likely to think of no sweeter joy than a... love affair"[17] expresses a moral attitude that turns the Catholic reliance on nature, in justifying monogamous marriage for men, too, on its head. The new research supporting the idea that homosexual orientation has a nontrivial biological basis[18] implies that the Church might have to concede that homosexual pleasure, desire, and behavior are also part of God's design. If having homosexual desire is little different from being green in the eye, the Church would find it a philosophical challenge to continue to withhold moral acceptability from homosexual love relationships.

This kind of nature/nurture/moral dispute (Are gays and lesbians the way they are by nature? By how they were raised? By their own moral defect?) has always proved difficult to resolve to everyone's satisfaction. The study, for example, of the origins and explanation of apparent racial and gender variations in mental functioning has always been a mess. Scientific solutions might be possible in principle, but they have been elusive in practice. Psychological and social factors influence the kind of scientific solution an individual prefers, and political factors play a large role in determining what solutions are reached and become socially accepted as knowledge.[19] Nevertheless, some gay and lesbian political activists like the idea of explaining their sexual orientation biologically. If their sexual preferences are caused by Mother Nature, if homosexual desire is a genetic trait, then gay and lesbian lifestyles become socially easier to justify and to defend legally. One lesbian made the point in a CNN documentary a few years ago, using Aquinas to her own advantage: it was God who made her the way she is. The Thomist will not deny that if God willed it, it is right; he denies only, in the case of homosexuality, that God willed it. But if it is illicit for the Thomist to argue from the unnaturalness of an activity to its being morally wrong, it is equally illicit for gay and lesbian activists to argue from the naturalness of homosexuality to the conclusion that their activities are morally permissible.[20] This kind of argument might be widely persuasive and politically useful[21] (the way in which state legislatures were convinced in the past by Thomist thought in constructing sodomy laws), but it is technically fallacious.

For Aquinas, there is one more mortal sexual sin: adultery, or extramarital sex, *when one already has children*, is unnatural and hence one of the sins of the worst kind.[22] He claims:

It is evident that the bringing up of a human child requires the care of a mother who nurses him, and much
more the care of a father, under whose guidance and
guardianship his earthly needs are supplied and his character developed. Therefore indiscriminate intercourse is
against human nature. The union of one man with one
woman is postulated, and with her he remains, not for a
little while, but for a long period, or even for a whole
lifetime.[23]

The hoary thought that monogamy is built into human nature,
into the design of the species, has for eons been the subject of
debate, nicely illustrating the problems in the investigation of
human nature and distinguishing the role of nature from the role
of culture in human sexuality. (Note the absence of argument in
Aquinas, beyond "it is evident.") These problems, however, have
not interfered with speculation and the dissemination of bold the-
ses among those who like to reason sociobiologically. For example, Anthony Walsh thinks that "nature had to capture [the
male] in love,"[24] that is, the love of the male for the female of the
species was selected for in an evolutionary process, through its
power to keep the father with the mother and the children who
passed on his genes. Walsh generalizes his thesis to both sexes:
the love that was selected includes the mother's "selfless and
unconditional care," since that was required for the survival of
the infants.[25] As a result of this process, "Nature has emotionally
enriched the human reproductive impulses with love, and in doing so she has immensely increased our enjoyment of both."[26]
"How convenient!" a cynic might reply; this link between sex
and love is not merely a piece of conservative religious teaching
or romantic ideology, but inhabits our very genetic code. Similarly, one can imagine a sociobiological defender of Aquinas's
natural law prohibition of the adultery of a father arguing that
monogamy, as Aquinas claimed, is built into the human design.
But there are so many cases of this sort of adultery that a contemporary Christian would be better off saying that the moral prohibition against this extramarital sexual activity is in order precisely

because men have a tendency to stray and need the encouragement of the moral law to remain faithful to wives and children. And, as against Walsh, Russell Vannoy thinks that the connection between sex and love is anything but natural; on his view, sex itself, *without* the entanglements of love, provides the highest sensual bliss.[27] Listen, too, to Richard Mohr praise raw sex:

> Sexual pleasure is... in intensity and kind unique among human pleasures; it has no passable substitute from other realms of life. For ordinary persons... orgasmic sex is the only access they have to ecstasy.... Sex as the most intense of pleasures is one of the central free-standing components of the good life.[28]

"Free-standing" here means that sexual activity is its own justification, and does not need to be linked with procreation or love or anything else to be the valuable experience it is.

PSYCHOLOGICAL PERVERSION

Thomas Nagel has devised a theory of human sexuality that distinguishes between natural and perverted sexuality but which, unlike Aquinas's view, focuses on the psychology of human sexual interaction instead of its biology.[29] Thus, in offering a psychological account of sexual perversion, Nagel emphasizes the distinctness of the human, and how humans differ from lower animals, in opposition to a biological or procreative approach that emphasizes the anatomy and physiology that humans and animals have in common.[30]

In human sexuality, consciousness and self-consciousness play a role that is absent from animal sexuality. Humans respond with arousal to the recognition that another is trying to arouse them with a properly timed or placed touch or glance (or by the wearing of clothing or perfume). Further, humans respond with arousal to the recognition that the other person is experiencing arousal in response to us—to our body, our mannerisms, and our touches. At the beginning of a sexual interaction, I am aroused by merely "sensing" (touching, looking at, smelling) you, and you are similarly aroused at this basic, even animal, level of sexuality. But as our interaction proceeds, I respond with arousal to noticing that you are aroused in response to sensing me, and in that response I perceive myself as the object of your sexual interest.

Before this point, while I am merely aroused by looking at or smelling or touching you, I perceive myself only as a sexual subject, but when I notice that you are aroused by sensing me, my conscious "expands" and I start to perceive myself as also a sexual object. (Think about holding hands sexually with another person for the first time. The tightness of the mutual grip increases as each person becomes aware of the other's arousal in response to the pleasure of the touch.) I am aroused by noticing that your looking at or smelling or touching me arouses you, and if the same is true for you, we both perceive ourselves at once as both subject and object in the sexual interaction. This makes human sexuality distinct from, and more interesting than, animal sexuality. Nagel's account thus implies that for sexuality to be psychologically natural (what he calls "complete"), a person must allow himself or herself to be an object in the consciousness of another, and to be aware of this feature of their interaction, in addition to being a sexual subject. Objectification, then, is in this sense not alien to human sexuality but essential to it.

Note the implications of Nagel's account for voyeurism; given his account of human sexuality, it is an excellent example of psychological sexual perversion. The voyeur does his or her best to remain at all times a sexual subject, keeping himself hidden from the look or the sensing of the other person, and so never descends into the self-conscious embodiment of being a sexual object of someone else's sexual attention. Nagel also suggests that what is perverted about sadomasochism is that one person, the sadist (or "top"), remains fully a sexual subject, never an object, while the other person, the masochist (or "bottom"), remains fully a sexual object, never becoming a subject.[31] (I think, as Nagel admits, that the psychodynamics of a sadomasochistic sexual encounter are more complex than this; it may well include reciprocal awareness of arousal.) Another illuminating implication of Nagel's account is how it captures what happens when a prostitute pretends to enjoy the sex for which he or she is paid (or when a husband or wife pretends, for the sake of the pleasure of the other spouse, to be enjoying the boring sexual activity in which they are engaged). To be rid of the client and conserve time, the prostitute wants the client to reach orgasm quickly. He or she feigns arousal, knowing that when this "arousal" is perceived by the client this will increase his arousal in a Nagelian spiral: he becomes conscious of himself as both subject and object. Finding this state of awareness blissfully arousing and pleasurable, the client then achieves orgasm.

There is one more notable feature of Nagel's theory of sex. In English, we often use the concept "sexually perverted" to speak about the type of sexual act performed; we also use it, just as often, to speak about the person who performs the action. The usual relationship between these two uses of "sexually perverted" is this: we speak of a person as a pervert or as sexually perverted if that person performs sexually perverted acts. That is, we take "sexually perverted," as applied to acts, to be logically primary, and "sexually perverted," as applied to persons, to be a derivative notion. Nagel agrees with this approach, but issues an important qualification: the sexual perversions, on his view, involve "sexual *inclinations* rather than... practices adopted not from inclination but for other reasons."[32] His point is that a person might perform a sexually perverted act yet not be properly judged to be a sexually perverted person (or pervert); it all depends on *why* the person performs the sexually perverted act. If act A is a sexually perverted act, because in doing it a person x remains a sexual subject and never becomes in his or her own consciousness a sexual object, the x who performs A is a sexual pervert only if A is what x really wants to do: x has an inclination for performing

A because A brings x sexual joy. But if x performs the act just because, say, x has been bribed to do so with a gift of jewelry, and x has no independent desire to do it, then x is not a sexual pervert.

Similarly, from the fact that a person has performed or does perform homosexual sexual acts (that is, engages in sexual activity with persons of the same sex), it does not automatically follow that this person is a "homosexual" or has a "homosexual orientation." In part, such a judgment depends on *why* the person performs these sexual acts.[33] A male who engages in sex with another male merely for money and not out of a desire for the act or person, because he is in prison and has no other sexual outlet (not having access to the women he prefers to have sex with), or because he has been dared to do so or is trying to win a bet, is probably not correctly judged homosexual. Homosexuality involves not just behavior (and maybe not even behavior at all) but, as Nagel says, inclinations (perhaps as revealed in one's sexual fantasies): a genuine desire to engage in same-sex sexual activity, even if that desire is never acted on. Of course, this is not to say that an inclination to engage in homosexual acts is sexually perverted. Indeed, on Nagel's account, the fact that two persons are of the same sex does not prevent them from being aroused by recognizing the arousal of the other person; their sexual interaction can be as complete as heterosexual interaction and hence just as psychologically natural.[34] Again we find little reason to distinguish between heterosex and homosex: in each case, the sexually interacting persons become aware of themselves as both sexual subject and sexual object.

A CONCEPTUAL FRAMEWORK

The ground we have covered in the Introduction and Chapters One and Two suggests that there are five central distinctions to be made within the conceptual philosophy of sex. Each of the following five categories can be used to ask distinct questions about the value, significance, or nature of sexual activity. That these categories mark *distinct* parameters of evaluation is the point to be emphasized; how we apply one category to a given sexual activity will not necessarily determine how we apply any other category. We can say, to use a mathematical metaphor, that these five evaluations vary independently of each other.

First, we can inquire about the *moral quality* of any particular sexual activity or sexual encounter. Is the act morally permissible (or morally obligatory), on the one hand, or immoral, morally wrong, on the other? An example of the first kind might be heterosexual coitus engaged in by a married couple; an example of the second kind is rape, forcing someone to undergo a sexual experience without his or her consent.

Second, we can ask a separate question about the *nonmoral quality* of sexual acts: does the act provide arousal, pleasure, and excitement (nonmoral goodness) or is it tedious, boring, and unenjoyable (nonmoral badness)? It is a simple matter to show that there is no equivalence between the moral and nonmoral quality of sexual acts, that these two evaluative categories are distinct: morally permissible sex might be dull (the sex engaged in by the long-married couple), while adulterous sex (let us assume it is morally wrong) might be very satisfying. Indeed, it is a phenomenon either much deplored or celebrated in literature, films, and television programs, that a disparity often exists between what is morally permissible in our sexual behavior and what is sexually fulfilling.

Third, we can ask about the *legality* of sexual activity: is it legally permissible or legally prohibited? This will, of course, vary by jurisdiction. Again, whether a sexual act is moral/immoral or pleasurable/boring has no necessary connection with its being legal or illegal. Homosexual acts are illegal in some states, yet they may well be both morally and nonmorally good.

Fourth, there is the category of the *pragmatic* evaluation of sexual acts. Some sexual acts are medically safe, useful, or effective in achieving certain goals, or in general have good consequences (for example, pregnancy, if one wants to be pregnant);

other sexual acts are medically unsafe, counterproductive, or in general have bad consequences (pregnancy, if one does not want to be pregnant).

And, finally, sexual acts can be evaluated, using either a biological or a psychological criterion, as being natural or unnatural (perverted). Given that these evaluative categories are distinct, one can put together a list of thirty-two (that is, 2^5) sexual acts, none of which repeats, in all five ways, exactly how any other sexual act on the list is evaluated. (Construct an example in which the sexual act being evaluated is morally wrong, nonmorally good for at least one participant, illegal, safe, and unnatural.)

One lesson to be learned from the distinctions we have drawn has been expressed by the philosopher Michael Ruse:

> If one agrees that homosexuality is not immoral, then surely one ought to persuade people not to regard homosexuals and their habits with loathing. Certainly, one ought to persuade people not to confuse their disgust at a perversion with moral indignation.[35]

That we consider a sexual activity to be unsafe for the voluntarily participating persons, illegal, unnatural and disgusting (again, see figure 3), and perhaps also boring, does not force us to conclude, as well, that it is morally wrong.

CHAPTER THREE

SEXUAL ETHICS

Anyone who looks at a woman lustfully has already committed adultery with her in his heart. If your right eye causes you
to sin, gouge it out and throw it away.... And if your right
hand causes you to sin, cut it off and throw it away. It is better
for you to lose one part of your body than for your whole body
to go into hell.

—Jesus [according to Matthew 5: 28-30]

CONTRACEPTION

I n the case *Griswold v. Connecticut*, which was decided in
1965 by the U. S. Supreme Court,[1] a Connecticut law that
prohibited persons from obtaining contraceptive devices
(condoms, diaphragms, and so forth) and information about how
to use them was struck down as a violation of the U. S. Constitution. Connecticut had prohibited a practice that many consider to
be contrary to nature (although, in arguing before the court, at-
torneys for the state claimed that the law served the purpose of
discouraging adultery).[2] The majority of the members of the Supreme Court contended that Connecticut had no right to interfere
with such an intimate, private matter as the sexual relations and
family plans of a married couple, and that the law also infringed
on the speech rights of Planned Parenthood.[3] This is a question
only of the legality of the practice of employing contraception;
the moral question (and, perhaps, the issue of the cogency of the
reasons that the state of Connecticut originally had in 1879 for
prohibiting the practice) is a separate matter. But that question
has been handled by Natural Law ethics largely the way it has
handled homosexuality.

Recall that, according to Aquinas in *Summa Theologiae*, sexual acts are mortal sins "when the act of its nature is incompatible with the purpose of the sex-act. In so far as generation is blocked, we have unnatural vice, which is any complete sex-act from which of its nature generation cannot follow."[4] Apparently, Aquinas means in part (see "blocked" and "generation cannot follow") that the use of contraceptive devices[5] during heterosexual coitus is unnatural and hence immoral. And in *Summa Contra Gentiles* Aquinas writes that "every emission of semen, in such a way that generation cannot follow, is contrary to the good for man. And if this be done deliberately, it must be a sin."[6] So, whenever the use of contraceptive devices involves a deliberate intention to prevent the emission of semen from having its natural fertilizing effect, as when the semen is collected in the end of a condom, the sexual act, even though it is done in the natural style (heterosexual coitus), is unnatural and hence morally wrong.

Scholarly opinion is divided, however, on the question of whether Aquinas meant to condemn the use of contraceptive devices during heterosexual coitus; for while laying out his two lists of sexual sins in *Summa Theologiae*, he does not explicitly use the term "contraception" or a synonym. The philosopher Susan Nicholson thinks that Aquinas extended his moral analysis of sexual activity between spouses, one of whom is infertile (and for whom, then, the natural act cannot issue in progeny), to contraception: both are permissible, if the act performed is heterosexual coitus, even though fertilization cannot occur.[7] If so, then why isn't homosexual sex (a kind of infertile sex) also permissible? In contrast, the theologian Margaret Farley claims that Aquinas "opposed contraception... because it was in intention nonprocreative."[8] Then the difference between the permissible sex engaged in by an infertile couple and the impermissible sex engaged in by those who use contraception is that in the first case the avoidance of procreation is not intentional. But, then, homosexual sexual activity would seem to be morally wrong only if it was engaged in deliberately to avoid procreation. Another theologian, Paul Simmons, argues that contraception was, for Aquinas, not unnatural but *still* wrong, since it falls into the same category of sin (venial) as incest, rape, adultery, and seduction[9] (see Chapter Two). But how is the use of contraception a violation of the proper relations among humans living in society? How does it harm our neighbors?

Regardless of how we read Aquinas, it is abundantly clear, from Augustine through much twentieth-century Catholic thought, that in this tradition the use of contraceptive devices (including the pill) is considered to be unnatural and morally wrong. For example, in his 1968 encyclical "Humanae Vitae," Pope Paul VI argued on the basis of Natural Law against the permissibility of the use of contraceptive devices. "Each and every marriage act... must remain open to the transmission of life"[10] and, therefore, "conjugal acts made intentionally infecund" are immoral.[11] But Paul VI offered another, different argument, one that is reminiscent of both Augustine and Kant (see Introduction and below): the use of contraception could make a husband "lose respect" for his wife. Since using contraception implies that the sexual act is being done for its pleasure, and not for procreation, the husband might come to see his wife as "a mere instrument of selfish enjoyment."[12] Karol Wojtyla (later to be Pope John Paul II) agreed. Contraceptive sexual acts are morally wrong, in part, on the grounds that this practice is degrading or leads to exploitation, since such acts make pleasure the goal and tend to reduce one's partner to a means:

> When the idea that 'I may become a father'/'I may become a mother' is totally rejected in the mind and will of husband and wife nothing is left of the marital relationship, objectively speaking, except mere sexual enjoyment. One person becomes an object of use for another person.[13]

Why does Wojtyla say that *nothing* is left except mere sexuality when procreation has been blocked? After all, Paul VI asserts that the expression or deepening of spousal love is one of the three purposes of sex in marriage (see his "inseparability thesis," Chapter Seven). Perhaps Wojtyla's idea is that love, too, is excluded when a couple deliberately interferes with the procreative function of coitus.

Does the ban on the use of contraception mean that Catholic spouses are doomed to having large families or, alternatively, being celibate?[14] Not necessarily. In "Humanae Vitae," Paul VI asserted that the "rhythm method," which attempts to regulate birth by restricting the conjugal act to the infecund times in the wife's cycle, is "licit."[15] Can this be an effective procedure, any more so than *coitus interruptus* or *coitus reservatus*? In a 1995 encyclical, John Paul II praises medical science for making it possible for husband and wife to know with accuracy when in her cycle they can engage in intercourse without risking pregnancy.[16] Still, can this practice be considered either natural or moral, given Catholic principles? One might argue that because heterosexual intercourse was designed by God for procreation, it is contrary to nature to restrict intercourse to those times of the month when fertilization is most unlikely to occur. Does not the rhythm method involve an intention to make the reproductive act not serve its natural purpose? In Aquinas's terms, a couple that employs the rhythm method seems intentionally to want the emission of semen—for its pleasure—but not the procreation that is the emission's natural consequence. In Paul VI's defense of the rhythm method, he asserts that there is an "essential" difference between the rhythm method and the use of contraceptive devices; "in the former, the married couple makes legitimate use of a natural disposition; in the latter, they impede the development of natural processes."[17]

BEYOND NATURAL LAW

It might be asked about homosexual acts, group sex, adultery, contraceptive coitus, bestiality, wearing costumes during sex, making and viewing pornography, and masturbation, that if any of these activities can be engaged in, without any harm befalling the participants or other persons, by consenting adults who can be presumed to know what they want and what they are doing, how could they be morally wrong? The question has often been answered in the twentieth-century West with "they're not." But the Natural Law ethics of the Catholic tradition answers, in the words of Aquinas, that "unnatural vice flouts nature by transgressing its basic principles of sexuality."[18] That is, even in the absence of harm to third parties and if, in this sense, no violation of "charity" or of the commandment to love our neighbor occurs, the fact that two adults freely engage in a sexual act together is not sufficient for their act to be morally permissible. For others in the sexually conservative tradition, even if Natural Law is not invoked, a similar conclusion follows: only in a committed relationship (marriage, usually) is sexual interaction permissible, since only here is it possible for sexual partners to avoid treating each other as objects.

Secular humanists, sexual liberals, and moral libertarians claim that the fact that the sexual partners participate in their activity voluntarily means that they are at least in part being treated as ends by each other and not merely being used; when participation is voluntary rather than coerced, each person is respecting the other as an autonomous agent capable of making up his or her own mind about the value of the activity. Hence mutual consent is sufficient, in the absence of harm to our neighbors, for the moral goodness of sexual acts. Opposed to this view is the claim that it makes perfectly good conceptual and moral sense to say that two people, x and y, could be merely using each other even when each participates freely. Both Kant and Wojtyla take this route; to allow oneself to be used is to make an object of oneself, and making an object of anyone is morally wrong. Kant concludes (for details, see below) that sexual activity is not use only when it occurs within marriage, since in this case the persons have exchanged their selves with each other and have achieved a "unity of will."[19] For Wojtyla, only longsuffering, patient, forgiving, altruistic, committed love, which truly exists only in marriage, "can preclude the use of one person by another."[20] Love, on this view, is a unification of persons achieved through the mutual gift of their selves (see Chapter Five).

Natural Law and Kantian philosophy thus disagree with the sexually liberal outlook that has been increasingly popular in the West. The sexual liberal justifies permissive sexual ethics by appealing to the important values of pleasure and autonomy, while the natural law theorist justifies prohibitive sexual ethics by appealing to the design of nature to which human behavior ought to conform. If sexual acts are unnatural, they are morally wrong, in this ethical system, just for that reason alone. Thus, to one standard list of reasons sexual acts might be wrong (they are dishonest, cruel, unfair, coercive, exploitative, unfaithful, or negligently dangerous),[21] a list that any respectable libertarian will largely endorse, Natural Law ethics adds "unnatural." Not so the sexual liberals, for whom fellatio and cunnilingus, anal intercourse, mutual masturbation, and, for the more radical liberals, consensual sadomasochism, can be performed with Christian "charity." Mutual consent that is free and informed, in the absence of third-party harm, guarantees the morality of sexual activity. No law of God or nature supplements this basic principle of proper relations among humans.

KANT

Immanuel Kant is important as the author of the ethics of respect. He states, in what is known among philosophers as the Second Formulation of the Categorical Imperative:

> Act in such a way that you always treat humanity, whether in your own person or in the person of any other, never simply as a means, but always at the same time as an end.[22]

To respect a person, to recognize the dignity of the human being, is to treat a person as an "end," never merely as an object, a tool, or an instrument by which we attain our own goals. Kant intends this moral principle to be taken seriously ("always"); on his view, there are no exceptions to the rule that we must treat others as full persons and not (merely) as objects to be used for our own purposes. Kant's view of the nature of sexual interaction meshes nicely with this general moral maxim. As we saw before (Introduction), human sexual interaction, for Kant, involves by its nature one person's merely using another for the sake of pleasure:

> There is no way in which a human being can be made an Object of indulgence for another except through sexual impulse.... Sexual love makes of the loved person an Object of appetite.... Sexual love... by itself and for itself... is nothing more than appetite. Taken by itself it is a degradation of human nature.... As an Object of appetite for another a person becomes a thing.... This is the only case in which a human being is designed by nature as the Object of another's enjoyment.[23]

Kant's position on sex, then, is this: (1) all use is morally wrong, and (2) all sexual interaction involves the use of at least one person by another, or of both by each other; therefore, (3) all sexual interaction is morally wrong. Thus, in reflecting on the claim that *"respect is absolutely essential.* In the sex that you have, treat your partner like a real person who, like you, has real feelings,"[24] Kant might say: "nice sentiment, and I applaud your ethics. But what you ask of sexual interaction is impossible."[25] Of course, it is possible to reply to Kant that his view of the nature of sexual interaction is unduly pessimistic, that (2) is false:

> By awakening us to the living presence of someone else, sexuality can enable us to treat this other being just as

the person he or she happens to be.... There is nothing in
the nature of sexuality as such that necessarily... reduces
persons to things. On the contrary, sex may be seen as
an... agency by which persons respond to one another
through their bodies.[26]

But it is illuminating to investigate Kant's position further in his
own terms, by conceding, *ex hypothesi*, that both premises of his
argument are true.

If Kant's argument is sound, and all sexual acts—not only
rape, or those acts in which consent is absent, and even those in
which consent is present—are objectifying and instrumental, is
not celibacy required? St. Paul thought that the celibate life was
ideal, although not required (1 Corinthians 7:1, 6-7); but, on his
view, sexual activity was permissible only in heterosexual marriage when the spouses agreed to take on the "marriage debt":

> 7:4 The wife hath not power of her own body, but the
> husband: and likewise also the husband hath not power
> of his own body, but the wife.
> 7:5 Defraud ye not one the other, except it be with con-
> sent for a time, that ye may give yourselves to fasting and
> prayer; and come together again, that Satan tempt you
> not for your incontinency.

Kant follows but embellishes upon Paul:

> The sole condition on which we are free to make use of
> our sexual desire depends upon the right to dispose over
> the person as a whole.... If I have the right over the whole
> person, I have also the right... to use that person's *organa
> sexualia* for the satisfaction of sexual desire. But how am
> I to obtain these rights over the whole person? Only by
> giving that person the same rights over the whole of my-
> self. This happens only in marriage. Matrimony is an
> agreement between two persons by which they grant each

other equal reciprocal rights, each of them undertaking to surrender the whole of their person to the other with a complete right of disposal over it.... If I yield myself completely to another and obtain the person of the other in return, I win myself back; I have given myself up as the property of another, but in turn I take that other as my property, and so win myself back again in winning the person whose property I have become. In this way the two persons become a unity of will.... Thus sexuality leads to a union of human beings, and in that union alone its exercise is possible.[27]

This is an astonishing passage, containing a philosophically intricate argument. Kant does not merely assert that, as ordained by God and nature, sex must be restricted to marriage. That would not solve the puzzle of how sexual use would be overcome by marriage. But what exactly is his argument?

Mary Ann Gardell, instead of sensing Paul's "marriage debt" in Kant's exchange of rights, reads Kant as benignly claiming that "marriage transforms an otherwise manipulative masturbatory relationship into one that is essentially altruistic in character."[28] But there is nothing about "altruism" in the passage. I grant you the right of access to my body in marriage only because I am going to get, in return, the right of access to your body. Kant's marriage agreement appears to be a self-interested, even if mutually beneficial, tit-for-tat exchange. The point is that Kant speaks of marriage as a *contract*, the specific *content* of which is reciprocal ownership. By this contract, the spouses become each other's property. The fact that in a Kantian marriage what is involved is not a contentless contract, the terms of which the spouses are free to negotiate between themselves, but a contract having a determinate, unchanging content, implies that Kant is also not arguing that any marital pledge, any voluntary assumption of the terms of an agreement, assures that the spouses are not treating each other only as means, but also as ends, in the marriage bed.

Kant's argument, I think, rests on the numerical logic of

"use" in a sexual interaction; in sexual activity, *one* person uses another person, and the *second*, in turn, uses the first. Kant, then, justifies marital sex as an exception to his general conclusion that all sex is morally wrong by abolishing in marriage the very possibility of instrumentality: after the union of two persons into one by marriage, there cannot *be* any use of one person by another.[29] When I grant to you ownership of me and my sexual organs, you then own both yourself and me; when you, in turn, grant to me ownership of you, I get myself back (as Kant says), but I also get you as well. As a result, you own me and yourself, and I own you and myself. In this exchange, we become an enlarged "I," a moral and ontological union of two-into-one. In the formation of this new entity that is the marriage person/body, the use, sexual or otherwise, of one person by another becomes logically impossible. (For this reason, Kantian union, as well as the Pauline marriage debt, also seems to make rape in marriage—a kind of use, a violation of the principle of respect—*logically* impossible.)

Thus, to read Kant as espousing a philosophy of love-conquers-the-badness-of-sex is wrong. Even though the word "love" is not in the passage in Kant's text where he presents his solution to the puzzle, Russell Vannoy interprets the *Lectures* as claiming that "love" cleanses sex of its corruption:

> Kant fails to understand that if sexual desire is inherently exploitative and if love is inherently altruistic, trying to combine the two [in a Kantian marriage] generates a contradiction rather than sexual love of persons.[30]

But there is no such contradiction in a Kantian marriage, for Kant never supposes that the relation between the spouses, a contract according to which they own each other as property, is one of love or altruism. Indeed, the notion of a marriage contract seems to presuppose that altruism—the glue that normally holds a marriage together (or gets it going)—is absent, or only unreliably present. This is why Paul, speaking about his similar proposal, *admonishes* the spouses who are tied together by the marriage debt to show "due benevolence" to each other (1 Corinthians 7:3), as if he does not think that benevolence would flow naturally between the spouses.[31]

Kant's idea that a marriage contract having this content cleanses sex of instrumentality apparently implies that homosexual marriage would similarly cleanse same-sex sexuality.[32] After all, nothing in the argument turns on the sex of the partners or the procreative nature of sex. Why couldn't two men or two women exchange rights of ownership forever, thereby also qualifying as an exception to Kant's general conclusion? And doesn't the sexual coalescence of two-into-one of Kantian marriage imply that solitary masturbation, too, is an exception to his general conclusion that all sex, as the use of one person by another, is morally wrong?[33] Only in some strange sense of "use" can it be said that a solitary masturbator is using himself or treating herself as an object. Kant, unlike some contemporary Kantians, sidesteps both implications, asserting in the next section of the *Lectures* that masturbation and homosexuality are wrong because they are *crimina carnis contra naturam*:

> Onanism... is abuse of the sexual faculty.... By it man sets aside his person and degrades himself below the level of animals.... Intercourse between *sexus homogenii*... too is contrary to the ends of humanity; for the end of humanity in respect of sexuality is to preserve the species without debasing the person.[34]

The masturbator, as well as the homosexual, "no longer deserves to be a person" (recall that, according to Leviticus, the latter must be put to death). Kant, as did Aquinas, condemns nonprocreative sex as unnatural, even if it might be, in his own sense, noninstrumental. In reply to Kant, we might want to appeal to recent developments or hypotheses in the evolution of human sexuality (which is one way we replied to Aquinas): "masturbation and homosexuality are among nature's ways of managing the competition of men for women," opines Richard Posner.[35] Both activities, then, are natural, not *crimina carnis contra naturam*. But this is a Pyrrhic victory; masturbation and homosexuality are, on such a view, the acts practiced by losers in the reproductive contest.[36] The most compelling objection to Kant's move here is that his condemnation of masturbation and homosexuality is an *ad hoc* patch-up job. Kant was attempting the philosophically ambitious task of making an exception for marital sex *without* appealing to Natural Law. That he eventually falls back on "nature" to condemn homosexuality and masturbation suggests that he was unwilling to accept all the implications of his sophisticated contract argument.[37]

Kant insists that the reciprocal exchange of rights, if sexual activity is to be permissible in marriage, must be for life. But why could there not be an exchange of rights for three years or for an evening, also justified by a consensual contract? Nothing in the idea of an exchange of rights of access to the body seems to entail that the exchange must be forever; nor does the idea of a contract exclude that it be temporary. Is there something irreversible about this particular exchange of rights? If not, Kant's defense of monogamous, lifelong marriage in terms of a "unity" would fail. Perhaps Kant means that when one grants rights of access to the *whole* person, which is an entity that stretches over time, one is granting rights of access to future selves at the same time; maybe future selves are somehow included in the present self. In any event, Kant would need to argue that without now granting access to future selves, there is now no genuine "union" of two into one.[38] Does this beg the question, or can it be independently supported? Karol Wojtyla also asserts that only marriage eliminates sexual objectification, since marriage includes the unification of persons orchestrated by the mutual *gift*—rather than a Kantian contractual exchange—of their selves. On this view, marriage might by its nature be indissoluble (irreversible) if, once a person makes a gift of self to another, that gift cannot, for logical reasons, be taken back or returned. It would follow that sex in a union planned in advance to be temporary is impermissible.

Suppose that in every sexual interaction between two people, they must have the sincere intention of satisfying each other, and must actually try to do so; otherwise at least one person would be merely using the other. In a one-night affair, we have no guarantee that we will ever have a later chance to erase an inequality or injustice that arises in the sexual exchange, say, if one person is satisfied but not the other. Hence, in a single sexual interaction we must ensure that no injustice occurs. Now we can construct another Kantian argument against the permissibility of casual, uncommitted sex. Perhaps Kant reasoned that the achievement of equality in one casual sexual encounter is unlikely, given the selfishness of human nature; in a brief affair, deception and manipulation are too tempting or easy. Given our natures, no guarantee of full reciprocity or equality in a night exists; that can be achieved only in the long stream of an open-ended and indefinite marriage. For Kant, then, it misses the point to argue that we should aim, when having casual sex, for equality in a single sexual encounter *because* we will have no chance to set things straight. For that we will have no chance to remedy a failure that is likely to occur is precisely the reason for not having casual sex at all. Construed in this way, Kant's argument would turn on the claim that human nature cannot be trusted to pledge and then attain sexual reciprocity in a union temporally limited in advance.

CONTEMPORARY KANTIANS

We have already come across Kantian themes in twentieth-century Catholic sexual philosophy (Pope Paul VI and Karol Wojtyla). In addition, both contemporary sexual liberals and secular sexual conservatives have fashioned their own brands of sexual ethics, each camp drawing on its preferred strand in the complex fabric that comprises Kant's sexual philosophy.

Libertarian sexual ethics. Kant's notion of marriage, in which a person obtains rights over a person and their genitals in exchange for granting the same rights of access to oneself, looks like a business deal that itself reduces the spouses to objects.[39] Perhaps the best answer to this objection is that the voluntary agreement of the spouses to their marital arrangement is sufficient to eliminate mere use. But if Kant were to emphasize for moral purposes the voluntary nature of the exchange, he would be relying mostly on the contract *per se*, and not its content, to justify marital sex. This is precisely the move made by some moral libertarians: the existence of a free and informed contract between the persons is what counts, and it is up to them to work out the particular content of their sexual agreement.[40]

According to this libertarian sexual ethic, consent is both necessary and (absent harm to third parties) sufficient for sexual activity to be morally permissible. Without consent (say, activity that occurs through force or deception or one person's mental impairment), one person would be using the other, taking advantage, or otherwise violating the personhood of the other. The paradigmatically wrong sexual act for the libertarian is, therefore, not bestiality or homosexual anal penetration (as in Aquinas), but rape of any kind, in which the absence of consent makes the mere use obvious. With consent, no matter what the parties decide to do together, be it homosexual oral sex or heterosexual petting, is unobjectionable. The reasoning is that as long as the persons involved are participating voluntarily, they are not *merely* using each other for their own purposes; the free and informed consent of each to the acts that occur is sufficient to eliminate mere use and thus to make sexual activity, of whatever flavor, permissible. When participation is voluntary, each person is respecting the other as a mature agent capable of making a choice about his or her ends. Since the persons themselves decide on the content of their contract, the acquisition of the right of bodily access can be temporary and reversible, and it can occur between persons of the same sex.

Conservative sexual philosophy. In the writings of the legal scholar John Finnis, we find a negative assessment of both masturbation and homosexuality, on the grounds that these modes of sexuality are nonmarital.[41] Finnis claims that there are morally worthless sexual acts in which "one's body is treated as instrumental for the securing of the experiential satisfaction of the conscious self," thereby explaining how it might be possible, after all, for a person to use himself or treat herself as an object during solitary masturbation. In masturbating, or in a man's being anally penetrated by another man, Finnis claims, the body is just a tool of satisfaction and, as a result, one undergoes "disintegration." "One's choosing self [becomes] the quasi-slave of the experiencing self which is demanding gratification." But, for Finnis, the worthlessness and disintegration attaching to masturbation and homosexuality attach to "all extramarital sexual gratification."

The question arises here: what is special about marital sex that allows it to avoid promoting disintegration? Finnis replies that worthlessness and disintegration attach to masturbation and homosexuality in virtue of the fact that in these activities "one's conduct is not the actualizing and experiencing of a real common good." Marriage, on the other hand,

> with its double blessing—procreation and friendship—is a real common good... that can be both actualized and experienced in the orgasmic union of the reproductive organs of a man and a woman united in commitment to that good.

But what if the friends do have a common good, their friendship as constituted by shared valuable projects, the same way a married couple has the common good that is their marriage and its shared projects? If "their friendship is not marital," Finnis replies, "activation of their reproductive organs cannot be, in reality, an... actualization of their friendship's common good." Finnis tries to explain this claim, and in doing so reveals the crux of his sexual philosophy:

> the common good of friends who are not and cannot be married (man and man, man and boy, woman and woman) has nothing to do with their having children by each other, and their reproductive organs cannot make them a biological (and therefore a personal) unit.

We now have an answer to the question we posed to Kant: why must marriage, and therefore sex, be heterosexual? It is because only the heterosexual act of coitus allows the spouses to become a genuine unity. Finnis begins with the Kantian intuition that sexual activity involves treating the body instrumentally, and he concludes with the Kantian view that sex in marriage avoids disintegrity since the couple becomes a unit: "the orgasmic union of the reproductive organs of husband and wife really unites them biologically." Perhaps Finnis's point here helps us to understand Gilbert Meilaender's view (see the Introduction) that heterosexual coitus is "the act in which human beings are present most fully and give themselves most completely to another." If Finnis and Meilaender are right, homosexual activity cannot create the genuine unity between the spouses that is required for overcoming the essentially manipulative or instrumental nature of sexual interaction. But the sexual metaphysics presupposed here, that a genuine biological unity is brought about by heterosexual orgasmic sex, is obscure.

The real problem with Finnis's view might lie elsewhere. Given the pluralism of sexual motives, why must we employ our sexual organs to achieve the single common good of procreation? And why must the burden of achieving a common good, if it is a valuable good, be centered on procreative activity, whether inside or outside marriage? Friends can "actualize" their common good in many ways, and the fact that they also have sexual relations with each other that are not part of their freely chosen valu-

able common good seems not to be a moral defect of their friendship or their sexual activity (see Chapter Seven).

UTILITARIANISM

It seems likely that the John Stuart Mill who wrote *On Liberty*
(1859) would have defended, on general utilitarian grounds, something similar to libertarian sexual ethics, proposing that the consent of the participating parties is morally sufficient as long as
significant harm to third parties is avoided. Do as you will in
your "experiments of living,"[42] he might have said; neither public opinion nor the law should be brought to bear on private, consensual sexual activity unless, say, violations of "distinct and as-
signable" duties occur.[43] Of course, Kantians and Thomists agree
that the interests of third parties and of society might be wrongly
affected by sexual activity; this is an important moral consideration for them even if the acts occurring between two persons
embody genuine respect for both and is fully natural. But, for
Mill and other utilitarians, possible harmful effects on third parties and society in general are the only considerations to be taken
into account in reaching moral judgments about behavior. Acts
in general, and sexual acts in particular, are to be evaluated morally only by asking whether they do more good than bad for all
affected.[44]

The difficult question concerns which of the ubiquitous effects on third parties or society are significantly harmful. Is a
person harmed by becoming nauseous when noticing two people,
either heterosexual or homosexual, kiss (or engage in intercourse)
in public? Is a spouse harmed by the adultery of his or her spouse
about which he or she knows nothing? Does the very fabric of
society require that strict sexual morality be enforced by either
the law or by public pressure? This area of social and political
philosophy has been especially contentious, since decisions about
"harm" have profound implications.[45] A narrow notion of harm
yields a permissive (sexual and nonsexual) ethic and provides

little justification for using the criminal law to interfere with sexual behavior; a broad notion of harm implies the opposite. In the nineteenth century, Mill and James Fitzjames Stephen (1829-1894) squared off against each other over the value and extent of individual freedom.[46] In the mid-twentieth century, the debate was revived by Lord Patrick Devlin and the British philosopher of law H. L. A. Hart.[47] Utilitarian sexual ethics can, in any event, be restrictive *or* permissive, depending on the truth of empirical assertions about the consequences of sexual behavior, or about the consequences of trying to prevent sexual behaviors. In addition to depending on contestable notions of well-being, the empirical claims underlying utilitarian judgments are difficult to verify.

For example, it might be argued on utilitarian grounds that the general use of contraception be encouraged, since that would serve to reduce population pressure. But the widespread use of contraception likely has other effects, perhaps promoting adultery, or damaging the bodies of those who use them, so that determining whether the good effects outweigh the bad effects, and deciding which effects, exactly, are the "bad" ones, is difficult. It might also be argued, on utilitarian grounds, that premarital sexual activity among young people ought to be discouraged, for their own sake as well as for the sake of the larger community. The empirical claims underlying such a judgment are notoriously controversial: can a connection between clothing or music and detrimental or unhealthy sexual behavior among teenagers be established? Similar problems plague the claim that the existence of pornography helps maintain a social environment inimical to the well-being of women. For some, these problems make the utilitarian approach nearly unmanageable.

Nevertheless, a case can be made that a *prima facie* right to engage in sexual activity (and all similar freedoms) can be derived from Mill's utilitarianism. Utilitarian reasons for a right to engage in sex surely exist: the value of pleasure *per se* and its role in the good and happy life, and the contribution shared pleasure makes to the intimacy and hence value of our personal relationships.[48] In this way, private, consensual sexual activity creates much good and, if harm to third parties is avoided, it creates no bad, and on this score would be blessed by utilitarianism.

SADOMASOCHISM

Sadomasochism has long been scorned by moralists. But in the absence of harm to third parties, is not the fact that two adults voluntarily engage in a sadomasochistic sexual act together sufficient for their activity to be morally permissible? For the Thomist, as we have seen, the answer is "no," at least because the act might be unnatural. Recall that in the category of mortal sins, Aquinas included "rather beastly and monstrous techniques."[49] And for others in the sexually conservative tradition, the answer is also "no"; perhaps such sexuality involves a "disintegration" of both persons, since they are employing their bodies for pure pleasure (and pain). Furthermore, a moral paternalist would claim that even when a sexual act is not harmful to third parties, it might be harmful to one or both participants, and it is morally wrong for a person x to harm another person y, or for y to allow x to harm y, despite the voluntary participation of both parties. The moral paternalist does not accept the libertarian *volenti* maxim: that to which one consents does not count as harm.[50] This view need not be religiously inspired, and it shows that there is room within Kantian and utilitarian frameworks to argue about the sufficiency of consent.

A Kantian might argue, for example, that in sadomasochistic sexual activity the "top" exhibits disrespect for the personhood of the "bottom," even when their chosen activity is perfectly consensual; humiliating and demeaning attitudes retain their character even when consent is present.[51] The utilitarian might conclude that such activity in the long run does more harm than good, both to the parties and society, as in some utilitarian arguments against active, doctor-assisted euthanasia, say, the procedures of Jack Kevorkian. According to other Kantians and utilitarians, however, sadomasochism can be engaged in affectionately, while fully respecting one's sexual partner, and without harm being done to nonparticipants. In the sadomasochist subculture, a slap to the face or the tush is often spoken of as one way a top can express love.[52] And the bottom makes "a total gift of self [that] requires... strength and courage,"[53] a phrase reminiscent of Wojtyla's philosophy of love.[54]

Some lesbian sadomasochists derive sexual pleasure from pornographic depictions of their preferred activity, so they oppose the censorship of pornography. Here is a reply to these lesbians:

> To the extent that pornography both maintains a normative order that legitimizes the eroticization of violence, and to the extent that it constitutes even a remote cause of violent, nonconsensual, nondesired sex, the "rights" of such adherents to acquire pornographic products important for their sexual gratification must take second place.... Such rights to pleasure must surely be subordinated to the more fundamental right to be free from serious harm.[55]

The argument is highly qualified. It does not state that pornography does legitimize violence against women, and it supposes only that pornography might be a remote cause of rape. The authors do claim, however, that "to the extent" these things are true, that is enough warrant for restricting or censoring pornography. Because the argument is so qualified, deciding which side is more persuasive does not turn on whether we grant to the lesbians a literal "right" to sexual pleasure. Simply recognizing that sexual pleasure is an important human good yields the nearly unresolvable dilemma between advancing or protecting the good of some people and the good of others. At least, the claim in the passage that the lesbians' pleasure "surely" takes a back seat is an overstatement. Many would give it more weight, while acknowledging that choosing between these two goods would be an agonizing exercise in casuistry.

Feminists differ greatly in their moral and political assessment of consensual sadomasochism engaged in by either heterosexual or lesbian couples.[56] Indeed, the debate over both pornography and sadomasochism has been, and continues to be, especially heated among feminists.[57] About lesbian sadomasochism in particular, Claudia Card says, on the positive side, that its "participants generally wish each other well and respect each other's choices." But Card also worries about such activities: "the only things distinguishing the behavior of [a top] from battery and other abuse may be the motivations of the parties and the consent of the [bottom]"[58]—and, for Card, neither the consent nor the motivation (e.g., to achieve sexual pleasure) seems to turn battery and abuse into anything other or better than battery and abuse. But what more could we want in distinguishing respectful sadomasochism from battery, other than the consent to experience mutual sexual and emotional pleasure? To say that consent is not enough, that something else is required, is to jeopardize all unconventional sex, not just sadomasochism.

LOVE

Alan Goldman has suggested that sexual partners, even if they are persons of the same sex or not married, can satisfy Kant's Second Formulation:

> Even in an act which by its nature "objectifies" the other, one recognizes a partner as a subject with demands and desires by yielding to those desires, by allowing oneself to be a sexual object as well, by giving pleasure or ensuring that the pleasures of the act are mutual.[59]

But Goldman's expression, "allowing oneself to be a sexual object," again suggests the question of whether the presence of consent to be used as an object by another sexually really guarantees that one is not merely being used as an object. Two people allowing themselves to be used as sexual objects by the other might multiply, not reduce, the instrumentality of their relationship. Similarly, Michael Ruse thinks that "by yielding oneself [to another], body and soul, one shows respect for the other as an end."[60] That might be true. In satisfying your desires, I treat you and your goals as intrinsically valuable; in offering myself to you, I recognize your personhood. But the claim has the same air of paradox. In giving myself to you, in devoting myself to your goals, am I not treating myself as a means or object for your benefit? Something else seems required, beyond yielding, for sexual acts to be morally permissible.

One straightforward account of the ingredient that is required beyond consent has recommended itself to many people. If the quest for sexual pleasure threatens the self's wholeness (Finnis), the other's personhood (Kant, John Paul II), and society's viability (Devlin); if it insults the human spirit (Augustine), the natural order of things, and God (Aquinas); then perhaps love—be it a dose of *agape* or *caritas* or an uplifting sort of *eros*—is the missing ingredient required for sexual relations to be licit. The idea that love, benevolence, or some other altruistic attitude is the required ingredient that prevents sex from being morally pernicious is very popular, even if vociferously rejected by libertarians. This idea is part of the standard picture of relationships described above (see Introduction)—a man and a woman fall in love, get married, engage in sexual activity, and build a family and a domestic life together, in which their early, passionate, romantic love deepens into genuine care and concern for each other. But the idea that love is the ingredient that makes sexual activity psychologically and morally wholesome and pleasing to both God and society has immediate and radical application to the use of contraception, sadomasochistic relationships, and homosexual marriage.

Love as the magical ingredient makes defending the use of contraception relatively easy: sexual acts, including those that are deliberately nonprocreative, express and bolster the love spouses have for each other. But as soon as contraceptive sexuality is blessed when it occurs within a loving relationship, a similar advantage accrues to other nonprocreative sexuality. Sadomasochism might genuinely express love or be carried out by a loving couple; at least, whether it can seems to be an empirical question, as long as we have a workable operational definition of "love." What kind of domestic arrangement do these unusual sexual partners have? Is it much different, aside from their sadomasochistic sex, from the marriage of Ozzie and Harriet, Archie and Edith, the Huxtables, or Lord Peter and Harriet? Similar reasoning can be employed to justify gay and lesbian sex when it occurs in a loving, monogamous relationship or marriage. "As gay men, we do not believe our love is of any less magnitude or importance than that of any other couples in a long-term committed relationship. For that reason we want the legal recognition of our Holy Union."[61]

Given the rhetorical and logical power of appeals to love to justify nonprocreative and nontraditional sexual arrangements, it makes sense that the Church has refused (officially) to budge on the question of the impermissibility of the use of contraceptive devices in heterosexual marital activity; for conceding that procreation might be curtailed in order that sexual acts better express and cement the love that the spouses have for each other is to begin to glide down a slippery slope at the bottom of which is homosexual marriage.

CHAPTER FOUR

SEXUAL POLITICS

Forget the realities of women's sexual/economic situation. When women express our free will, we spread our legs for a camera.

—Catharine MacKinnon, *Feminism Unmodified*

Free and genuine consent is widely recognized to be a necessary condition not only for the moral goodness of sexual activity but for the permissibility of most other activities as well. The libertarian thinks that freely given consent is also sufficient, in the absence of harm to third parties. Whether consent is only necessary or also sufficient, any moral principle that relies on consent to make moral distinctions among different sexual events presupposes that we have a clear understanding of consent—what it is, how to recognize it, and how to distinguish the real thing from the bogus.

For example, does the presence of *any* kind of pressure put on one person by another amount to coercion that invalidates or negates consent, so that the subsequent activity, be it sexual or nonsexual, is morally tainted? Depending on the example we have in mind, it might be reasonable to say either that some pressures do not count as coercion at all (the husband who nags his wife for sex) or that some pressures are coercive but not an unfair or otherwise morally objectionable kind of coercion (a woman who marries in part for economic reasons). But these examples are controversial, and they show that how we understand the notions of the voluntary and the involuntary will influence our particular judgments about sexual interactions and arrangements— hence the debate about prostitution. Are some (or all) prostitutes ex-

posed to unfair economic pressure? Do men who pay the prostitute money to perform a sexual act coerce her, or is she coerced
by the structure of society? Are these objectionable sorts of coercion?

PEDOPHILIA

Sexual activity between an adult and a child, what some call
"intergenerational" sex, is considered morally wrong in many
cultures. The arguments against it are two-fold. First, sex between
an adult and a child is physically and psychologically harmful to
the child. Second, intergenerational sex violates canons of consent. Children are not able to consent to sexual activity the same
way they are not able to consent to surgery or to what school they
attend; in these areas parents are empowered to decide for them.
The apparent verbal agreement of the child, when it exists, cannot be taken at face value. The point is not that we should paternalistically worry that the child might not make a wise selection
of partner or act, but that children are not ordinarily equipped to
give or withhold consent to begin with. Defenders of intergenerational sex reply that depending on the age of the child and the
acts performed, sexual activity need not be physically harmful,
and it is psychologically harmful only to the extent that their parents and society condemn it. After all, there are cultures that practice ritualized homosexual intergenerational sex, and the children
seem not to be harmed in any way by it.[1] Further, children are
able to consent to sexual activity the same way they are able to
give consent, or withhold it, to what they eat, wear, or to which
movie their parents take them: "any child old enough to decide
whether or not she or he wants to eat spinach, play with trucks or
wear shoes is old enough to decide whether or not she or he wants
to run around naked in the sun, masturbate, sit in somebody's lap
or engage in sexual activity."[2] Finally, we do many things to and
with children to which they do not consent, but which they obviously enjoy. So consent may not always be a requirement of per-

missible sex at least, say, when the child has expressed a credible desire for the activity. Whether children of a given age are able to give meaningful consent to sex, and whether their inability to do so amounts to a crucial objection to intergenerational sex, depends, in part, on what we take the significance of sex to be—whether sex is more like eating pizza or contributing to the Grand Design—and, in part, on how we understand and weigh consent.

Perhaps we patronize children by discounting their interest in engaging in sex among themselves or with adults; maybe children have *bona fide* sexual needs that should be attended to by those who are concerned for their well-being; and perhaps children express real desire for sexual activity with adults, even if this desire is not fully formed and is shown in ambiguous ways. To object to adults' attempting to satisfy the inchoate sexual desires and sexual curiosity of children by claiming that the desires children express are not (yet) their own desires sounds convincing—until we ask, When is it ever the case, not only for developing children but also for adult women and men, that one's desires are "one's own"? The legal scholar Ruth Colker worries that the sexuality expressed and exhibited by adult women, which surely feels to them to be their own sexuality, is not "authentic," not really their own. Women's genuine sexuality, on her view, can be known only after women "peel away" all the layers of the patriarchal "social influences" that "limit [their] freedom."[3] Whereas Colker views authentic sexuality as lying beneath the construction of women's sexuality by an oppressive, sexist culture, as something that has not been imposed on women by outside forces, John Stuart Mill thinks that social factors play an unavoidable and benign role in the genesis of our genuine natures:

> A person whose desires and impulses are his own—are the expression of his own nature, as it has been developed and modified by his own culture—is said to have a character. One whose desires and impulses are not his own has no character, no more than a steam engine has a character.[4]

The problem of how to distinguish sexual desires that are our own from those that are not will arise several times in this chapter.

PROSTITUTION AND MARRIAGE

Whether prostitution is morally wrong also in part depends on our view of the significance of sexuality. If sexual activity is holy or inextricably tied with our spiritual being, it seems reasonable to conclude that sexual activity should not be bought or sold. What would also be morally suspicious, on such an account of sex, would be the practice, common both throughout history and in our society, of marrying, and as a result engaging in sexual activity with one's spouse, for economic or social reasons. But if sexuality does not have this profound significance—if providing sexual services to strangers can be characterized as being similar to conducting any menial service activity for strangers (filling out tax forms, taking deposits and cashing checks in a bank, performing a professional massage, helping a customer try on shoes)—then prostitution may be, on this score at least, faultless. Further, we might add to Richard Posner's claim, that masturbation and homosexuality are nature's ways of compensating the losers in the competition among males for females (Chapter Three), that prostitution is one of society's ways of smoothing out the rough edges of the same competition. Or suppose that sexuality is a "basic human need."[5] If having sex is like eating, satisfying a natural and important need, then this fact might vindicate prostitution. It would not justify rape, as if we had full freedom to take a person's sexuality by force, at least because we can live, even if unhappily, without sex (while we cannot live without food). Thus, those who cannot obtain sexual satisfaction otherwise than through prostitution should not be condemned for buying it, and those who provide this service are equally blameless—as long as their transaction is entered into by both parties with freely given, genuine consent.[6] Could that be true? Is the prostitute compelled unfairly by a need for money? Is the client compelled unfairly by sexual desires or needs he cannot otherwise satisfy?[7]

The British philosopher Bertrand Russell (1872-1970) wrote, back in the 1920s, that

> The intrusion of the economic motive into sex is always... disastrous. Sexual relations should be a mutual delight, entered into solely from the spontaneous impulse of both parties.[8]

Russell suggests that if prostitution is not morally wrong, it is at least not an ideal form of sexuality; Russell's "should be" is normative, but not necessarily moral. But to this postulate of sexual philosophy, Russell adds a Kantian moral rule:

> Morality in sexual relations... consists essentially of respect for the other person, and unwillingness to use that person solely as a means of personal gratification without regard to his or her desires.

In prostitution, the client uses the prostitute for his own selfish sexual pleasure, and perhaps she, too, uses the client and manipulates his sexual needs to extract money from him. Russell, in applying his Kantian rule, decided that "prostitution sins against this principle"[9] of respect.

The libertarian philosopher Igor Primoratz has replied to Russell that prostitution "does not offend against the principle of respect for human beings" as long as prostitution "is free from coercion and fraud."[10] Primoratz's reason for rejecting the way Russell applies his Kantian rule to prostitution should be familiar enough by now (see Chapter Three): "informed and freely given consent absolves the relation of any such charge."[11] Russell reflected, at the same time, on the sexual activity of married couples and concluded that much of this sex *also* sinned against his principle: "the total amount of undesired sex endured by women is probably greater in marriage than in prostitution."[12] This suggests that Russell was not impugning the moral power of consent to justify sexual activity, but was insisting, instead, on a more critical account of genuine consent.

The implication of Russell's view of marriage, as involving sexual relations tarnished by an "economic motive," is that social changes are needed to allow genuine consent to occur: marriage by women for economic reasons must be socially engineered out of existence. The Marxist philosopher Friedrich Engels (1820-1895) had earlier reached the same conclusion. Engels proposed that whatever occurs among persons in their love, marriage, and sexual relationships is fine, if their choices are made freely, and this meant, for Engels, that economic and political domination must be absent from their lives:

> Full freedom of marriage can... only be generally established when the abolition of capitalist production and of the property relations created by it has removed all the accompanying economic considerations.... For then there is no other motive left except mutual inclination.[13]

The idea that personal relationships should be governed only by Engelian "mutual inclination" or Russellian "spontaneous impulse" was a long time coming. Social and religious imperatives, economic and other pragmatic considerations, and the wishes of parents directed the course of marriage (see Chapter Seven). Nowadays the idea is popular in the West, that autonomous agents can freely choose their partners on the basis of individual preference or inclination, even if the reality of our arrangements does not fully match this expectation.[14]

Engels's and Russell's idea is, arguably, fundamentally sound: ideally consensual participation in sex requires substantial economic and social equality between the persons involved. If some groups (blue-collar workers, women, children, blacks, and other minority persons) have less economic and social power than others, their members will be relatively more exposed to sexual coercion, among other kinds. In particular, a society that contains poverty and deprivation is one in which some people are exposed to obvious economic pressure, even as it appears that they freely consent to what they do. And if there is no substantial opportunity for employment outside the sex industry, prostitutes and others working in this industry might be said to be socially compelled into their vocations.[15] We can therefore understand why Andrea Dworkin claims that in the prostitution relationship, the man has all the power: "he pays money, he does what he wants" to her.[16] But others have denied that this is always or mostly the case; some prostitutes set strict limits and, in virtue of their experience and knowledge, control the men who come to them.[17] What divides the two classes of prostitutes may be their state of economic need and their education and intelligence. If so, to conclude that all women (and men) who engage in prostitution, either now or in a more egalitarian future society, do not or would never genuinely consent because they have economic motives, is implausible. The "intrusion" of money as a reason to engage in sex instead of the plain desire for sensual delight does not always destroy consent or make sexual activity morally corrupt, just as the presence of a wide variety of other motives to engage in sex (wanting to have a child, needing the exercise, or getting revenge) does not always destroy consent.

Russell's observation about sexual coercion in marriage was prophetical; he was ahead of his time. In objecting to the economic pressure experienced by women for acquiescing to the sexual demands of their husbands, Russell was voicing something close to Robin Morgan's feminist definition of rape:

Rape exists any time sexual intercourse occurs when it has not been initiated by the woman, out of her own genuine affection and desire.... How many millions of times have women had sex "willingly" with men they didn't want to have sex with?... How many times have women

> wished just to sleep instead or read or watch the Late
> Show? . . . Most of the decently married bedrooms across
> America are settings for nightly rape.[18]

The woman who is nagged into engaging in sexual activity by her husband, and does so when she would prefer not to, is worrying that if she says "no" to him too often or at all, he will abandon her—an abandonment that she fears for economic, social, and psychological reasons. Posner has claimed, "Marital rape may be uncommon, since few wives will refuse their husband's demand for sexual intercourse."[19] But Posner overlooks Morgan's point: the fact that wives do not refuse the sexual *demands* made by their husbands is evidence that this marital sex *is*, rather than is *not*, rape. By contrast, the man who gives in (or not) to his wife's nagging him for sex, when he would prefer to watch television, has less (if any) fear of being abandoned as a result of refusing. (The content of the "marriage debt" in patriarchal society is that women owe sex to their husbands, but not *vice versa*.) Women will be free to leave men, and to refuse them sex if they want to, only when they are the economic and social equals of men.

Thus sexual activity in marriage is often rape because women are financially compelled to give in. Further, women's sexuality, even their felt desires to engage in sexual activity with their lovers or husbands, may not be, as Colker suggested, "their own" but the result of oppressive social influences. As Sandra Harding says, "There can never be objectively consensual [sexual] relations between members of oppressor and oppressed groups."[20] Rape, according to Morgan, can be avoided in heterosexual relations only when the sexual activity is "initiated by the woman, out of her own... desire." But given the culture of male dominance in which heterosexual activity occurs, when would it ever be the case that a woman knows what "her own" desires are, let alone having her own desires? This would be true even if a woman has a well-paying job and economic security. Her sexual freedom or "liberation" in a sexist society, the freedom to behave sexually as if she were men, is a sham. The economic solution to women's sexual plight must be supplemented with more extreme measures of social engineering.

But instead of saying, with Morgan, that in virtue of economic or other pressures women are routinely raped by their husbands, we could make a less dramatic point, in agreement with Posner, that women do consent to this sex, and the pressure they accede to does not amount to coercion; yet because they do not always genuinely desire this sexual activity they are *harmed* by it. This argument has been advanced by the legal scholar Robin West. A woman might consent to undesired sex, according to West, because she and her children are financially dependent on a man; or she does not want to experience the "foul humor," anger, or abuse that might result from refusal; or she has sex with him in order to gain protection from the unwanted advances of other, "more dangerous" men; or she has sex with him because she thinks it is her duty or "lot in life" or because of "peer expectations."[21] West does not take Morgan's route of saying that in these cases the pressure felt by women is coercion and the sexual acts are rapes because the women do not participate "willingly." West claims, to the contrary, that a woman's participation in sexual activity in these situations is both consensual and, given her situation, rational. Nevertheless, women's participation in undesired sex harms them: it damages "their sense of selfhood"; they "sustain injuries to their capacities for self-assertion"; they "injure their sense of self-*possession*"; "they injure their sense of autonomy"; and they injure "their sense of integrity." West's view has the advantage of refusing to see ordinary marital sex as rape; still, she alerts us to deep problems in heterosexual relationships that might require, to be overcome, a good deal of social engineering. The personal, as we learned from feminism, is the political.

COMPULSORY HETEROSEXUALITY

Adrienne Rich once asked this beguiling question:

> If women are the earliest sources of emotional caring and physical nurture for both female and male children, it would seem logical... to pose the following questions: whether the search for love and tenderness in both sexes does not originally lead toward women; *why in fact women would ever redirect that search.*[22]

If women are the earliest and most reliable love-objects for both men and women, that boys become heterosexual men who seek bonds with women is not surprising; but it is surprising that girls become heterosexual women, erotically attached not to other women, their mother-substitutes, but to men. Or suppose that infants are born polysexual, not having any inborn leaning toward or preference for any particular sexual acts or objects, but just those capable of triggering the sexual pleasure system. In either case, it would not be homosexuality that required explanation, but also heterosexuality.[23] In Chapter Two, we more-or-less assumed that heterosexual desire was natural, and we wondered whether reasons existed for thinking that homosexual desire, too, was natural. But now we must consider the possibility, with Rich, that it is the failure of women to be homosexual that requires explanation. At the very least, we are forced to provide explanations of both homosexuality and heterosexuality.

Rich answers her question by invoking the socialization of our sexuality. Indeed, Rich asserts dramatically the depth of the social coercion that infects personal feelings, attitudes, and relationships. She claims, as did Ti-Grace Atkinson before her (see Introduction), that heterosexuality is a "man-made institution" that is "forcibly and subliminally imposed on women" and "designed to keep [them] within a male sexual purlieu."[24] Women by their natural history, having been mothered by women, would, if left to their own resources, gravitate toward women as providers of love. Lesbianism, we might say, is the "authentic" female sexuality Colker was searching for, hidden beneath layers of women's socialization into compulsory heterosexuality. Their heterosexual desires are not their own. (I wonder, though, whether compulsory heterosexuality is merely like compulsory showering. We are culturally imposed on to shower, on pain of being ostracized.)

Other feminists also emphasize the deep conditioning of women's sexuality. According to Andrea Dworkin, much of the sexual activity women engage in with men involves physical and psychological surrender to the man's power. Even in "normal" intercourse, when forcible rape is absent, women are possessed by a man who owns her. Women, for their part, experience this possession as "deeply erotic," assuming that what feels natural to them is indeed their own authentic sexuality. Remaining heterosexual, then, is "collaboration," against their interests as women, with their oppressors.[25] The feminist philosopher Christine Overall seems to hold out some hope for heterosexuality:

> There is an important sense in which a woman can genuinely and even sanely choose to be heterosexual, although the conditions and opportunities for that choice may be fairly rare. Beyond the claim that... heterosexuality is coerced (which seems true in regard to the heterosexual institution as a whole) there is [another] possibility: that heterosexuality is or can be chosen, even—or especially!—by feminists.[26]

This is small consolation for the millions of women who are powerless to resist the indoctrination into heterosexuality. The socialization is so thick that chances to escape it by peeling off the layers of compulsory heterosexuality are "rare."

In order to save women from the unfairness and oppression of compulsory heterosexuality, Ti-Grace Atkinson champions a biomedical technology of extrauterine prenatal life.[27] Only when human reproduction is purely mechanical will women be able to escape compulsory heterosexuality. To make sure women never have to depend on men economically, another contemporary feminist, Shulamith Firestone, also insists on fully artificial reproduction.[28] Never again would a woman have to interrupt her career or take a dead-end job just because she wants to become pregnant. And since sexual "intercourse is the pure, sterile, formal expression of men's contempt for women," it is a godsend for Andrea Dworkin that technology is bringing it about that "intercourse is not necessary to existence anymore."[29] Hence the sexual liberation of women, or the moral refurbishment of heterosexual relations, requires biological equality. It follows that either men must be bioengineered to be able to get pregnant or women must be relieved of that burden, or both. The theologian Gilbert Meilaender worries, about such proposals, that fully artificial reproduction

> may be an exercise of freedom that eliminates something fundamentally human from the act of begetting: the way in which (as with the animals) it involves our bodies, not just our minds.[30]

The feminist proposal to eliminate the body (both male and female) from human reproduction is to embrace a Cartesian dualism of mind/soul and matter/body and to insist, as did Augustine, on the inferiority of the flesh whose ways must be overcome by the will (through science). Meilaender suggests that such an Augustinian victory of mind over flesh through the artificial reproduction of the species would make us less human, or would destroy our humanity altogether.

The views of Morgan, Rich, and Dworkin on coercion seem extreme, but other writers find value in similar accounts of coercion. For example, the social psychologists Charlene Muehlenhard and Jennifer Schrag provide a list of ways "women are coerced into having unwanted sexual intercourse" that are "more subtle" than being violently raped.[31] Among these are compulsory heterosexuality, "discrimination against lesbians" (which compels women into sexual relationships with men), "status coercion" (women are coerced into sex or marriage by a man's fame, occupation, or money),[32] and verbal pressure (the husband who badgers his wife for sex). Similarly, Mary Koss's category "sexually coercive men" includes those who obtain sex "after continual discussions" or by false avowals of love.[33]

Such claims are difficult to evaluate, likely because all claims about consent are ultimately value-laden.[34] Still, we might be able to arrive at some tentative conclusions in a wide variety of cases. Consider these four possible scenarios in heterosexual relationships:

(1) A man gets a woman to go to bed with him, having promised or given her a diamond;
(2) A man gets a woman to go to bed with him, having promised or given her a stone she was led to believe, falsely, was a diamond;
(3) A man gets a woman to go to bed with him through false avowals of love and devotion; and
(4) A man gets a woman to go to bed with him by announcing that their non-marital relationship will be over if she does not.

Which of these cases involves unfair coercion? Which involves, instead, unobjectionable pressure?

In case (1), we might want to say that the woman freely and knowingly made a deal, and that as long as consent is sufficient to justify sexual activity, we cannot object to his offer, her acceptance of it, and their subsequent sexual activity. Matters would be different, however, were the woman homeless or barely making it, financially, from day to day. Then their sexual arrangement, if it was made possible only by the woman's vulnerability, looks like exploitation. In this respect, not much difference would exist between cases (1) and (4), *if* the woman in case (4) was extremely needy. If so, the man's ultimatum appears to be exploitation. But if the woman has a base (even if low) level of economic security, what Jeffrie Murphy says about such cases seems reasonable:

> [I]t is sometimes permissible... morally... to obtain sex by the use of threats and offers. "Have sex with me or I will find another girlfriend" strikes me... as a morally permissible threat, and "Have sex with me and I will marry you" strikes me... as a morally permissible offer. We negotiate our way through most of life with schemes of threats and offers.... I see no reason why the realm of sexuality should be utterly insulated from this normal way of being human.[35]

In case (2), a deal was struck based on an attractive offer, but the man did not keep, indeed never intended to keep, his part of the bargain. Not even the libertarian would condone the use of deception, since lies of this sort negate consent. However, notice that in Plato's *Symposium* (184e), Pausanias asserts that if the pursued person y gives in to the pursuer's, x's, sexual desire *because* y believes (falsely) that x is rich, y is "disgraced" in showing himself or herself to be a shallow person attracted to superficial properties, willing to engage in sex just for a share of x's wealth. About the third case, one of Koss's examples of "sexual coercion," we might say that the woman should have known better (her mother probably told her repeatedly that men's declarations of love should not be taken seriously) or should have conducted herself more cautiously. Whether and to what extent this piece of deception on the part of the man is blameworthy depends, in part, on a moral judgment about the woman's own responsibility for knowing certain things about men and sex.[36]

PORNOGRAPHY

In order to determine, among other things, what effects pornography has on heterosexual relationships, the sociologist Diana Russell asked nine hundred women in the San Francisco area this question: "Have you ever been upset by anyone trying to get you to do what they'd seen in pornographic pictures, movies, or books?" In effect, Russell is seeking empirical confirmation of Robin Morgan's thesis (see Introduction) that pornography is the theory, rape (in marriage, too) is the practice. Morgan had claimed that women sense "pressure... from their boyfriends or husbands to perform sexually in ever more objectified and objectifying fashion as urged by porn movies and magazines."[37] Ten percent of the women answered "yes" to Russell's question.[38] In terms of finding support for Morgan's thesis, it is not clear whether we should emphasize that *only* 10% answered "yes" or that a *full* 10% answered "yes."

In any event, because husbands often try to persuade their wives to do things in bed, a wife has difficulty knowing whether any particular attempt had been encouraged by his looking at pornography.[39] If so, we cannot conclude from Russell's data that pornography harms relationships. Do men nag more frequently now than they did twenty-five years ago for competent fellatio? Perhaps they rely on pornography as part of a persuasive argument (their badgering), rather than having been incited by pornography, or they would request the act anyway and drag in pornography as a last-ditch effort to put together a case. But, alternatively, perhaps some men are too timid to ask directly for what they desire and use pornography as a ploy, leaving *Playboy* or *Penthouse* on the television under her *Vogue* or *Cosmopolitan*. Russell presents no data indicating that these uses of pornography are unlikely, but if they are common ways men use pornography to get their wives or lovers to vary their sexual activity, it cannot be concluded on the basis of Russell's study that pornography is responsible for any harmful effects on women. Further, to object to pornography on the grounds that it encourages husbands to pressure their wives into engaging in sexual activities presupposes that it is wrong for men to exert such pressure or that women have a right not be pressured. This objection to pornography is therefore consistent with Morgan's definition of rape, as any sex not initiated by the woman out of her own desire. But if, as many have observed,[40] women are socially trained to be sexually passive, then the badgering of husbands might be seen, in part, as helping their wives by attempting to persuade them to overcome their sexual inhibitions.

The major problem regarding pornography, however, might not be that pornography helps men apply pressure on women to engage in unwanted or undesired sexual activity, but that the women (and the men?) who are paid to pose or model for nude pictures or to engage in sexual activity in front of a camera or video recorder are unfairly coerced to do so. One of legal scholar Catharine MacKinnon's major complaints about pornography is the way it is produced: "the pornography industry... forces, threatens, blackmails, pressures, tricks, and cajoles women into sex for pictures."[41] This is why, in constructing their Model Anti-Pornography Law, Andrea Dworkin and MacKinnon included clauses designed to prevent the coercion of persons into making pornography:

> Section 3.1. *Coercion into pornography*: It shall be sex discrimination to coerce, intimidate, or fraudulently induce... any person... into performing for pornography."[42]

The proposal to legitimize civil suit for coercing someone into making pornography (that is, for *rape*) seems fine. But how "coercion" and its sibling "consent" are understood is crucial in evaluating the production of pornography. Arriving at anything near a consensus about their meaning is difficult, and what the Model Law proceeds to assert about "coercion" is controversial. The Model Law characterizes coercion negatively: "proof of one or more of the following shall not... negate a finding of coercion"— at which point the Model Law lists thirteen conditions that, if proven to obtain (singly or together) by a defendant accused of coercing someone into the making of pornography, would *not* prevent a court or jury from deciding that coercion of the complainant had occurred.

The clauses of the Model Law that have drawn critical attention are these:

Proof of one or more of the following shall not, without more, negate a finding of coercion:... (xi) that the person signed a contract, or made statements affirming a willingness to cooperate in the production of pornography; or (xii) that no physical force, threats, or weapons were used in the making of the pornography; or (xiii) that the person was paid or otherwise compensated.

The Model Law's provision that the items mentioned in clauses (xi)-(xiii) should not *automatically* rule out a judgment of coercion may be technically right. The facts that a check was written and cashed, the woman signed a contract, and no force is visible in the film or photographs, do not make *impossible* her having been psychologically or physically forced into the affair. If the woman can display wounds or bruises, some reason exists to be suspicious that she voluntarily, without any force or coercion, signed the contract. When explaining this part of the Model Law, MacKinnon describes Linda Marchiano (Lovelace) as "systematically beaten," "kept under constant psychological intimidation and duress."[43] Clauses (xi)-(xiii) are designed to thwart this coercive abuse.

But because a signed contract, the absence of force in the content of the pornography, and a check deposited by the woman into her bank account do not imply that she consented to the sex in which she took part in making pornography, the Model Law apparently "creates a strong presumption" that all women who make pornography are coerced to do so.[44] By voiding these three things, even if combined, as reasonable or *prima facie* evidence of consent, the Model Law apparently puts the burden of proof on the accused to show that he or they did not coerce anyone into making pornography. Since a contract, the absence of force, and a check made out to a woman do not "negate a finding of coercion," one might scratch one's head pondering what a defendant in a civil suit could do or show in order to exonerate himself. How could he establish that he did not psychologically coerce ("cajole") the woman? What if he promised to make her the number one female porn star in the country (status coercion) or declared his love for her?

The Model Law, in this respect, resembles philosopher Lois Pineau's treatment of rape. For Pineau, we can reasonably presume that a woman would not consent to certain unpleasant sexual acts. Pineau means, in particular, sex that is aggressive on the man's part, noncommunicative, and unpleasurable: the man is pushy; silence replaces discussion about what will occur between them; and she feels no sexual desire for him. If a woman does engage in this nonmorally bad sexual activity, the presumption is that she did not consent to it, that is, that the sex was also morally wrong. Hence the man bears the burden of showing that she did consent.[45] Gayle Rubin finds the same theme in the Model Law:

> Dworkin and MacKinnon appear to think that certain sexual activities are so… distasteful that no one would do them willingly, and therefore the models… must have been forced to participate.[46]

The argument that group fellatio and anal intercourse are so universally repugnant that no woman would freely participate in them is silly, of course; so, too, is the weaker claim that the disgusting nature of these sexual acts creates a presumption that women who participate have been coerced to do so. Dworkin's harsh words about heterosexual coitus ("pure… contempt for women") does suggest that this is her position. And when MacKinnon writes:

> I will leave you wondering, with me, why it is that when a woman spreads her legs for a camera, she is assumed to be exercising free will.[47]

her point seems to be that when women spread their legs for a camera, they do not do so freely; nude spreading is so dehumanizing that any consent a woman gives to doing it must be bogus.

But MacKinnon offers a second argument, one that turns not on the "distaste" of making pornography, but on economic considerations. Suppose we asserted, given the plurality of motives one might have for engaging in sexual activity, that doing so for money is not necessarily objectionable. Of course, in some situations engaging in sexual activity (or selling a kidney, serving as a subject in biomedical experiments, or selling blood) smells of exploitation when one direly needs the money. We would also have reason to doubt that consent was genuine when a woman has no skills or the economy provides no opportunity for earning a living some other way. But a money motive is not always coercive or objectionable. MacKinnon's second argument, in effect, is a rebuttal to this line of reasoning. After mentioning the occurrence of the kind of physical and psychological abuse experienced by Linda Marchiano as one reason for the "coercion into pornography" section of the Model Law, MacKinnon goes on to say:

> The further fact that prostitution and modeling are structurally women's best economic options should give pause to those who would consider women's presence there a true act of free choice.[48]

As Carole Pateman makes the point, "economic coercion is involved since the sex industry pays better wages than most occupations open to women."[49] Hence no woman participating in the making of pornography does so freely; if she is not physically or psychologically abused into it, or if she is not compelled by deprivation, she is coerced by the lure of good money, more money than she might get working in a fast-food restaurant. MacKinnon, that is, does not restrict economic coercion to poverty and the lack of other job opportunities. Even when a woman has skills and could have worked elsewhere, she is coerced by the better (indeed, in some case, excellent) pay she gets by making pornography.[50] It follows, on MacKinnon's view, that every act of sex in the making of pornography is rape. It also follows that clause

(xiii) of the Model Law, according to which payment does not negate a finding of coercion, is misleading; the payment *proves* coercion. Payment cannot ever negate a finding of coercion because payment *is* the coercion. An alternative view, suggested by West, is that a woman's participation in the making of pornography, when she receives good pay for doing so, is both rational and consensual, even if in some ways it might be harmful to her (just as voluntarily working in a fast-food restaurant is also harmful to her).[51]

There is yet a third argument MacKinnon offers, one that depends, as does the first, on the nature of sex. "No pornography is 'real' sex in the sense of shared intimacy," she writes; "this may make it a lie, but it does not make it 'simulated'."[52] Pornography lies, on her view, because genuine sex is shared intimacy, while pornographic sex is quite the opposite, the sexual domination and economic exploitation of women by men. MacKinnon's claim is normative: the best sex, or the only sex worthy of the name, is sex that occurs within, or expresses, shared intimacy. The cold, loveless sexual activity of pornography is dehumanizing, beneath human dignity. In continuing her description of the abuse suffered by Linda Marchiano, MacKinnon writes:

> Men... don't want to believe what she says happened.... Men... don't want to know that she didn't like it. She loved it, see, she was paid. Never mind that consent in sex—and pornography is a form of sex—is supposed to mean freedom of desire expressed, not compensation for services rendered, which is what it means in commodity exchange.[53]

Consent in sex is "supposed" to mean "freedom of desire expressed," not material compensation for actions. On MacKinnon's view, then, offering a woman money or jewels or marriage or some other compensation to engage in sexual activity is coercive and wrong—not only by the nature of coercion, but also by the nature of what sex is "supposed" to be. To claim that there could be genuine consent to prostitution, then, is to make a kind of category mistake. Consent is also absent in the making of pornography, since that activity involves commercial sex. But where does MacKinnon's "should" come from? Why does MacKinnon assume that sex for money excludes "freedom of desire" or that a "freedom of desire" for money itself is offensive (assuming that poverty is not the cause)? The motives for sex arc legion: consider the freedom of desire in having sex in order to get a good night's sleep, or the freedom of desire to have a child, or the freedom of desire to make someone happy. No nonarbitrary way seems to exist to exclude, as incompatible with the nature of sex, a desire for compensation of one sort or another, including money but maybe just some body- and ego-stroking. MacKinnon's "supposed to mean" places too narrow a limit on respectable reasons to engage in sex.

PART TWO

LOVE

CHAPTER FIVE

VARIETIES OF LOVE

Parents are youthful, beautiful, perfected, and live joyously no longer than they can beget eggs and fecundate them. They are never more brave, sprightly, valiant, pleasant, or beautiful than when coitus is about to be performed.

—William Harvey
Disputations Touching the Generation of Animals (1651)

WHAT IS LOVE?

The complexity of this question is reflected in the fact that many different answers to it exist and debates about the nature of genuine love seem impossible to resolve. But there is a methodological principle to apply in approaching an answer: if an assertion about what love is entails that too many (a vague notion, to be sure) cases of what we ordinarily call "love" are not love at all, that is a reason (although not necessarily decisive) for believing the assertion false. For example, it is possible to claim that genuine love lasts "forever," that it endures as long as the lover and the beloved both exist. However, imagine that two persons love each other during their senior year in college, but get jobs after graduation in different cities. They live too far apart to continue to nourish their love, which eventually fades away. By accepting these jobs and moving apart, the lovers were deciding, in effect, not to continue to love each other. Are we not reluctant to say that just because their love ended, it had never been love? As much as we might hope that love lasts forever, we realize that many occurrences of genuine love do end. Our methodological principle would have us reject the constancy thesis. Similarly, it is implausible to assert that when one person x loves another person y, x's actions always serve to benefit only y, or that if x loves y, then x could not love another person z at the same time. If these claims were true, the world has seen very little love. And if so, how do we reliably come to know what the word "love" means? (The rub is, maybe we don't.)

In many respects, "love" is like other complex concepts: "work of art" is a good example.[1] What love is, and what art is, are equally perplexing questions. Yet we are able to apply "art" to a large number of noncontroversial cases; the same is true for love. The concept "automobile," by contrast, possesses a simplicity that "art" and "love" lack. It does so, however, because our making mistakes as to what counts as an automobile is ordinarily not as momentous as confusing love with, say, lust or infatuation, because the emotions have profound effects on our lives. Mistakes in love are as pivotal, if we are investors, as mixing up works of art with garbage.

One reason we disagree about the application of "love" to specific cases might be that the word refers not to one thing but to many things.[2] Leo Buscaglia, to the contrary, tells us that "there are not 'kinds' of love. Love is of one kind. Love is love."[3] Buscaglia probably means that all the phenomena we call "love" (for example, loving one's mother, loving chocolate, loving God, and romantic love) have something in common in virtue of which they are all cases of love (the "fine gold thread" of love). A problem with this view is that specifying the ingredient common to all loves is difficult. For example, if the common ingredient in all love is that the lover is concerned for the well-being of the object of his or her love, it would turn out to be nonsense to say that a child loves its mother, since children do not yet have a concerned attitude toward their parents. Some loves contain more need for their object than benevolence toward it. Or if the desire to form a bond, a unity, with the object of love is the common ingredient, then although a child might have an inchoate desire to merge, or remain merged, with its mother, and so love her, to say that because the child loves (needs) its milk, the child wants to merge with it, stretches too severely the notion of merging.

The many kinds of love that humans experience can be differentiated and categorized in several ways. First, we can distinguish loves in terms of its *objects*, those pieces of the world that are the recipients of our love. We can love our spouses, parents, siblings, children, friends, pets, country, abstract ideals, geometrical theorems, God, personal belongings, food, movies, books, and nature. In some cases it is possible for these items to return our love. Second, loves can be differentiated by their *basis*, that which accounts for the existence of the love or "grounds" it. Below we shall categorize loves according to their basis as being "e-type" and "a-type" loves. Loves can also be differentiated by their typical or constitutive causal effects, whether, say, the love leads to a desire to benefit the beloved, or to a desire for union with the beloved, or to a desire to possess the beloved.

Some languages partially distinguish different loves by using different nouns. The ancients made a linguistic, philosophical, and theological distinction among the Greek terms *eros* (erotic, yearning love, sometimes called "romantic love"), *agape* (Christian giving love), and *philia* (friendship-love). In Hungarian, the word "szerelem" means romantic, erotic love, while "szeretet" stands for almost everything else: parental love, brotherly love, and God's love. English uses the same word, "love," for all these phenomena, employing adjectives instead of nouns to mark differences among them. This linguistic fact about English acutely raises the question whether a common feature occurs in all these things we call "love."

LOVE AND VALUE

We commonly both want something and like it. We want it, usually, *because* we like it; we do not like it because we want it. There are times, however, when we do like something just because we want it; these are psychologically interesting and puzzling cases. Similarly, there is a correlation between our loving something and our finding value in it. Do we love this thing because we find value in it, or do we find value in it because we love it? In particular, the correlation between our love for persons and the value they have can be understood in two ways: (1) one person x loves another person y *because* x finds the properties of y to be valuable or attractive, or (2) x finds the properties of y to be valuable, or x finds value in y, *because* x loves y.[4] We can also ask, in the same fashion, whether a person x hates another person y because y has an annoying property, or x finds the properties of y annoying because x hates y. Indeed, about many emotions (for example: fear, anger, and admiration) we can wonder whether a person x has the emotion toward another person y *because* y has some property P, or x believes y has P *because* x is experiencing the emotion toward y.

Henceforth, loves that exhibit relation (1) between love and value will be called "e-type" loves, while loves that exhibit relation (2) will be called "a-type." The theory of e-type love derives from Plato's doctrine of *eros* in the *Symposium*, according to which a person x loves a person (or object) y in virtue of the beauty and goodness of the beloved y. The theory of a-type love derives from descriptions of Christian *agape*, God's or Jesus's love for human beings, in the New Testament. *Philia*, which is the word the Greek philosopher Aristotle (384-322 B.C.) used for love in his *Nicomachean Ethics*, is a special kind of e-type love that includes concern for the sake of the other (as theorized about a-type love), but is based solely on the moral and intellectual virtue of its object (hence is e-type). *Philia* is often said to be friendship-love.

In e-type love, first the value of y, the object of love, exists, then x's love for y arises as a response to this antecedent value. Hence love is the dependent variable, and its occurrence is explained by the valuable properties possessed by the beloved y. What is not explained in the theory of e-type love is the existence of this value, the basis of x's love for y. That is the independent variable, and requires explanation by factors that must be ap-

pended to the theory of e-type love. Note one immediate implication of this theory of love. If a person x loves another person y
because y has the valuable set of properties P, we should not expect x to love only y, but to love any other person z (and even z′,
z″, and so forth) who also exhibits the same valuable properties.
Plato noticed this implication, and rejoiced in it, calling it "great
folly"[5] for a person x *not* to value other people who also possessed P as much as x valued y; with so much beauty on the
landscape, there is no reason to focus on a single instance to the
exclusion of all the others (*Symposium* 210a-b). The contemporary philosopher Robert Brown, by contrast, does not rejoice. On
his view, to love someone is "to value the person... as irreplaceable,"[6] and so he rejects the supposition that the beloved's valuable properties are the basis of the lover's love for him or her.
(See Chapter Six.)

In a-type love, the love exists first, and then the value of the
beloved, as far as it figures into love, comes into existence. Hence
the beloved's value for the lover is the dependent variable, and
its existence is explained by the lover's love for the beloved. What
is not explained in the theory of a-type love is the love itself. The
love is the independent variable, and requires explanation by factors that supplement the theory of a-type love. Later, several bases
for a-type love will be mentioned. A-type love must be kept distinct from a very common mixed case that is ultimately an e-type
phenomenon. Suppose that some value V_1 in the beloved exists
first, and the lover x loves the beloved y in virtue of this value he
or she has. The love is based on, depends on, and is explained by
V_1. But in virtue of loving y, x attributes some other value V_2 to
the beloved y. This aspect of x's love for y is a-type. But x's love
is essentially e-type, since the attribution of the further value V_2
and x's love for y are both explained by x's responding to y's V_1.
These cases would be a-type only if x's love for y was not
grounded in V_1 or any other valuable property of y.

Relation (2) between a person's love for another person and
the former's evaluation of his or her beloved is commonly as-

serted. Robert Kraut, for example, says that "someone's love for a specific person is not 'based upon' the belief that the person has superb qualities; if anything, it is the other way around."[7] Kraut offers no argument for his view, except to defend it by observation: "Walter might judge Sandra to be the most marvelous person in the world, and these judgments might evoke feelings. But it seems to work precisely the other way around. The amorous feelings often come first; the favorable judgments... are already 'guided' by—that is, are a consequence of—the emotional responses."[8] W. MacLagan also claims that "person x loves person y because y has valuable P" gets things backwards; he cites one of F. H. Bradley's (1846-1924) *Aphorisms*: "We may approve of what we love, but we cannot love because we approve. Approbation is for the type, for what is common and therefore uninteresting."[9] The argument here against relation (1) and in favor of (2) is that e-type love is incompatible with love's being exclusively directed at one beloved. Were the lover x to love the beloved y because x merely approved of y, then x would have reason to love any other person z of whom x also approves. Approbation is for properties commonly shared by many people, that is, is directed at *types* of people, while genuine love is for the ineffably unique individual. (See Chapter Six.)

If a person x loves another person y because y is beautiful or good, x's love for y is straightforwardly explained as an everyday emotional phenomenon. It would be no different from other e-type phenomena—for example: x's hating y because y has done something nasty to x, or x's fearing a bear because the bear's claws pose a threat to x's life and limb. The only questions that remain are about the source of y's beauty or goodness in the first place, and why x responds to these properties and not others. But these questions admit of relatively uncomplicated answers. By contrast, if x judges y to be beautiful or good because x loves y, we have an answer to the question about the source of y's value. But x's love for y is left dangling, unexplained. Consider an extreme case. If x judges y to be morally good just because x loves y, despite the fact that all the evidence indicates that y is a liar and a cheat, then the attribution of value to y by the lover x looks mysterious; and answering the question, why x loves y, is difficult. The cause of or reason for x's loving y, in this case, cannot be something familiar, but must be something esoteric, since x's love has such a profound effect on x's cognitive faculties. If x believes y to be good *because* x loves y, and there are no other merits in y that explain x's love as, at bottom, an e-type phenomenon, or if x believes that y has done something nasty A_1 to x *because* x hates y, and y has not already done something else nasty to x, A_2, that grounds and warrants the hate, then explaining the existence of x's emotion, be it love or hate, is going to be difficult. This is why the theory of e-type love provides an appealing, if not commonsensical, analysis of love. The fact that anyone (for example, Kraut and MacLagan) thinks that the a-type relation applies typically to love shows, I think, that we have adopted a special attitude toward love that we do not adopt toward other emotions; we want to treat love as something special, not to be comprehended along the lines of other, less ethereal, emotions.

In the paradigm case of a-type love, the Christian God's love for humans, the attractive and unattractive properties of the object, the object's value, are entirely irrelevant:

> God does not love that which is already in itself worthy of love, but on the contrary that which in itself has no worth acquires worth just by becoming the object of God's love. Agape has nothing to do with the kind of love that depends on the recognition of a valuable quality in its object; Agape does not recognize value but creates it.[10]

Why, then, does God love humans? What is the basis of this a-type love? "The 'reason' why God loves men is that God is God, and this is reason enough."[11] As Anders Nygren says, "There is only one right answer.... Because it is His nature to Love.... The only ground for it is to be found in God himself."[12]

Love's not being based on the merit of its object is also characteristic of Christian love of one's neighbor, which demands that humans love each other with the goodness of God's love for humans. This kind of love, the basis of which is obedience to the commandment to love, is in some translations of the New Testament rendered as "charity." It is patient, selfless, giving, and long-suffering; it never fails and endures all things.[13] Hence we are commanded to love the sinner, the stranger, the sick, the ugly, and the enemy, as well as the righteous and one's kin. Given this list of appropriate objects of love, it is clear that individual attractiveness plays no role in neighbor-love. As the Danish philosopher Søren Kierkegaard (1813-55) says, while speaking about *agape* for one's neighbor,

> The task is not: to find—the lovable object; but the task is: to find the object already given or chosen—lovable.[14]

When we ask, what objects are we to choose and then find lovable?, Kierkegaard answers: "True love is precisely [to find] the unlovable object to be lovable."[15] In contrast to "that simple wise man of ancient times," Socrates, who taught that to love is to desire the beautiful, and joked about loving the ugly (Plato's *Symposium*), Kierkegaard announces that we should love "the ugly."[16] Kierkegaard does not mean that a person x should love another person y in virtue of y's ugliness if *that* property arouses x. Rather, we are to love those who are unlovable in the worldly sense of "lovable" exactly because they are unlovable in this sense, not because they turn out to be lovable in our subjective perception of them.

But neighbor-love can be interpreted not as an a-type love but as an e-type love. If humans are not worthless precisely because God has bestowed value on them, then neighbor-love could be construed as one person's response to this value in another person.[17] Or perhaps neighbor-love is a response to the valuable piece or spark of God that exists in all humans.[18] Hence neighbor-love is a "universal" e-type love. Here we should distinguish the claim (about the *basis* of love) that in x's neighbor-love for another person y, x loves y because y has the valuable property "contains a piece of God," from the claim (about the *object* of love) that in neighbor-love what one loves is not the human *per se* but that very piece of God that dwells in the human being.[19] This complication is analogous to one that arises about Plato's doctrine of *eros* in the *Symposium*; does a person x love another person (or object) y because y possesses the valuable properties P, or does x really love P itself, for which y is merely the vehicle?

It is interesting, given these ways of understanding neighbor-love as either an e-type or an a-type love, that *agape*, too, can be characterized as an e-type love. J. Kellenberger claims that *agape* is a response to "the inherent worth of persons as persons."[20] His view seems to be that whereas *eros* responds to the accidental values in a person, *agape* is a response to a person's necessary (inherent) value, value that is not lost regardless of changes in his or her accidental values. If this is right, how are we to understand responding to a person in virtue of his or her valuable properties that define the person's character and constitute his or her identity? These properties are accidental but also necessary, since without them the person would lose his or her identity as that person. Further, the idea that *agape*, as a response to a person's inherent value, is a universal e-type love, has odd consequences when applied to God's *agape*. It implies that God loves human beings in virtue of precisely the value that He has bestowed on them as their creator. This generates a circle, if God bestowed that value on humans just because He loved them.

Similarly, although the human love for God is typically seen as an e-type love, since we love God (if we do) in virtue of his infinite magnificence,[21] it is possible to understand it, instead, as an a-type love. On this view, we love God no matter what He does or what happens to us in His world; we continue to love God with all our hearts, constantly, enduring all things, despite the bad we get in life that must ultimately be due to Him, the creator of everything. In this way, the human love for God appears to be a-type.[22] However, suppose that we are able to love God, no matter what, only because we do not genuinely believe that the bad that befalls us is genuinely bad—after all, God is perfectly good and everything is, in his plan, for the best. If God never really does bad, our loving God "no matter what" is vacuous. This is not the unconditional love that loves in spite of genuine bad (for example, God's *agape* for us, we who sin), but is a love that loves constantly because it has faith that there is no bad. So our love for God is e-type, after all; we love God in virtue of his infinite goodness and the indecipherable wisdom of His plan.

In other e-type loves, the attractive properties of the object also account for the existence of love and determine its course. This is true of Plato's *eros*; the beauty or goodness of an object (body, soul, mathematical theorem, work of art, or piece of philosophy) grounds our love for it, even though Plato likely considers beauty itself to be love's object, instead of or not only its basis. In courtly love, the lover chooses "one woman as the exemplar of all significant virtues and [uses] that as the reason for loving her.... The inherent excellence of her total personality... elicits his love,"[23] rather than his love eliciting her excellence. In sexual love, the properties of the object play an important role, even if sexual desirability is subjective and some lovers are less discriminating than others.

Parental love seems to be an e-type love, too: the parent loves the child not on the basis of the child's mere existence but because the child has the property "is a child of mine" ("contains a piece of me") which is, from the parent's perspective, meritorious. The parent's reason for loving the child is both general and selective; if this is why the parent loves and cares for child x, the parent has equal reason for loving and caring for child y, yet has no reason for loving and caring for someone else's child. That is, parental love is preferential in a way that God's *agape* and neighbor-love could (or should) never be. This preferential, special concern in parental love appears also in adult personal love; when a person x romantically loves another person y, x lavishes a kind of care on y that is not lavished on those x does not love. Parental love, then, differs significantly from *agape*: God loves all His children, but everyone is one of His children (God's love is general but not selective), and God loves all His children equally (all worldly meritorious properties are irrelevant). But again we stumble on a paradox. Does this imply that God's love for human beings is e-type after all, if God loves humans in virtue of their possessing the property "is a child, or creation, of mine"? If God loves human beings at least in part because they contain a piece of Him, the soul, then God is like the e-type lover Narcissus who falls in love with the beauty of his own reflection in the water.

EVALUATING LOVE

That personal and romantic love between adults is e-type, or is instead a-type, is not a necessary truth about the basis of love. Nor is it empirically obvious which type is more common. This should not disturb us, since it is plausible to interpret the debate between proponents of these two theories or traditions as a debate over what love ideally is. This suggests that we should invoke other considerations in discussing the relative merits of these loves: their rationality and morality.

John Brentlinger has argued that there may be "no general answer" to the question whether personal love is better understood as e-type or a-type. Brentlinger begins his treatment of this question by noting that *eros* "proceeds from" value and *agape* "creates" value.[24] He then suggests that the distinction between *eros* and *agape* derives from a logically prior philosophical difference between conceiving of values as objective (values exist independently of the lover's attitudes and emotions and hence are the kind of thing love could "proceed" from) and conceiving of values as "relative" or subjective (values exist in virtue of the lover's attitudes and emotions and hence are the kind of thing that love could "create"). If so, we would now have to resolve one of the great issues in metaethics: are values objective or subjective? However, the distinction between values being objective

and being subjective does not correspond to the difference between e-type love and a-type love; in e-type love, a person x might
love another person y quite because x merely subjectively evalu-
ates y as beautiful or good. Brentlinger acknowledges this point
and proposes that deciding between *eros* and *agape* reduces, instead, to deciding whether x's believing y to have value leads x to
love y, or x's loving y leads x to believe y has value (which is
where we began). At this point, Brentlinger declares the problem
unsolvable: "*Neither* concept is by itself sufficient to explain all
cases of love. Rather, some lovers and loves will be cases of *eros*
and some of *agape*.... Both have existed and... both are possible."[25]
This is why Brentlinger concludes that there is "no general answer" to the question of which type of love is "preferable."

E-type love may be "preferable," however, because it con-
forms to a standard according to which we can and should have
some idea why we select particular persons as beloveds. Our acceptance of this standard is shown by the fact that the lover is
commonly called on to justify loving a particular beloved; the
beloved might press the lover with the question, "why *me*?" The
lover must provide to a beloved (and to those not loved) something more convincing than "that's just the way I feel" or "dunno,
just do" (or "just don't"). For Brentlinger to say there is "no general answer" to the question of whether e-type or a-type personal
love is preferable is as unconvincing as saying that there is "no
general answer" to the question of whether e-type hate is preferable to a-type hate. When we hate someone, or are angry, we
usually have and know the reasons why; hate without reasons
violates our standard and thus strikes us as irrational or patho-
logical and maybe even morally blameworthy.

Brentlinger mentions that for proponents of a-type love, "it
is *better* to love without a reason, than with a reason."[26] But why
think so? For example, perhaps only a-type love is constant. Constancy, however, is not necessarily a virtue of love, for either the
lover or beloved. And constancy, as already argued, might not be
required for love to be what it claims to be. The fact that the

termination of love might cause the beloved pain is not, in general, a moral defect of love. Love is risky business, and beloveds know in advance that they might get hurt. Further (and theoretically the most important point), why think that a-type love, or the lover's inability to offer reasons for the love, secures any more constancy than e-type love? Of course, in e-type love, in which a person x loves a person y for y's attractive properties P, y's losing some or all of P puts x's love for y in jeopardy; e-type love can only be as constant as its basis, y's value. But if x has, instead, *no reasons* for loving y, the constancy of love would seem to be in equal jeopardy. Suppose that a person x loves another person y constantly, undaunted by domestic discord, but not because x's love is based on y's merit. Instead, the constancy of x's love is due to something about x, something in x's nature, and not to something about y (the way God's love for humans is due to His nature, not ours). The constancy of x's love might result from x's determination to continue to show concern for y's well-being despite significant disagreements about matters that affect them both. This determination is the basis of x's a-type love. Or suppose that x's love is or results from a promise that x has made to y and is grounded, thereby, in an act of will[27] (the way God loves humans, by His will alone). In either case, whether determination or will grounds a-type love, the same principle applies: love will be only as constant as its basis. The constancy of a-type love will depend on the often unpredictable and uncontrollable vicissitudes of one's determination or will. Our will and determination, unlike God's, are not perfect. Which, then, is more constant: that the beloved continues to have the P that grounds the lover's e-type love for him or her, or that the lover's will or determination remains "ever-fixèd"?[28]

INTENTIONALITY

Suppose (story 1) that you are sitting at home, watching television and eating pizza. The telephone rings; the person on the line says she is a friend and neighbor of your grandmother and that your grandmother has just collapsed and died. As a result of hearing this news, you experience shock and tremendous grief. The emotion grief is brought about by your belief that your grandmother is dead and your desire that she be alive—after all, you love your grandmother and have long been attached to her. You immediately get into your car or on your bicycle and go over to your grandmother's. But as you enter the house, you feel strange: no one, no other member of your family, is in the parlor or dining room, but all the lights are on, and there is a familiar rattle of pots and pans in the kitchen, from which the scent of your grandmother's stew is flowing. When you investigate, you find your grandmother in the kitchen. Now you are overcome by relief and joy and embrace her tightly. Here your emotions are brought about by the same desire you had earlier—that she be alive, since you love her—but a different belief, that she is, after all, alive. Story 1 can be fancifully extended. Suppose that as you embrace your grandmother, she pulls away from you and rips off the rubber and plastic mask that has been covering "her" face to reveal a ghoulish monster. Again you are thrust into grief (and other things), since now you believe, once more, that she is really dead. (Shall we extend the story even further by imagining that the ghoul rips off another mask to reveal that she is really your grandmother?)

There is another scenario (story 2); your emotional responses might play out differently. On hearing the news on the telephone that your grandmother was dead, you experience joy instead of grief. Why? Because you have the same belief, that she is now dead, but you have a different desire: you want her to be dead so you can inherit her fortune. And when you go to your grandmother's house and discover her in the kitchen making stew, you now experience anguish and anger, because you have the same desire you had earlier—that your grandmother be dead, so you can collect—but now a different belief, that she is, unfortunately, alive and kicking. Finally, when the mask is ripped off to reveal the ghoulish monster, you feel joy again as you hightail it out of the kitchen, realizing that your dream of inheriting her fortune will come true after all, if only you survive.

There are a number of lessons to be learned from these stories. First, which emotion a person experiences is a function of the beliefs the person has. In story 1, when you believed that your grandmother was dead, you experienced sadness, but when you later believed that she was alive, you experienced relief and joy. Indeed, the radical change in your emotional state, from grief to joy, was directly due to a change in your belief. Second, there is no doubt that while you believed that your grandmother was dead, your sadness and grief (or your joy) were real, that is, genuine instances of these emotions. The fact that a person's emotion is dependent on a *false* belief does not mean that the emotion is bogus or some other emotion pretending to be that emotion. Emotions, we can say, are *intentional*: they depend on beliefs and these beliefs need not be true. To some extent, then, our emotions are "about" us, not "about" the world. The third lesson to be learned is this: do not count your chickens until they hatch. You could have, maybe should have, tempered your emotional response, your joy, to hearing the "news" from a stranger on the telephone that your grandmother was dead. For good prudential reasons, at least, you could have quieted joy (or sadness), by considering that you had to check whether the caller was telling the truth. In the same way, we might have control over our loves: a person could temper his or her response to meeting an attractive person until he or she knows that person better and ascertains that he or she really has those attractive properties (and has no significant offsetting liabilities). Such tempering is important not only for prudential reasons, however; declaring your love for another on the basis of incomplete knowledge or false beliefs might be morally faulty, since the declaration creates expectations that you might not be able to fulfill.

One more lesson comes from the contrast between story 1 and story 2: the genesis of an emotion, and the particular emotion it is, is not only a matter of one's beliefs, but of an interaction between one's beliefs and desires. The only difference between reacting with sorrow and reacting with joy to the news that your grandmother has died is that in one case the operative desire is that she be alive, and in the other that she be dead. Now we are in a position to analyze "mixed" emotions, when we feel two, often contrary, things at once. In one type of mixed emotion, a person believes both B and not-B at the same time, and has either a desire that B or a desire that not-B (in other words, that B be true or that it be false). For example, suppose that after receiving the phone call, you partially believe that your grandmother is dead, but also partially believe that she's alive; you haven't quite suspended belief, but have given some credence to both possibilities. In this situation, your emotional state may be a mixture of sadness that she is dead and perplexity about what is going on, perhaps being troubled that someone might be trying to trick you. In another type of mixed emotion, a person both desires B and desires not-B, and believes either that B or that not-B. For example, suppose you have conflicting desires about your grandmother; out of love for her, you'd like her to be alive, but out of greed you'd like her to be dead so you can inherit her fortune. When you receive the telephone call and believe that she is dead, you feel both sadness and elation. Or suppose that your grandmother has a terminal illness that she experiences as painful and degrading; out of love for her, you both want her to continue living and want her to die, for her own sake. In this case, too, you will experience sadness and relief if you believe what you are told on the telephone.

In e-type love, we said, one person x loves another person y because y has a set P of attractive properties, while in a-type love the merit of the object is irrelevant. But now we must take into account the complications surrounding intentionality. We should characterize e-type love more precisely this way: a person x loves another person y because x *believes* or *perceives* that y has P. In the sequence leading from y's having P to x's loving y in virtue of P, we have to insert between them x's belief or perception that y has P. Indeed, e-type love will exist even if y does not have P, as long as x *thinks* that y has P. To say that e-type love is intentional is to say that, just like grief based on the false belief that your grandmother is dead is real grief, love based on the false belief that y has P is genuine. Intentionality also figures into a-type love, but not as a factor in its basis. In virtue of loving a person y, a person x attributes value to y, and so x comes to believe or perceive that y has this value. The intentionality involved in a-type love is a consequence of love and not, as in e-type love, part of the antecedent cause of love.

If a person x loves another person y because x believes that y has P, whether x's belief is true or false can influence our assessment of x's love. X's belief that y has P might be due to a suspicious psychological process—for example, rationalization, projection, or idealization. In this case, x's love-grounding belief is not only likely false but also irrationally-formed, and x's love is defective. At least, we expect this "blind" love to dissipate as soon as x wakes up to the reality. Alternatively, maybe x has made a culpable mistake about y's properties; x believes that y has P, but x did too little "research" about y to warrant believing, firmly, that y has P. If x fears an object because x believes that the object is dangerous, but x's belief is founded on weak, too little, or no evidence, then x's fear is epistemically irrational. A love based on insufficient evidence about the value of its object is similarly defective.[29] Perhaps the person x believes falsely that the other person y has P not as a result of a psychologically suspicious process, or through negligence or recklessness in arriving at beliefs about y, but, which might be just as common, because y has deliberately deceived x into believing that y has P. In this case, if x's love ends when x wakes up to the reality, we are more prone to blame y than x and perhaps to judge y immoral for the deception. People who exaggerate their own merits, verbally or through their actions and appearance, are often attempting to induce love in another person. This tactic is often not successful in the long run, because when x comes to know y better, x discovers, if x objectively looks at the evidence, that x had been deceived.

If a person x loves another person y in virtue of believing falsely that y has P, is it correct to speak of x's emotion as love? Or even if x does experience love, is it y that x loves—as opposed to loving a figment of x's imagination? W. Newton-Smith, for example, claims that if a person x loves another person y falsely believing that y has P, then x's emotion is love only if x's emotion continues after x corrects his beliefs about y; if x does not feel the same after exchanging his false beliefs for true ones, then x "never loved anyone at all."[30] Indeed, if x loves y first believing falsely that y has P and later believing correctly that y does not have P, x's love is a-type, since it is not a function of y's having P.[31] Consider another emotion, hate. Suppose that one person x believes that another person y has done something especially vicious to x (say, x believes that y has been telling bare-faced lies about x) and that, in virtue of this belief, x begins to hate y. Simply because x's belief is false—as a matter of fact, y has been saying only nice things about x—do we want to deny that the emotion that x experiences is genuine hate? Probably not. Do we want to deny that it is y that x hates? Again, probably not. Note, too, that we expect, when x corrects his or her belief about y, that x's hate will dissipate, and properly so; the dissipation of the emotion is due to a change in x's beliefs about y. Hate, that is, is a fully intentional emotion. Still, some would say that if a person x loves another person y in virtue of believing falsely that y has P, then x's emotion is not love; or if x loves y falsely believing that y has P, then the object of x's love is y-qua-possessor-of-P, which is a nonexistent being. X's love has no object, except the one in his or her head (what some call "the intentional object" of love). But if love, like hate, is fully intentional, we should analyze them the same way, not treating love as a special case.

MORAL LOVE

A person x can love another person y on the basis of almost any property that x finds valuable or attractive; the theory of e-type love does not by itself place any limit on what P in y might elicit love in x for y. But perhaps we can make a moral judgment about x's loving (or hating) someone on the basis of some properties rather than others; the logical "anything goes" does not entail a moral "anything goes." It is difficult to decide for which properties people should love others, and in this area one can slide from doing philosophy into blandly moralizing. There are, however, several suggestions worth considering.

One line of argument goes like this. Properties, when considered as the basis of love, can be divided into two types, the superficial S properties and the significant T properties. Then a distinction can be made between x's loving y for S properties and x's superior love for y on the basis of T properties. For example, suppose that the beauty of one's face or body, one's income or wealth, or one's power and position, are S properties, while intelligence, grace, wit, and moral virtue are T properties, as claimed by Pausanias (*Symposium* 180d-181a, 183e), who distinguishes between "vulgar" *eros* of the body and "heavenly" *eros* of the mind. Then a person x could love a person y for her beautiful hair and her sexual attractiveness (or for her usefulness in helping x achieve his or her goals, as in Aristotle's use-friendship), but if x loved her instead, or in addition, for her intelligence and courage (or for her moral and intellectual virtue, as in Aristotle's genuine friendship), x's love would be superior. But why is a person's loving another person on the basis of the latter's T properties a superior style of love? Perhaps x's loving y for T is more likely to produce constancy in x's love, thus showing it to be the real thing, while x's loving y for S is unlikely to endure. Or if x's love is based on T rather than on S, then perhaps x will exhibit more reliably the behaviors connected with love, especially, say, being unselfishly concerned for the well-being of y. Finally, perhaps

x's loving y for T means that x is loving y on the basis of properties more closely associated with the person that y is. Loving someone for his or her beautiful hair and feet or economic resources
might seem to be a shallow love, while loving on the basis of
intelligence and virtue seems more substantial. But distinguishing between those properties that are in fact superficial and those
that are significant is at least a value-laden and maybe even an
arbitrary project.

The important matter, on this view, is to come down on the
right side in the battle between the variable and unreliable physical attributes of human beings and their more constant and respectable psychological and ethical characters. That is, according to this view we should love each other not for our firm bodies, but in spite of our flabby bodies and in virtue of our attractive
minds. This might be just a hedge; for our characters are often
ugly, at least in part, if not in whole. Does our moral and intellectual beauty or goodness really attract others to us and successfully overcome their perception of our badness? Have we been
able to conceal the bad components of our character well enough,
so that our mental flab is not too visible? The badness in our
characters likely surpasses the ugliness of our bodies. To solve
this problem, in turn, we would have to learn to love each other
not in virtue of our good characters, but in spite of our having
none. Having already risen from loving on the basis of the body
to loving on the basis of the mind, however, to what do we rise
one more time? To the spark or piece of God within us all or, as
in Kellenberger's *agape*, to the "inherent worth of persons as persons"? Perhaps the only nonsuperficial value, literally and meta-
phorically, of a person is his or her "deep" value as a person and
which all persons have equally; if anything is going to provide
the basis for love, it should be this. But now we have lost all
possibility of preferring or selecting one person instead of another to be our beloved, since we *all* have the inherent value that
attaches to personhood. Maybe we should just admit, given the
corruptness of our characters, that our fleeting, youthful physical

beauty is our only beauty and the major provocation of love (see the epigraph). Loves based on the silly traits of our beloveds need not be failures.

According to a different approach, the best love is based on the lover's autonomously chosen or formed preferences. The point is that it is not the type of value in y, the beloved, that counts, but why x the lover is pulled to some properties and not to others. Thus, the best love exists in virtue of y's properties, whatever they are, that mesh with x's preferences that are not superficial, that is, are not unreflectively and uncritically allowed to operate in x's choices. (Recall Colker's wish that we, but especially women, be guided by our "authentic" desires; see Chapter Four.) The normative value of the preferential choice made by the lover flows from the value of autonomy, not from the value of the object of that choice or the specific properties involved. But for lovers to have control over their preferences and their ability to distinguish in a reflective fashion worthy from unworthy objects of love is not a matter merely of inner strength; social and economic conditions (as Colker warned us) must be such as to encourage lovers to develop and modify their preferences freely. And if this requires the absence of economic, social, and political inequality or oppression, social engineering may be necessary to refurbish not only our sexual relationships but also our loves.

Loving on the basis of autonomously formed preferences, or focusing only on the significant properties of beloveds, if you favor that view, are not the only requirements for avoiding defective or shallow love. As mentioned above, a love may be irrational if the lover's belief that the beloved has P is irrational, not well-founded on the evidence. This irrationality is not merely a cognitive defect; it can also be a moral fault. Suppose that a person x loves another person y, believing that y has P, and that this belief was formed carelessly. In some cases of this sort, x knows (or can be expected to know) that x has not had enough opportunity to gain the knowledge of y required for a rational belief that y has P (or that y's attractive properties outweigh y's unattractive properties). X's loving y on the basis of negligent beliefs about y is a moral wrong to y, for x now leads y to believe that x loves y, makes commitments to y, and creates expectations in y about x's future behavior. X leads y to believe that x has certain love-related desires: to spend time with y, to share some delicacies and experiences exclusively with y, and so forth. Further, x creates in y the expectation that y is and will be an object of x's special, preferential concern. Creating all these beliefs in y on the basis of negligently false beliefs will harm y, since x will likely discover later that x's beliefs that y has P are false, and x's love-related desires and concern will disappear. Loving someone while having well-grounded and accurate knowledge of one's beloved is, in this way, a moral dimension of love.

Pausanias says that it is "discreditable" for a pursued beloved to give in (sexually) too quickly to his or her desirous lover (*Symposium* 184a5). The beloved must discern, with adequate evidence, whether the lover is motivated by vulgar or by heavenly *eros* and whether the lover is even feigning the heavenly to hide his or her vulgar *eros*. If the beloved gives in too quickly, he has only himself to blame; he has negligently allowed himself to be someone's beloved in not waiting long enough to make sure that he has rational and true beliefs about the lover's motivation and character. Aristotle, too, thinks that the beloved is to blame if "a person has erroneously assumed that the affection he got was for his character, though nothing in his friend's conduct suggested anything of the sort" (*Nicomachean Ethics* 1165b7-9). Pausanias also says that if y, the beloved, gives in to x, the lover, because y believes that x is rich, y is proceeding incorrectly, whether y's belief is rational or irrational, true or false; y in this case is "disgraced" in showing himself to be the sort of shallow person attracted to superficial properties. On the other hand, if the pursued y gives in to the pursuer x believing that x is wise and virtuous, "it does him credit," regardless of the truth of the belief (*Symposium* 184e-185a). But what Pausanias should say is that if y believes falsely but on good evidence that x is wise, y's giving in to x's pursuit is praiseworthy, since y's giving in reveals y's commendable motivation (to become virtuous); but if y believes falsely, due to negligence or not waiting long enough for the evidence, that x is wise, then despite y's motivation y is a "discreditable" beloved. For y has not seriously attempted to sort out the heavenly from the vulgar lovers.

THE FINE GOLD THREAD

What does it mean to say that something, C, is the central ingredient of love? Of course, C is common to all loves, not only to all the instances of one type of love but also to all the various types of love. But C must not be something that is only trivially present in all cases of love. "Occurs in the Milky Way" is present in all cases of love that we know about, but it is not relevant to our understanding of love. Nor will it do to say that in all cases of a person's loving something, he or she likes it; that might be true (is it?), but that idea, too, is not illuminating. The central ingredient of love should be something that is able to explain why a case or type of love *is* love. By reference to C we must be able to point out the essential difference between love and other things, all of which also "occur in the Milky Way." C must provide a way to distinguish love not only from things that are wildly different from it (dogs, meatballs), but also from things that are closer to love but either pretenders or mildly associated phenomena (infatuation, respect, admiration, sexual desire).

Because of the apparent multiplicity of love—the types of love include "vulgar" sexual love, "refined" or "heavenly" erotic love, romantic love, courtly love, brotherly and neighborly love, parental love, love for one's country or one's god or chocolate—discovering one common, significant element in all cases and types of love would be a magnificent feat. Such a fine gold thread is bound to be elusive. If some C is proposed as the central ingredient of love, one must argue that (1) this C *is* common to all cases and types of love, especially regarding those cases or types in which C intuitively seems not to be present at all or present only incidentally, *or* (2) that cases of love in which this C is absent are not cases of love at all, or not "true" cases. Alternatively, a weaker claim about the scope of the central ingredient might be advanced, in which (3) the applicability of C is restricted to one prototypical kind of love or to only those types of love that most strongly demand elucidation. In this case, the attempt to uncover the fine gold thread of love has been abandoned, and we are asked to settle for the fine gold thread of only some loves, the "important" ones.

The sorts of problems that arise in this project can be illustrated by discussing Plato's account of love and contrasting it with Aristotle's and Paul's. Plato set out in the *Symposium* to establish his own view about the fine gold thread that runs through, without restriction, all cases and types of love, including love for the gods, persons, and inanimate objects. For Plato, the generic formula, that love is the desire for the perpetual possession of the beautiful and the good (*Symposium* 204b, 204e, 205d), expressed that fine gold thread. This purported central ingredient does a good job of illuminating love by explaining some its common features. It explains why love is so often, if not by temperament, nonexclusive, directed at many persons and things, refusing to be faithful to any one of them. It explains why love is dispositionally inconstant, switching from one focus of attention to another, abandoning the first for the second: some earthly beauties deteriorate with time, thereby showing their inferiority to other beauties that do not fade as quickly. Or the lover's love for the beloved is not constant because the lover realizes in advance that the beloved's beauty *will* fade (*Symposium* 210b-c). The lover's love for the beloved dies even before the beloved's beauty starts to diminish, because the lover knows that this beauty, vulnerable like all earthly things to diminishing and disintegration, is an inferior sort of beauty. Besides, once a person has achieved satisfaction by possessing many instances of one type of beauty, this person has had his or her fill; a higher level of happiness through love is attainable only by possessing higher types of beauty. And Plato's formula explains the burning possessive passion of love (*Symposium* 204d-e): making the beautiful and good our own, part of our selves, is a goal we must relentlessly pursue, on pain of not fulfilling our potential or of not achieving genuine happiness. For Plato, the exclusivity of the object of love and the constancy of love are eventually secured, but only when the lover progresses to the highest stage of the ladder of love; here the lover contemplates Absolute Beauty itself, a unique, unchanging, infinite beauty, Beauty unalloyed with any mundane vehicle (*Symposium* 211e). This beloved, however, unlike the similarly infinitely good Christian God, is an impersonal thing and so does not reciprocate the human being's love for it.

The way Plato expresses his doctrine suggests that love may be a desire directed at an inanimate *thing*, for goodness and beauty are properties, inanimate items existing among the furniture of the universe. Hence, if one loves a beautiful horse, the beauty of the horse is the beloved, the object of one's desire, not the horse itself; the horse is only the "target" or the "occasion" of love, the particular that carries the genuine object of love. This dimension of Plato's account of love is, in many cases, not problematic; his view holds up well when applied to a large number of possible targets of love: love for the gods, love for art and music, even sexual love in which the lover is entranced by the physical beauty displayed by the arousing body. But it has been complained about Plato's view of love, originally and implicitly by Aristotle (in his criticism of two inferior kinds of love, use-friendship and pleasure-friendship, in which a person's usefulness and pleasantness themselves are the object of love [*Nicomachean Ethics* 1165b1-5]), more recently and vigorously by Gregory Vlastos, that when we apply Plato's doctrine of *eros* to the love of one person for another person, the account yields unacceptable results: when person x loves person y, x does not really love y but only the goodness or virtue that y manifests, a goodness that has an independent existence of its own and for which y is only the vehicle.

As Vlastos put it, this is "the cardinal flaw in Plato's theory. It does not provide for love of whole persons, but only for love of that abstract version of persons which consists of the complex of their best qualities."[32] The alternative superior style of love that Vlastos has in mind is an a-type love. The love we should strive for is an unconditional acceptance of the other person; only then is the "whole" of us loved.

A Platonist can make three moves here, given the above strategies. First, the Platonist could say that Plato's view does apply to personal love in exactly the way suggested by his formula—a person x loves just and only the beauty and virtue x finds in the beloved y—and we need to deflate our sentimental belief that in some delightful sense x loves y "in himself" or "for himself" or "as a whole person." For Plato, we love the person's courage and intelligence, but in no sense he, himself. We must wake up to this fact about even the most happy of our loves. Second, the Platonist could contend that personal love, insofar as it does not fit under Plato's generic definition of love, is not a case of genuine love at all, but only a vaguely-related pretender. But to claim that personal love is not a kind of love to begin with, but only a pretender, is unappealing. Third, one could restrict the scope of Plato's definition, admitting that the formula does not apply to personal love (which is a real kind of love), and then claim that the formula is meant to illuminate only a subset of the domain. This strategy is hardly commendable; it eviscerates Plato's theory of *eros*. The first strategy is the most ambitious; it grips the bull by the horns and encourages us to redescribe and re-evaluate personal love.

After Plato, Aristotle placed the love for persons in a predominant spot, driving the point home by using the word *philia* in preference to Plato's *eros* when talking about personal love.[33] For Aristotle, Plato's concentration on the love for things was wrongheaded, since on Aristotle's view inanimate things could not be beloveds in the true sense:

> Love for a soulless thing is not called friendship, since there is no mutual loving, and you do not wish good to it. For it would presumably be ridiculous to wish good things to wine; the most you wish is its preservation so that you can have it. To a friend, however, it is said, you must wish goods for his own sake.

A thing cannot reciprocate the feelings or desires we have for it and, more significantly, we cannot, in virtue of its dumb nature, wish it well for its own sake (*Nicomachean Ethics*, 1155b30). This phenomenon—a person's desiring for another what is good for that person, for that person's own sake, and pursuing that person's good specifically for his or her benefit and not one's own—is Aristotle's central ingredient of genuine love. But Aristotle did not intend the formula to be taken as an umbrella definition covering all cases and types of love. Rather, with this emphasis on this "robust" concern, Aristotle was portraying personal love at its best. Aristotle recognized other types of love among persons (use-friendship and pleasure-friendship), but he did not expect them to fit with everything implied by his formula for perfect love.

The implications of *eros*—the lack of exclusivity and constancy in love—reappear in Aristotle's account of friendship,[34] which is no surprise, given that all three forms of friendship are e-type loves in which the basis of love is the other's usefulness, pleasantness, or, in friendship at its best, the other's excellence, his or her moral and intellectual virtue. For Aristotle, if a person x loves another person y because y is pleasant or useful to x, x's love is self-interested (*Nicomachean Ethics* 1156a11-17). These friendships will not be constant or exclusive; the basis of the friendship, y's being pleasant or useful, is widespread and not something that lasts (*Nicomachean Ethics* 11156a20-1156b5, 1157a5-10). In these two kinds of friendship, the object of love is really the usefulness and pleasantness of the person who is useful or pleasant. This is also partially true about Aristotle's perfect friendship. He claims that in perfect friendship, a person x loves another person y because y's character is good and that this goodness is not something incidental to y but part of y's nature (*Nicomachean Ethics* 1156b10). But if x loves y for y's good character, and that good character is partially constitutive of y, then y's good character is both the basis and (at least part of) the object of x's love. Aristotle does not expect genuine friendship-love to be exclusive; even though men of good character are rare (*Nicomachean Ethics* 1156b25), one should, if one can, have many such friends. But in contrast to an inferior friendship that is based on the usefulness of the other person in terms of securing one's own goals, Aristotle does expect ideal friendship to be constant: moral virtue (as opposed to usefulness or pleasantness) is something that usually endures, so love that is based on goodness will be correspondingly constant (*Nicomachean Ethics* 1156b2). Yet Aristotle's *philia*, unlike a-type love, is conditional on its object's remaining good (*Nicomachean Ethics* 1165b12-22). When Aristotle says that a person x should abandon *philia* for his or her beloved y if y changes from being good to being evil (should that be possible), he is not asserting that x's love ends for a self-interested reason. Rather, x realizes that x can no longer do anything to benefit y for y's own sake.

Several hundred years later, Paul and the authors of the New Testament gospels registered their disagreement with Aristotle on the alleged perfection of *philia*. It is not perfect, they claimed, because, like Plato's *eros*, Aristotle's *philia* is conditional on the beloved's merit: a person x is drawn to another person y in response to y's antecedent virtue, even if x later pursues y's good purely for y's sake. Aristotle's *philia* is not perfect because it grants benevolence only to those who are judged to be worthy of it; *philia* is not a universal love but preferential.[35] For Paul, a perfect love would graciously bestow value on its beloveds, not respond to their variable, unreliable, doubtful pre-existing value. It would love, and continue to love, despite the faults of its beloveds, endlessly forgiving the sinner and trusting the enemy and the stranger, full of hope for the best. God's *agape*, shown in the sacrificial gift of his only son for the sake of all humanity, as unworthy of such an infinitely valuable blessing as humans were, is perfection. Is this *agape*, the freely-bestowed creation of value by the lover in the beloved, the only kind of (true) love for the Christian tradition? A dilemma arises here. If the answer is "yes," that other types of love can never be the real thing, it becomes difficult to understand, let alone name, the human love for God, which apparently could not itself be *agape*. But if the answer is "no," that *agape* is not the only kind of (true) love, then the unconditional and creative bestowal of value cannot be the fine gold thread of love.[36]

Perhaps what we should emphasize about *agape* is not its bestowal of value, but its more general benevolence, "the works of love,"[37] that is, benevolent acts done for the sake of others without any thought of benefit accruing to the self. If we pay more attention to this aspect of *agape*, Aristotle—from a Christian perspective—did not make such a big mistake. He still asserted, with Plato, that benevolence was to be distributed according to antecedent merit, but he made an advance over Plato by seeing that concern for the well-being of the beloved for the beloved's sake was essential to love at its best. But even Plato in his own truncated way recognized that love motivated us to perform virtuous acts. Phaedrus's contribution to the *Symposium*, in which he praises the power of love to cause us to do brave and noble self-sacrificial deeds (178d-179c), as well as Diotima's teaching Socrates that the main effect of love was the begetting of beauty and goodness (*Symposium* 206b-e), show that Plato's *eros*, even if it aims ultimately at the lover's own happiness, is not selfishly egocentric. Hence in all three philosophers—Plato, Aristotle and Paul—there is the idea, emphasized to a greater or lesser degree, that benevolence is a feature of love. Perhaps, then, benevolence toward the beloved is the fine gold thread of love. Even if benevolent concern, however, is not the central ingredient of all love (because the human love for God might be an exception, as well as the child's need-love for its parents), it is plausible that concern for the well-being of the beloved for the beloved's sake is a necessary feature of personal love at its best.

CONCERN

The social psychologists Donn Byrne and Sarah Murnen opine that "we should be able to learn to treat loved ones with as much politeness and kindness as we do strangers."[38] This cannot be right, as a rule. If we should treat loved ones as nicely as we already treat strangers (Ethiopians in need) or our neighbors (the elderly woman down the street to whom we never offer help), then we would not treat our beloveds well at all. Byrne and Murnen implicitly admonish us to be nicer to our beloveds, as if our love for them did not express itself naturally as concern but as destruction. But anyone who needs to be told to be nice to a beloved is not a lover. It seems, that is, to be a truth of some sort about personal love that when a person x loves another person y, x wants to benefit y, and to benefit y in particular. If x does not love y, there is less reason to think—unless we construct elaborate stories—that x would be especially concerned for y's well-being. Perhaps x's desire to benefit y, when x loves y, can be conceptualized as a causal, nearly nomic, consequence of love. But because it is difficult to make sense of the claim that x loves y when x does not care at all about the happiness, prosperity, or flourishing of y, the connection between x's love for y and x's wanting to benefit y might be tighter: x's wanting to benefit y might be either a logically necessary condition for, or partially constitutive of, x's loving y.

Suppose, then, that when a person x loves another person y, x wishes the best for y and acts, as far as he or she is able, to pursue the good for y. But how much is x concerned for y, or to what extent is x concerned to help y flourish, if x loves y? What or how much of or how often must x be prepared to sacrifice his or her own good for the good of y, if x loves y? A common argument between two persons, x and y, both of whom claim to love the other, goes like this: one person says, "if you loved me, you would do act A," and the other person replies, "if you loved me, you wouldn't ask me to do A." These lovers disagree about the extent or nature of the beneficial acts entailed by love. Who is right? Does that depend on what act A is, or is that beside the point? These are interesting questions and, if we ever love and want to understand what we are doing, important ones.

Some things can be said about love's benevolent concern without much fanfare. A person's loving another person is not incompatible with the former's not sacrificing his or her life in order to secure a much less valuable good for the beloved, although never sacrificing anything for his or her benefit likely negates the lover's claim to be a lover. If the only thing that x's beloved y desires is that x have all x's desires satisfied, x will satisfy all y's desires, as soon as he satisfies his or her own desires, but x will not necessarily be benefiting y or pursuing y's good. And x as a lover will sometimes be divided between seeking what y the beloved wants or desires and seeking something else for y, what x thinks is best for y. Here a conflict arises between y's autonomy and x's concern for y's well-being. For the lover to abide by the beloved's autonomous preferences is to jeopardize one part of the latter's well-being by foregoing what is good for him or her, even though the beloved protests otherwise; and to pursue these other aspects of the beloved's well-being might paternalistically violate the beloved's status as a person. Further, there is often a conflict between love, on the one hand, and morality or justice, on the other. Singling out one person, the beloved, to be the recipient of one's special, preferential concern might violate a moral principle of equality. If it is difficult to decide how much of the lover's own good the lover x must be willing to give up for the sake of the beloved y, it is also difficult to decide how much of z's good the lover must not give up in pursuing the beloved's well-being, where z might be a close relative (parent, child) or a needy stranger.

A person x can hate another person y even if x respects y and finds y attractive. Hating the attractive, hating that which is ordinarily lovable, is possible. Our reaction to the worldly successful is often envy rather than love. Our response to a beautiful, witty, friendly, educated person might be dislike. When a person x hates another person y in virtue of y's attractive properties, this is not necessarily because in x's subjective world these properties are unattractive; x might admit that they are attractive. Similarly, rather than respond with hate or anger, a person x might love the person y who abuses x; loving a despicable or hateable y is also possible. Further, even though x would usually hate y if y has harmed x, sometimes x hates y because y has done something to benefit x. Loving behavior can generate not return love or even gratitude, but annoyance.

What these observations lead to is the question of how love and hate are to be differentiated. Love and hate can be inspired by the same properties; further, love and hate can be accompanied by similar behaviors toward their objects. Sometimes we do cruel things to our beloveds, and such mistreatment is often indistinguishable from the harm done by a hater to the one he or she hates. If the desire to spend time with the beloved is a typical result of love, that may not distinguish love from a perverse hate in which a person relishes opportunities to be with the one he or she hates just in order to provoke that person. So where is the essential difference between love and hate? One answer is that love and hate can be differentiated only by their phenomenal feels, by how they register in the consciousness of the person experiencing them. But then the only person who can distinguish a person's love from that person's hate is that person himself, for only he has access to his conscious states. But how did this person learn to label these different internal states, if not by the example of the external behavior of other persons? We might rely on the nature of a-type love to differentiate love and hate: when a person x loves another person y, x is caused to evaluate y positively; when x hates y, x is caused to evaluate y negatively. But this will not work for e-type love, and it works for a-type love and hate only because in a-type love and hate we have no obvious explanation why love and hate arise in the first place.

One way of identifying emotions is by referring to their characteristic beliefs. For example, a person experiences fear when he or she believes that something is dangerous; or a person experiences gratitude toward another person when he or she believes that that person has benefitted him. Yet if a person can either hate or love someone when he or she believes that the other has the same attractive P, this way of distinguishing love and hate apparently fails. Accordingly, the philosopher D. Hamlyn claims that love and hate are "not differentiated by beliefs [but] by factors other than beliefs."[39] Nevertheless, if we do want to rely on a person's beliefs about the object of his or her emotion, perhaps the distinction can be made this way: love occurs when the attractive properties outweigh or make insignificant the unattractive properties of its object, while in hate the relationship is the other way around. If so, e-type love and hate would be a function of the interplay between the attractiveness and unattractiveness of their objects.

Robert Brown has suggested, alternatively, that

> if we are to distinguish love from hate, the former must embody recognizable good will toward the beloved and the latter ill-will toward the victim. A lover who over the long term wished only ill-will toward his consort would be as much a definitional absurdity as a man who, filled with hate for his consort, would wish her only good.[40]

Hate with no ill-will and only goodwill is not hate at all; love with no goodwill and only ill-will is not love. Brown's idea, then, is that love and hate can be distinguished by certain desires (and the behaviors that follow from them) that are constitutive of or nomic causal effects of love and hate. This way to distinguish love and hate might be better than distinguishing them by pointing out that in love, but not in hate, one person believes that the other's attractive properties outweigh his or her defects. But Brown's proposal provides only a weak criterion: no goodwill at all means no love. Brown's suggestion seems to handle adequately the case of the lover who occasionally hurts his or her beloved. This person at least shows some goodwill toward his or her beloved, and so counts as a lover. But a stronger criterion is required, something like this: as long as the general pattern of a person's desires over the long haul is mostly a string of goodwill desires, that person is experiencing love; if the general pattern is one mostly of ill-will desires, then it is hate. But is the "mostly" here quantitative or qualitative? We have not come any closer to settling how much, and of what kind, the lover x must be willing to give up for the sake of the beloved y, if x loves y.

UNION

According to the "union theory" of love, the central component of love is a physical, psychological, or spiritual union between the lovers in which they form a new entity, the *we*. The union theory goes back at least as far as the Hebrews (Genesis 2: 23-24):

> The man said, "This is now bone of my bones and flesh of my flesh; she shall be called 'woman', for she was taken out of man." For this reason a man will leave his father and mother and be united to his wife, and they will become one flesh.

In the *Symposium*, Plato put a tragicomical version of the union view into the mouth of Aristophanes, who tells a romantic story about two half-persons wanting to be welded together into the whole they had once been (*Symposium* 189c-193e). Diotima replied in the dialogue that Aristophanes' union view of love was misleading: "Love is not desire either of the half or of the whole," Diotima teaches Socrates, "unless that half or whole happens to be good" (*Symposium* 205e). Plato, for whom generic love consisted of the desire to possess the beautiful and good, himself advanced a union view of love, in the sense that possessing the beautiful and the good, for Plato, involved the inclusion of that beauty or goodness into one's self.

Michel Montaigne (1533-1592), inspired by his friendship with Étienne de La Boétie, proffered a union view in his famous essay on friendship, claiming that, in love, "each gives himself so entirely to his friend that he has nothing left to share with another."[41] G. W. F. Hegel (1770-1831), in much the same spirit as Montaigne, wrote that "love is indignant if part of the individual is severed and held back."[42] In our day, the theologians Paul Tillich and Karol Wojtyla have contributed their own versions of the union view of love; the psychoanalytic philosopher Erich Fromm has argued that love, as union, was the answer to the major problem of life (aloneness); the psychiatrist Willard Gaylin made union the central theme of his book on love; and the secular analytic philosophers J. F. M. Hunter, Mark Fisher, and Robert Nozick have proclaimed that a union, fusion, or merging of two beings into one lies at the heart of love.[43]

Suppose that concern for the well-being of the beloved is an important ingredient of adult personal love, even if not the fine gold thread of love. Can the union theory of love allow that, say, Aristotelian robust concern or the concern of *agape* is a common feature of personal love?

Consider Hegel's philosophy of love. Love "proper," he says, is "true union."[44] "In love, life is present as a duplicate of itself and as a single and unified self."[45] Of what does this union consist? "To say that the lovers have an independence... means *only* that they may die" separately.[46] Hegelian lovers are unified except in the sense that, being physical creatures, they might not die at the same time and so one might live, disunified, without the other. Hegel apparently means this literally, for he asserts that "consciousness of a separate self disappears, and *all* distinction between the lovers is annulled."[47] Hegel's suggestion that love destroys the consciousness of separate selves is implausible about adult persons who love each other and who normally do retain consciousness of themselves as distinct persons. Of course, all human relationships involve some loss of our independent existence; whenever one person becomes closer to another person, both gain beliefs from the other, or abandon beliefs, and both gain and lose options for behavior. There is also some reciprocal modeling of personality traits. This is ubiquitous in the human condition. But Hegel's loss of consciousness of the self and other as separate, the annulment of all distinction between the lovers, means that the independence of the lovers radically drops out of the picture. If so, how could one person in the union-love be concerned for the well-being of the other for the other's *own* sake?

Karol Wojtyla attempts to make room for concern in a union model of love. He argues that because two *I*s merge into a single *we* that is the fused entity of love, "we can hardly speak of selfishness in this context."[48] His idea is that if the persons remain separate, then there are two distinct foci of interest or well-being, in which case selfishness is logically possible; but when two lovers merge into a single entity, selfishness is logically ruled out, since a single entity cannot be selfish toward itself or treat itself selfishly. Hence, Wojtyla seems to imply, love as union, in ruling out selfishness, must instead contain genuine concern for the beloved.

The argument, however, supports the contrary thesis that the loss of independence in union-love is incompatible with robust concern. If a union of two people into a single entity eliminates the possibility of their being selfish towards each other, it also eliminates the possibility of their having robust concern for each other, since wishing the other well for his or her own sake, just as being selfish, presupposes that the other is an independent focus of well-being. If, as Hegel says, two people in union-love form "a single and unified self,"[49] then in love there is only one entity acting on its own behalf. We might try to imagine a single entity or person that wished itself well for its own sake, as a single person might respect himself or herself. This concern aimed at one's self, however, would not be robust concern; it would be only self-interest. Further, were one person x to (try to) sacrifice x's good for the sake of the other person y, x could only be sacrificing the x-y joint good for y's sake, not x's own good, since x no longer has any good of x's own that x could sacrifice. So the logical possibility of self-sacrifice is also eliminated. The well-being of the lovers *not* being joined together is logically necessary for one lover to exhibit either selfishness toward the other or sacrificial concern for him.[50]

We do have a need to overcome our existential or metaphysical aloneness; without an intimate union with another person we often feel distressingly incomplete.[51] Thus we desire to join our life with the life of another person, to mingle or merge our self with the self of the other. And once this union has taken root we have a motive for continuing and nurturing the interpersonal connection that has alleviated our Angst. Yet, at the same time, we also require a secure sense of ourself as a distinct individual, and this depends on maintaining separateness from our lover or beloved. We must be able to glory in the independent exercise of our abilities and to be responsible in our own right for acting in the world in accordance with our individual natures. We can often, or at least partially, satisfy both needs at roughly the same time or alternatively; yet resolving the tension between the need for closeness with another person and the need for independence is challenging.[52]

So Aristophanes cannot be right (he was joking, after all) that what lovers want more than anything else is to be welded together. We undergo the strenuous process, we take on the task, of separating ourselves from our parents and other powerful significant others precisely in order to become our own (hopefully "authentic") persons. Why would we want to forsake the fruit of that onerous and exhausting labor by establishing ourselves once again within a union? Why would we want to give up that hard-gained autonomy for the sake of a union-love, thereby abandoning our prize? If women in our culture have more difficulty than men individuating themselves from Mother, and so achieve whatever autonomy they do achieve more precariously and painfully, why should they be so willing to throw it away? One answer is that women are not interested in autonomy in the first place; autonomy is a masculine value and trait. The union theory of love, that is, in emphasizing the merging of selves at the expense of autonomy is true to women's nature and their experiences. On this view, to criticize the union theory of love by invoking the importance of autonomy at the expense of the merging of the lovers is to appeal to a masculine value to deflate women's values or nature.

Still, it must be said that union-love may not be good for women. Although in the theory of union-love, both people merge into each other and become a single *we*, in practice it has been the woman who merges herself to the man, losing her identity in the relationship while he maintains distance from it. The French philosopher Simone de Beauvoir, in expressing the union view of love, claims that "the supreme goal of human love... is identification with the loved one." But then de Beauvoir proceeds to describes "the woman in love"; she

> tries to see with his eyes.... When she questions herself, it is his reply she tries to hear.... She uses his words, mimics his gestures.[53]

This description strongly suggests that the woman in love undergoes a substantial loss of self. Perhaps if the man were to merge equally to or with the woman, all would be well; but, on the other hand, maybe the woman should be more concerned, as the man is, to maintain her autonomy and independent identity.

CHAPTER SIX

FEATURES OF LOVE

When two beings fall in love with one another and begin to suspect that they were made for each other, it is time to have the courage to break it off; for by going on they have everything to lose and nothing to gain. This seems a paradox, and it is so for the feeling, but not for the understanding.

—"A" (Søren Kierkegaard,
"The Rotation Method," *Either/Or*, vol. 1)

A nalyzing the exclusivity, constancy, and reciprocity of love is of fundamental importance in being able to understand and evaluate various theories of love. Some philosophers have even suggested that these three notions are pivotal in characterizing the central cases of genuine love. Romantic love, for example, is often claimed to be exclusive, constant, and reciprocal by nature, and marital love is equally commonly taken to exhibit these three features. But what do exclusivity, constancy, and reciprocity amount to, and are they essential to love?

A common charge made against the theory of e-type love is that it does not secure these three features of love. A love based on the attractive properties of its object will exist only as long as the beloved possesses these properties; a lover who responds to P in the beloved y will also respond to P in some other person z and thus will not love y exclusively; and if both x and y are concerned only with merit of each other, nothing guarantees that when x loves y, y also loves x. But failing to secure constancy, exclusivity, and reciprocity is not a disadvantage of an account of personal love, if these features are not viewed as definitional of love. Further, there may be ways of construing e-type love so that it does secure some constancy and exclusivity. At any rate, a-type personal love may not exhibit much constancy or not fare any better in this regard that the theory of e-type love (see Chapter Five). Søren Kierkegaard claimed that "Christianity's... task is man's likeness to God. But God is love; therefore we can resemble God only in loving.... Insofar as you love [only] your beloved, you are not like unto God, for in God there is no partiality."[1] But if God's *agape* extends to all humans, and if Christian neighbor-love, as a copy of God's *agape*, extends to all people without partiality, then any attempt to fit personal love within this tradition will also have difficulty securing exclusivity.

The most important thing to do is to state clearly what we mean when we say that love, or this particular type or example of love, is exclusive, constant, or reciprocal (or, to the contrary, is not any of these). In fashioning our definitions, care must be exerted to keep separate logical or semantic claims about the exclusivity, constancy, and reciprocity of love, from both psychological claims about these features and ethical claims about them. For example, the difference must be recognized between saying (1) that a person x's love for another person y cannot *be* love if y does not love x in return, and (2) that x *will not*—given his or her psychological nature, our nature as human beings, or the nature of the relationship in question—love y unless y loves x too. Further, when defining exclusivity, the other features, constancy and reciprocity, must not be mentioned (and vice versa): the definitions must be independent of each other. Our definitions must not rule out in advance the possibility that a person x loves *only* another person y but this love fades away, or that x loves *both* y and z and these loves endure.

EXCLUSIVITY

The logical claim "love is exclusive" can mean that love is *timelessly* exclusive, or exclusive "for all times"; the very recurrence of an emotion toward a second person at any time entails that it is not love. This is exclusivity in its strictest sense; love is an emotion that a person can experience only once in a lifetime and toward only one person. Hence, in this sense of exclusivity, after a person x's loving another person y begins, x can love no one other than y, and before x's loving y began, x could not have loved anyone else; x's first beloved y is x's only beloved, and if y dies, x will not love anyone else. Note that this is not a psychological thesis about the state of mind of the lover, but a claim about the nature or logic of love.

"Love is exclusive" can also mean that love is *timed* exclusive, or exclusive "at one time." If an emotion is directed at two people at the same time, it cannot be love; having two objects at the same time is ruled out by the exclusivity of love. Timed exclusivity allows (but does not require) serial, multiple loves: a person x loves a person y and only y at t_1, yet x may love another person z and only z at some other time t_2. Whereas the doctrine that love is timelessly exclusive prohibits multiple loves altogether, the doctrine that love is timed exclusive prohibits only multiple loves that overlap in time. Someone who asserts that love is exclusive might mean either that a lover can love only one person *period* or that a lover can love only one person at a given time; and someone who denies that love is exclusive might mean either that multiple loves occurring at different times are possible, or even that multiple overlapping loves are possible, depending on which notion of exclusivity is being denied. Serial, nonoverlapping loves can be conceived of as either exclusive or nonexclusive, depending on which doctrine of exclusivity is assumed.

If love is timelessly exclusive, it would be an anomalous emotion, since other emotions typically admit of multiple objects. Further, were this analysis taken as an empirical claim about what we ordinarily call love, it would be false; it implies that the world has not known much personal love, since many people claim to have loved at least two people. One virtue of the timed exclusivity analysis is that it implies that if a person x loves a person y at t_1 and y dies or runs away, then x's loving yet another person z can be true at the later t_2; the doctrine does not entail that x's first beloved is x's only beloved. Timed exclusivity also avoids the other extreme: it conceptually allows x to love y and z at different times of x's life without giving x conceptual *carte blanche* to love w, y, z, and their siblings all at the same time. But the doctrine of timed exclusivity gets caught in the middle, attacked both by defenders of strict exclusivity and proponents of the view that love has no logical constraints of this sort at all. In principle, timed exclusivity places no limit on the number of loves a person can have, as long as they are temporally separated from each other. But is there not a point at which the sheer number of serial loves (even if temporally bracketed) implies that not all these instances are love? We might try to put a theoretical limit on the number of loves by requiring that (a) some amount of time elapse between a person's different loves (we would set a minimum length of time to gaps between sequential loves) or that (b) any bracketed love last a minimum amount of time. Filling in the details of (a) seems arbitrary and futile. Route (b) implies that the fuzziness of the idea of timed exclusivity is to be patched up by the idea of constancy—but that concept may be no less fuzzy. Alternatively, defenders of the doctrine of timed exclusivity might insist that what matters, in deciding whether or which of a person's attachments count as love, is the quality of his or her love, that is, the benevolent concern the person displays for his or her beloveds, not the number or duration of these instances of love. But timed exclusivity then gives way to nonexclusivity, because that view claims that what matters is the quality of the love, not the triviality that a person x's love for y temporally overlaps with x's love for z. The purists, however, step in: *that* is not trivial; if you want the quality of genuine love, the special sacrificial concern lavished on the beloved, love must be timelessly exclusive.

The philosopher Robert Brown claims that

> a relationship of affectionate care... is limited in its number of participants by the limitations imposed by the re-

quirements of interest, attention, committal, and intimacy. Because we cannot be equally interested in, attentive to, committed to, and intimate with, a large number of people, we cannot enter into relationships of equally affectionate care with them. To have close and affectionate relationships with a few people ensures not having such relations with any larger number.[2]

Brown's point is that there are material, economic, temporal, and psychological constraints on our ability to carry out multiple loves. Notice that love is not, on this view, exclusive solely by *its* nature, but in virtue of its surrounding environment. Yet it might be asserted that these pragmatic considerations are powerful enough that our loves must be timelessly or timed exclusive in order to be genuine. No one argues that practical constraints place powerful limits on the number of people we can admire, respect, or hate. Thus we would have to claim that the nature of the benevolent concern in love requires it to be exclusive in some sense; since sacrificial concern is a feature of love but not of other emotions, it follows that only love can be expected to be exclusive.

A different sort of defense of exclusivity is advanced by the philosopher Robert Ehman:

Although [the lover] might put two or more persons ahead of all others, he cannot put two persons absolutely first in his life; and this is what love demands.... When the lover admits that his beloved is merely one of several whom he counts as equal, he takes back his claim to love her.[3]

Whereas for Brown the concern involved in love implies that love for pragmatic reasons cannot be extended equally to too many people, for Ehman this concern logically can have only one person at a time as its object. The lover might be able to extend superlative concern to two people, but he had better not, on pain of negating his claim to love anyone. Ehman's view has an interesting implication: if a person loves and hence has concern for the well-being of y, his or her spouse, then the spouse must be "absolutely first" in the person's life—but, then, what about his or her love and concern for their children? Do they come "second"?

In contrast to Ehman, another philosopher, W. Newton-Smith, claims that "there is *nothing* in the concept of love that rules out" a person's loving two other people at the same time, and that exclusivity "cannot be presented as a fact about the nature or essence of love."[4] Newton-Smith's interlocutor is Karl Jaspers, who claimed that "he only does love at all who loves one specific person." Newton-Smith offers the diagnosis that Jaspers's claim is a "normative" claim disguised as a conceptual truth, a "legislative" decision. In arguing that love is not by its nature exclusive, Newton-Smith begins by acknowledging what Brown asserted—that the nonexclusive lover "is apt to find himself spread a little thin if he attempts to provide the sort of concern, interest, commitment and so on which we take love to involve." This may be seen as an admission that defending nonexclusivity will require some work; for if love does involve concern and commitment, the right conclusion to draw, along with Brown, might be that thin-spreading is incompatible with these features of love. Newton-Smith's rejoinder is this: "That it will be difficult to bring it off," that is, for a person to love two other people at the same time, "does not show it is in principle impossible." But Newton-Smith must do more than this. He must offer some account of the kind or amount of concern that is involved in love and then argue that, given this kind or amount, when a person x attempts to provide concern to both y and z, x will not be spread so thin that x ends up loving neither. That account would explain, surely much better than the mere assertion that "difficult" does not entail "impossible," why "nothing" in the concept or nature of love rules out overlapping loves.

The way Newton-Smith continues this discussion confirms the weakness of his argument. "Difficulties [in a person's bringing it off] are most apt to arise if the set-up is not mutual all round": when a person x loves both y and z, and y and z do not love (perhaps even hate) each other. In this case, Newton-Smith worries that x's loving y will distress z, and x's loving z will distress y; x's causing them both distress may be incompatible with x's loving them, since in causing distress x might not "really be concerned for both." His answer to this quandary is simple: "Probably all that is required for [x] to be thought of as loving both [y] and [z] is that he [is] distressed at their distress." But to say that in causing y and z distress, x is nevertheless *adequately* concerned for them, as a caring lover, as long as their distress distresses him, is to appeal to an implausible notion of the concern of love. Why not say, instead, that if a person is genuinely concerned for two other people, he will desire to remove the cause of their distress? As if realizing his answer may not be convincing, Newton-Smith ultimately handles this case another way: "To show that love is not so exclusive as to rule out multiple love relationships we need only imagine a set-up that is mutual all round," that is, x loves y and z, y loves x and z, and z loves x and y. In this fully mutual situation, no distress arises to bring into doubt x's love for y and z. This "argument" begs the question. If, in order to show that love is not necessarily exclusive, all we need do is to "imagine" a love-triangle in which x loves y, x loves z, y loves x, y loves z, z loves x, and z loves y, then all we need to do in order to show that x can bring off loving both y and z is to imagine that two other persons, y and z, *are* able to bring it off. But whether anyone can is the question.

UNIQUENESS

It is often said that one person x loves *only* another specific person y because y has some unique set of valuable properties: no other person z does or can match the quality of y. This thesis is weak, because the significant uniqueness presupposed does not exist. The properties in virtue of which we are unique (fingerprints) are not the valuable properties we have in virtue of which we are loved; and the valuable properties we have that do ground love are ubiquitous (beauty, intelligence, kindness). But even if we grant that each person has a unique set of valuable properties that grounds love, it is still a *non sequitur* to conclude from this uniqueness that a person will love only one other person. The valuable properties might explain why a person x loves another person y in the first place; but the fact that these properties make the beloved y unique does not allow us to insert the "only." That x loves y for y's unique set of properties P_1, P_2, and P_3 does not logically prohibit x from loving a second person z for another unique set of properties P_4, P_5, and P_6 that only z has.

Unless a person's possessing the specific set of properties P_1, P_2, and P_3 is necessary for a person x to love anyone at all, the fact that y's having this set grounds x's love for y has no bearing on whether x loves some other person z when z does not have this set. Exclusivity, then, is secured by the uniqueness of the beloved only when (1) a person x loves another person y in virtue of y's having this set of valuable properties, (2) the possession of this set of properties makes y unique, and (3) the possession of this set by a person is necessary for x to love anyone at all. But how likely is it that the possession of a specific property or set of properties is absolutely necessary for x to love anyone at all? Most unlikely: we often do love one person y for his or her beauty and wit, yet find another person z equally appealing and lovable in virtue of his or her wisdom and courage. True, anyone I love must have the property "has never killed my mother" (or something similarly monstrous), but this sort of trivial property is exhibited as frequently by potential beloveds as "has body hair." Uniqueness, then, cannot be appealed to generally in accounting for exclusive love.

Our discussion so far has focused on exclusivity in e-type love. But given the impartiality and universality of *agape* (see Kierkegaard, above), exclusivity would also seem to be difficult to derive from the theory of a-type love. Agapists might maintain that the exclusivity of, say, marital personal love is not a conceptual requirement but, instead, demanded by the ethics of love. The fulfilling of this duty, through a promise to love exclusively, is what secures exclusivity. But what is the basis of this promise initially and what keeps it in place? If determination and will are inadequate as a secure foundation for the constancy of a-type love, or serve no better than the basis of e-type love (see Chapter Five), they will also be inadequate, for the same reasons, to secure its exclusivity.

There is nothing incoherent, however, in one person's saying to another: "You're not like any other lover" *because* "you're my lover." The lover admits that the beloved is significantly unique only insofar as the beloved is "loved by the lover" and no one else has that property. But saying that a person x's loving a person y exclusively *makes* y unique is different from claiming that x loves y exclusively because y is unique. Uniqueness is now the *explanandum*, not the *explanans* of exclusivity. Further, the lover in his or her rational mind knows that the beloved is not otherwise significantly unique, but the lover still acts as if the beloved were. This bestowal of uniqueness is not necessarily (although it might be) a psychologically suspicious overestimation of the beloved's merit or the wish-fulfilling attribution to the beloved of excellences the beloved does not have. Nor must it take the form of pedestalism or of denigrating other possible beloveds in order to think highly of one's actual beloved. The lover embellishes the beloved's merits in order to build the beloved's confidence and sense of self-worth and to express the important meaning the beloved has in the lover's life.

IRREPLACEABILITY

Perhaps a loving sexual desire, as opposed to generalized horniness, latches on to a particular object (I want *Jennifer*), in a way hunger does not (I want a sausage, and *any* juicy one covered with mustard will do). As the British novelist C. S. Lewis says,

> Eros makes a man really want, not a woman, but one particular woman... in some mysterious but quite indisputable fashion.[5]

Heavenly sexual love makes us desire one special person; vulgar desire, as Pausanias says (*Symposium* 181b), is satisfiable by any one of a number of fungible bodies. But the distinction between heavenly sexual desire and simple lust is a fine one, and in many instances doubtful. We often deceive ourselves that we are experiencing a lofty sexual desire instead of base lust; we just as often merely imagine that this person is not replaceable by others as the object of our desire or affection. Still, in genuine love, according to Shulamith Firestone, a man would love a woman, and *vice versa*, as an "irreplaceable totality,"[6] not as a collection of attractive properties or on the basis of these properties.

In claiming that the object of love is "irreplaceable," Firestone does not necessarily mean that genuine love is exclusive or that every beloved is unique in a substantive sense. "Irreplaceable" is close to both "unique" and "loved exclusively," but it is not the same thing. Two items, for example, two 1909S-VDB pennies, might, both of them, be irreplaceable for their owner(s), yet neither penny is unique, and a person who loves his or her 1909S-VDB penny might also and equally love the much less scarce 1950D Jefferson nickel. And items might be unique, yet replaceable by something else that satisfies us and is appreciated, but not exclusively: my dog is unique, and I might be attached to the dog, but I might at the same time like another dog just as well and be equally happy with some other dog, should my dog die. What, then, is irreplaceability? And can Lewis's "mystery" survive Ronald de Sousa's cynicism that our belief in the irreplaceability of our beloveds is nothing but cultural "ideology"?[7]

The philosopher Thomas Nagel argues that a desire for an omelet is conceptually different from sexual desire: the object of omelet-desire, but not of sexual desire, is replaceable. I might desire an omelet for its "combination of aroma and visual aspect," and any other "omelet with the crucial characteristics would do as well."[8] In contrast, if I sexually desire Jennifer "it is not similarly true that any person with the same flesh distribution"— and now we expect Nagel to complete the sentence with—"would do as well." But Nagel says instead, "can be substituted as object for a particular sexual desire that has been elicited by those characteristics." Is "cannot be substituted" equivalent, for Nagel, to "would not do as well," so that I will eagerly consume the second omelet but will not be happy with, or even refuse, the second person? No. Nagel means that another person who is just as sexually attractive *logically* cannot be substituted for the first; while in the omelet case, he means that the second dish of eggs can be *psychologically* substituted for the first. I think, however, that the psychological sense of "irreplaceable" is more interesting and germane to love than the logical sense.

Nagel is concerned to make a point about the individuation of desire: "It may be that" the crucial flesh characteristics "will arouse attraction wherever they recur, but it will be a new sexual attraction with a new particular object, not merely a transfer of the old desire to someone else." By contrast, omelet-desire is *not* individuated by its object; my desire for the second omelet is not a new omelet-desire, but the same desire transferred from one omelet to another. Since sexual desire *is* individuated by its object, my desire for the second person, should it exist, is a new sexual desire. I cannot agree that there is necessarily this difference between omelet-desire and sexual desire. It is not obviously wrong to say that my desire for the second omelet is historically or spatiotemporally a new omelet-desire; and my sexual desire for the second person may simply be a continuation of my desire for the first person. It is not obvious that when I become aroused by Jasmine after having been aroused by Jennifer, we must count these as two separate sexual desires.

Furthermore, even if my sexual desire for the second person is a new desire, that does not mean that I will not be, psychologically speaking, equally as happy with the satisfaction of that desire for Jasmine as I would have been with the satisfaction of my original desire for Jennifer. It is true, we can grant, that I have not transferred one and the same sexual desire from Jennifer to Jasmine, if we individuate sexual desire as Nagel recommends. Yet

I *have* transferred sexual attention from one to the other; I have transferred the goal of achieving satisfaction with Jennifer to achieving it with Jasmine. Since I might be just as happy satisfying my sexual desire for Jasmine as I would have been satisfying my sexual desire for Jennifer, the logical individuation of sexual desire places no limit on what might "do as well" psychologically. Yet, if the distinction between omelet-desire and sexual desire is of any significance for love, it would have to be that the second omelet will, but the second person will not, "do as well," that is, that the object of sexual desire is psychologically irreplaceable.

The British philosopher Roger Scruton repeats one of these criticisms of Nagel's view as a question:

> Is it not *merely a convention* that leads us to say that, when I transfer my appetite from this dish of carrots to that [dish], there is only *one* appetite, with two successive objects, while, when I transfer my attention from Elizabeth to Jane, there are two desires, differentiated precisely by their successive objects?[9]

Scruton, in defense of Nagel's view, responds to the objection:

> Sexual desire is unlike my appetite for these carrots, in being *founded upon* an individuating thought. It is part of the very directedness of desire that a *particular* person is conceived as its object.[10]

In support of this thesis, Scruton points out that there can be "mistakes of identity" about the object of sexual desire, but not about the object of carrots-desire. Suppose that a person x sexually desires a person y, but spends the evening in bed with another person z believing that z is y.[11] How is this situation to be described? "In a crucial sense," says Scruton, x "does not desire [z], but the other" person y. Hence, x's evening with z has not satisfied x's desire for z, since x has no such desire. But x does have a desire for y, and we can say either that (1) z has helped x satisfy x's desire for y (since during the evening x believed z was y) or that (2) x's desire for y was not satisfied by x's evening with z (since x did not sleep with y). If we assume some desire of x's has been satisfied (x enjoyed himself or herself), we should opt for description (1). Description (2) claims that x's desire for y has not been satisfied, and we already know that x has no desire for z that could have been satisfied, so (2) forces us to say that no desire of x's has been satisfied, despite x's pleasure.

Scruton does opt for (1): x's "desire for [y] seemed to be satisfied by his night with [z], only to the extent that, and for as long as, [x] imagined it was [y] with whom he was lying." Thus, x's desire for y *is* satisfied when x does not know that z, instead of y, is in x's bed; and x's desire for y is *not* satisfied when x knows that z is slipping into bed with x. By contrast, according to Scruton,

> the desire for a dish of carrots is not similarly dependent upon an individuating thought, and does not therefore give rise to errors of identity. To eat the wrong dish of carrots may be a social howler, but it is not a mistaken expression of desire—I really did desire the dish of carrots I consumed.

Scruton claims that the possibility of mistaken identity in sexual desire, and its absence from carrots-desire, can "dispel [the] immediate force" of the objection to Nagel's view.

Scruton's argument, however, does not show that when a person x sexually desires a person y and then *later* sexually desires another person z, we should individuate x's desires in such a way that x's sexual desire for z is a new desire. For in Scruton's mistaken identity example, x never sexually desires the second person z at all. X has only one sexual desire to begin with—for y; x never has a sexual desire toward z about which we could ask,

"Is this the same or a new sexual desire?" Scruton originally posed his question as about how to individuate (count) a person's sexual desires when he *knowingly* is first attracted to Elizabeth and later to Jane, but in the mistaken identity case x never desires the interloper z, so there is nothing to count.

Perhaps satisfied that he has established his thesis about the individuation of desire, Scruton also claims, speaking psychologically, that "the person in love wishes his beloved to want him as the unique irreplaceable individual that he is."[12] In another passage, he again emphasizes irreplaceability: "if John is frustrated in his pursuit of Mary, there is something inapposite in the advice 'Take Elizabeth, she will do just as well'."[13] Why "inapposite"? Perhaps immediately giving that advice is irrelevant to what John is experiencing. But eventually that advice is excellent (with "she will do just as well" tactfully omitted) if John, lonely and depressed, is still self-destructively yearning for the unattainable Mary. Sure, John's desire for Elizabeth, if it develops, is not the same desire as John's desire for Mary, but that it is a logically new desire means not that the old desire has not been replaced by the new one, but that it has been replaced, along with its object.

After this, it comes as some surprise to discover that Scruton in effect agrees with de Sousa that the intuition that as lovers or beloveds we are irreplaceable is a bit of ideology, although Scruton calls the belief "a metaphysical illusion."[14]

> We regard each other as irreplaceable in arousal, just as we do in love, and individualising thoughts are in each case central to our endeavor.... Those thoughts have a large illusory component.... Individualising thoughts are... mystifications.[15]

Sexual passion and romantic love mislead us; they make it appear, falsely, that we are ontologically more than we are, that we are transcendental selves rather than mere material beings.[16] If this is right, Scruton should find the advice, "take Elizabeth, she will do just as well," acceptable. But Scruton resists, arguing that the illusion is beneficial:

> It is by such mystifications that we live. They are the necessary salve to the pain of incarnation.... In so far as we could give an explanatory account of what one person gains from another in love and desire, it is clear that he might have gained that benefit equally from someone other than the person to whom he directs his attentions. But it is imperative that we do not think of this. If we do so, our enterprise is jeopardised. By such thoughts we threaten the possibility of any lasting human attachment.[17]

What must not be thought is the truth that the beloved is, after all, replaceable, that someone else would have done, or could do, as well (or that we, as lovers, are replaceable). Why not claim, instead, that all sorts of things threaten love, that love is risky and fragile, and that a rational recognition of replaceability is the salve to the pain of abandonment or lost love? Further, there is something odd in Scruton's *telling* us that "it is imperative that we do not think" the destructive thought that our beloveds are replaceable. For if there are thoughts that must not be thought (which Scruton himself thought), these thoughts must not be spoken or written; maintaining the illusion requires silence. Exposing illusions, even to defend them as necessary, is hazardous. Like all illusions, sustaining the belief in the beloved's irreplaceability requires self-deception or other mental tricks. Hence love founded on such beliefs are (as argued in Chapter Five) defective.

CONSTANCY

When analyzing the concept of exclusivity, we had a choice between a restrictive notion (a person x timelessly loves only the person y) and a fuzzy notion (serial, nonoverlapping loves) that left open the number of beloveds a person could have and still be a lover. Regarding constancy, the choice is between a restrictive notion (if a person x loves a person y now, x will always love y) and a fuzzy notion that leaves open the length of time x's emotion must last in order to be love. The fuzzy notion of exclusivity got caught in the middle between proponents of the doctrine of strict exclusivity and proponents of nonexclusivity; the fuzzy notion of constancy is similarly situated.

The doctrine of *strict constancy* claims that "love is constant" means that love lasts forever: if a person x begins to love a person y at t_1, x will love y at all times t after t_1, as long as both x and y are alive ("until death do us part"). Thus, if x's emotion toward y ever ends, it had never been love. This is not quite precise enough: hardly anyone expects x to love y if x is alive but irreversibly comatose. The point of this analysis, however, is that if x loves y, then x's love continues if y, instead, is irreversibly comatose.

The doctrine of strict constancy can be employed critically: if a person x's emotion toward a person y ends, it had never been love—despite x's protests to the contrary. The doctrine thus connotes a negative evaluation; something was wrong with x's emotion such that it did not measure up to genuine love. But the doctrine of strict constancy can also be used defensively: if x's emotion ends, then it had not been love—which relieves x of the burden of having had to do those things that are expected of lovers. And if x's emotion ends, x is now free to pursue genuine love once again, a love that might itself be strictly constant. The escape clause of strict constancy thereby makes it easier to embrace the doctrine of timeless exclusivity. For a person x's loving now only the person y and later loving only another person z does not violate the conditions of timeless exclusivity as long as (by the doctrine of strict constancy) the termination of x's first love for y means that x had never really loved y at all. In this way, the latecomer z becomes x's first and only beloved.

If a person x's loving a person y means that x will love y at least until y dies, then x's loving y also means x will love y at least as long as y remains the person that y is. X's loving y until y dies and x's loving y as long as y remains y are equivalent under the assumption that y's identity as y is only a matter of bodily integrity: the later person y is the person whose body is the causal descendent of the body of the earlier y. Strict constancy requires the lover x to love this bodily identified beloved y for as long as y exists; in particular, y's undergoing dramatic personality changes does not count as y's no longer being y and therefore does not count as y's no longer existing ("dying"). The doctrine of strict constancy insists that if a person x really loves another person y, this love will continue toward this changed y. But if we make a different assumption about the beloved's identity, another version of the doctrine of strict constancy emerges (*identity constancy*): if x loves y at t_1, then x loves y at all times after t_1, as long as y remains morally and psychologically the same person y. This analysis of constancy does not require x to love y if y has undergone a change in identity and has become z, where z's body is causally continuous with y's, yet z's character, morally or psychologically, is drastically different from y's. That is, if x's love toward y ends when y becomes z, its termination does not put into doubt that x had earlier loved y. If x no longer loves y when y becomes z, x's love is gone only because its object is gone (y has, in effect, died), not because there is some fault in x's love. Indeed, were x to love this brand new z that y has become, merely because x had loved y, we may doubt that x had loved y at all, since who y was had little to do with x's states of love. If x loves this z, who is qualitatively different from y, because z is attractive to x independently of z's bodily continuity with y, x may be accused of loving nonexclusively (x's loves for y and z are two separate loves), but x cannot be accused of failing to love y constantly. For example, if x no longer loves y because the characteristically hedonistic y has become celibate (or *vice versa*), the doctrine of strict constancy implies that this cessation of love constitutes a failure of x's love to be constant and puts into doubt x's claim to have loved y. Identity constancy, by contrast, implies that the cessation of x's love is not a failure of constancy but the absence of an object to love. The difficult question faced by the doctrine of identity constancy, but avoided by strict constancy, is this: when does a change in y count as either an internal, smooth development of y's enduring moral-psychological identity or as a trivial change having no relation to y's identity; and when, on the other hand, does a change in y count as a development beyond y's character, significant enough to constitute the appearance of the new z on the scene?

The fuzzy analysis of "love is constant," the doctrine of *indefinite constancy*, does not require that the lover x love the beloved y forever, yet claims that x's emotion must last "some" length of time for it to be love. On this view, love is like grief and resentment. It makes no sense to suppose that one experiences only momentary flashes of these emotions (unlike pain or a bolt of blind rage); their enduring for an indefinite amount of time is logically necessary for experiencing grief or resentment at all. Strict constancy must give way to a less restrictive analysis, as timeless exclusivity had to give way to a weaker notion. The trick, however, is to say something more precise than that love must last "some" length of time to be love, otherwise the doctrine of indefinite constancy degenerates into the thesis that love logically admits of no time constraints. For to claim that love must last some vague length of time seems not to put any time constraint on love.

The doctrine of indefinite constancy can be made less vague by distinguishing in another way among strict constancy, indefinite constancy, and the claim that love does not admit of any time constraints. Let us say that an R_1 reason for the end of love is a reason that negates the emotion's claim to have been love (say, a person x "loved" a person y for y's beautiful breasts, and x's emotion ends after y gave birth or had a mastectomy). And let us say that an R_2 reason for the end of love does not call into question the claim that the emotion earlier had been love (say, x loved y until y suddenly ran off to Paris with z). The doctrine of strict constancy, then, is the thesis that the set of R_2 reasons is empty (or that there are only R_1 reasons for the end of love). Since, for this doctrine, love to be love must last as long as the beloved exists, it makes no difference why love ends, if it does; all reasons for the end of love (except the death of the beloved) challenge the claim that love had existed earlier. On the other hand, the doctrine that love has no time constraints at all is the thesis that the set of R_1 reasons is empty (or that there are only R_2 reasons for the end of love). Since there are no time constraints on love, its genuineness is never put into doubt if it ends, regardless of the reason. The doctrine of indefinite constancy, then, can be understood as the specific thesis that both R_1 reasons and R_2 reasons exist, rather than as the vague claim that love must last "some" length of time to be love. The point is that in investigating the constancy of love we now ask questions about *why* love ends, rather than about love's duration *per se*.

The distinction between R_1 and R_2 reasons for the end of love can be usefully employed to investigate views about love. Karol Wojtyla, for example, says that love

> is put to the test most severely when the sensual and emotional reactions... grow weaker, and sexual values... lose their effect. Nothing then remains except the value of the person.[18]

Why, for Wojtyla, is a severe test of love the death of sexual desire? Given his philosophical and theological project, it makes sense:

> There exists... a problem which can be described as that of 'introducing love into love'. The word as first used in that phrase signifies the love which is the subject of the greatest commandment, while in its second use it means all that takes shape between a man and a woman on the basis of the sexual urge. We could look at it the other way round and say that there exists a problem of changing the second type of love (sexual love) into the first, the love of which the New Testament speaks.[19]

Wojtyla does not mean that the *only* severe test of love in marriage comes when sexual excitement between the spouses declines, for on the very next page (see below) he proposes another severe test. But it is clear that, for Wojtyla, a love that ends when sexual desire ends is not genuine love. Hence he acknowledges R_1 reasons for the end of love. Does he also admit R_2 reasons? Since *agape* "endures all things" (1 Corinthians 13:7), and Wojtyla thinks that the personal love of marriage is agapic, he should not. Consider, however, this passage:

> We love the person complete with his or her virtues and faults, and up to a point independently of those virtues and in spite of those faults. The strength of such a love emerges most clearly when the beloved... stumbles, when his or her weaknesses or even sins come into the open. One who truly loves does not then withdraw his love, but loves all the more, loves in full consciousness of the other's shortcomings and faults.... For the person as such never loses its essential value. The emotion which attaches itself to the values of the person remains loyal.[20]

On the one hand, the beloved y has the inherent value of the person "as such" that never changes or diminishes.[21] Always having this value, the beloved y should always be loved by the lover x, whose "emotion... remains loyal." X loves y in virtue of the unchanging essential value of the person, even when y sins. Indeed, this is the real test of x's love, its enduring when y sins, thereby showing itself to be attached to the value of the person as such. Wojtyla seems to buck current popular ideas about love; hardly anyone expects one person to continue to love another person who becomes, for example, physically and emotionally abusive. On the other hand, Wojtyla is not comfortable requiring a person x to love another person y despite *any* of y's sins. For, as he seems to suggest at the beginning, love must endure only "up to a point." Here he might be allowing the possibility of R_2 reasons. But he fails to fill in the details and thereby gives the impression that no R$_2$ reasons exist. This is confirmed by his claim that marriage is indissoluble.[22]

The doctrine of strict exclusivity entails that if a person x has loved another person y, and y dies, x logically cannot later love z; and Wojtyla's strict constancy might entail that x must continue to love y even after y's body dies, since the value of the person as such would seem to be eternal. But Wojtyla's position on x's loving and marrying z, if x's spouse y dies, is complex.[23] On the one hand, he claims that it is "justifiable" and "permitted" for x to marry a second time, since "marriage is strictly a feature of man's physical and terrestrial existence, so that it is naturally dissolved by the death of one of the spouses." Yet Wojtyla also says that not to marry again is "altogether praiseworthy." The reasons are that not marrying again "emphasizes more fully the reality of the union with the person now deceased" and, more important, not marrying again recognizes that "the value of the person... is not transient, and spiritual union can and should continue even when physical union is at an end." This makes sense; if the beloved's essential value is spiritual, it never diminishes. The love that endures despite the beloved's sins, and which attaches to the beloved's essential value, is a love that endures despite the death of the beloved's body. Wojtyla's view of marrying a second time if one's spouse dies is similar to Paul's view of marriage itself. Paul had claimed (1 Corinthians 7:6-7) that it was permissible to enter marriage and engage in sexual activity there, although the best and praiseworthy state is to remain unmarried and celibate.

RECIPROCITY

Kierkegaard claimed that the death of one's beloved—not, as in Wojtyla, the loss of sexual excitement in marital love or the beloved's sins—is the test of the genuineness of love. After the death of the beloved, the lover can no longer get anything from him or her, so the continuation of love shows that the lover's attitude toward the beloved was genuine love and not merely instrumental (as in Aristotle's use-friendship).[24] Regarding love for an inanimate thing (say, a 1950D Jefferson nickel), Robert Brown says something similar: "The test of genuine love [is] that the love continues after all possible use of the object merely as a means... ceases."[25] Is not the object's being useless guaranteed only when it no longer exists? We should infer, then, that if a person x's love persists when the beloved y does not reciprocate that love (Kierkegaard: cannot reciprocate, because dead), this is also an excellent sign that the love is genuine, for here, too, the lover's love does not depend on his or her getting something from the beloved. No wonder that in some theories of courtly and romantic love, unrequited love is given the highest praise. But there must be ways to determine whether a person x loves another person y that do not depend on the beloved's death or not reciprocating the love—the quality of the lover's benevolent concern for the beloved or the depth of their intimacy—since we often believe a person when he claims to love someone who is alive and who does reciprocate his love. The intriguing idea is that because there is no reciprocity from an inanimate object, our love for it is pure, inspired only by the beauty or goodness of the object itself. Compare, then, Plato's *eros* for the form of Beauty, which kind of love necessarily lacks reciprocity, and the human love for the Christian God, which is by its nature reciprocal. Is it not a convenient psychological advantage of Christianity (an advantage eschewed by Plato) that it promises that one's love for God will always be returned, along with all the benefits of reciprocity?

Reciprocity is relatively easily defined: a person's love for another person is reciprocal, or reciprocated, if the latter also loves the former. Of course, we must be more precise: if the lover x loves the beloved y only at t_1 and y loves x only at some other time t_2, their love is not reciprocal. Thus, reciprocal love is x's loving y and y's loving x at the same time. If two persons' love is reciprocal, the two persons have the same emotion toward each other. But what does having the *same* emotion mean? Love comes in many varieties: there is e-type love and a-type love; there is e-type love based on physical properties, and e-type love based on personality properties; there is romantic, sexual love and there is agapic, selfless love. Hence, two persons' having the *same* emotion toward each other can mean two different things. In "broad" reciprocity, x's and y's having the same emotion toward each other is their having personal love of *any* kind toward the other. In "narrow" reciprocity, by contrast, many details of their respective loves are the same: they both love each other for their beautiful bodies, or they are both a-type lovers, and so forth.

The thesis that love is by its logic or nature a reciprocal emotion is the claim that if one person x has an emotion toward another person y, and y does not have the same (broadly conceived) emotion toward x, then neither x's nor y's emotion is love: a necessary condition for an emotion to be love is that the object of the emotion has the same emotion toward its subject. Love is not by its nature unilateral; either x and y love each other in some way, or neither x nor y love each other. This logical thesis must be distinguished from a psychological claim about some people, that they are not able to love another person unless they are loved in return (if not first), or that they would immediately stop loving the other when the other's love starts to waver. When Alastair Hannay writes, "Unrequited love, or parental love which is not... returned as such, are familiar phenomena, so no one could reasonably assert that [reciprocity] was necessary for love. Indeed, the suggestion that you could only love another if the other loved you... implies a... conditionality that is... incompatible with genuine concern,"[26] we are not quite sure he keeps distinct the conceptual and the psychological claims. His latter claim—if the continuation of my loving you is conditional on your loving me, then I do not genuinely love you—might state only a psychological fact about me, while Hannay's former claim—unreciprocated loves exist and therefore reciprocity cannot be necessary for love—is a conceptual point.

The logical thesis, if true, would make love an anomalous emotion. Other emotions are not by nature reciprocal: one person can unilaterally hate, admire, or resent another person. Further, many varieties of love are not, or not expected to be, reciprocal: (a) God loves all humans, but some humans do not love God; (b) a person might love chess or the Beethoven Violin Concerto, and of course chess and the Beethoven Violin Concerto cannot reciprocate; (c) a person might love an irreversibly comatose or dead person; (d) a parent may love his or her infant child, who does not yet have the ability to love anyone; (e) I might love a cat, and my love is not bogus just because a cat has a different kind of affective life; and (f) my neighbor-love for you is genuine love even when you hate me.

The response to this objection can be piecemeal or general. The piecemeal response explains away each counterexample: (a) God's love generates reciprocity, or to love God a human must only believe in God; (b) we may like the Beethoven Violin Concerto, but we cannot love it, because we cannot be concerned about an inanimate thing for its own sake; (c) a person's loving a comatose or dead person is a limiting case of a previously reciprocal love, or this comatose or dead person cannot really be loved; (d) parental love is another limiting case, since it aims toward or develops into reciprocity; further, infants might exhibit a rudimentary need-love for their parents; (e) either my emotion for animals is only affection, or animals (like infants) exhibit emotions close enough to love; and (f) neighbor-love may work like God's love to evoke reciprocity. Clearly, the piecemeal response is not compelling.

The general response is that love is, after all, an anomalous or special emotion. Hence, most of the counterexamples are irrelevant to the thesis that personal love requires reciprocity. But this will not do. Many cases of reciprocal personal love must have been, at least briefly, not reciprocal; it is unlikely that one person's loving another and the latter's loving the first begin simultaneously. The thesis that personal love is logically reciprocal, however, prohibits nonsimultaneous beginnings. There is another way to make the point. The logical thesis that love is reciprocal means that a person x cannot love a person y unless y, too, loves x; but, then, it is also true that y could not love x unless x loves y. This makes love look impossible. One might handle the problem of x's loving y and y's loving x not starting at the same time this way: *either* x's love, which begins before y's, is not "fully" love until y reciprocates (and y's loving x is not "fully" love unless x already "non-fully" loves y), *or* x's emotion can be love as long as, shortly after it begins, y also loves x. The former solution rests on a tenuous distinction between x's "not fully" and "fully" loving y; the latter solution blurs the distinction between (permanently) unrequited love and not-yet-reciprocal love. Further, why does fully loving, but not non-fully loving, require reciprocity? Perhaps if fully loving requires reciprocity, then non-fully loving also requires some reciprocity: x cannot non-fully love y unless y, too, non-fully loves x. All we need to do to generate a regress here is to point out that x's non-fully loving y and y's non-fully loving x do not start at the same time. Shall we solve this problem by saying that x's less-than-non-fully loving y cannot become x's non-fully loving y unless y reciprocates?

The thesis that love is by its logic or nature reciprocal seems supportable neither by observation nor by theory; for example, one person's finding another person attractive enough to love does not entail that the second finds the first attractive enough to love. Such is the stuff of tragedy. Yet some writers do claim that love is reciprocal. Robert Ehman says, "While reciprocity is not a condition of our desiring a person... it is nevertheless a condition of genuine love."[27] Ehman's argument is the same as his argument that "there is in the strict sense no love at first sight" (which makes sense, since "love at first sight" is a kind of "love" that initially exists without reciprocity). On Ehman's view, love requires knowledge of the beloved's character; not only must a person x have true beliefs about the person y that are formed rationally (that is, there is no idealization in x's love), but x's knowledge of y must be extensive. Hence, love at first sight is never love, since x could not know nearly enough about y at their first meeting. Similarly, "there is no purely unrequited love." Never having had "the opportunity to share his life with his beloved," a person cannot base his emotion on "the qualities of the person that are at once most unique and most permanent." Instead, "the unrequited lover may make a show of loving, but in fact he loves a mere unrealized ideal."[28] I do not find Ehman's argument convincing. Even if a person's loving another person requires the first to know the second well, it does not follow that a person cannot love another unless the other also loves in return. The knowledge that a lover must have to love a beloved might be available only if the beloved spends a good deal of time with the lover, but this condition is satisfiable without the beloved's loving the lover.

Karol Wojtyla also claims that personal love "is by its very nature not unilateral but bilateral."[29] Like Ehman, Wojtyla thinks that unrequited love is not "genuine" and psychologically unsound: "onesided" love does not have "the objective fullness which reciprocity would give it.... If a love of this kind persists,... this is because of some inner obstinacy." But Wojtyla's argument in defense of the logical thesis is different from Ehman's. "Love is not just something *in* [a person x] and something *in* [a person y]—for in that case there would properly speaking be two loves—but is something common to" x and y, Wojtyla asserts.[30] Love is a (third) thing to which both people contribute; it is not their separate loves for each other, but "something 'between' two persons, something shared." Hence, without either one person's love for the other or the other's love for the first, there is no love, that third thing, at all. But it is not clear why the love "between" the two people, x and y, is not merely x's loving y and y's loving x. We would not say that when x and y mutually hate each other, there is only one hatred rather than two. And if we find odd the metaphysics that joins two people into one in a union-love (see Chapter Five), we will find odd the metaphysics that creates one love out of two.

Wojtyla's thesis is surprising, coming from an agapist. Neighbor-love is not by nature reciprocal: one turns the other cheek in the face of abuse or a failure of reciprocity and continues to love.

One would never say of neighbor-love, as Wojtyla says of unrequited personal love, that it is psychologically unsound in having "some inner obstinacy." Indeed, the obstinacy of neighbor-love is a virtue. Given the role that *agape* plays in the constancy of personal love for Wojtyla, it would appear to be impossible for him to argue that love is by nature reciprocal. If the lover's love for the beloved is expected to endure beyond the point of the beloved's sinning, surely the lover's love for the beloved must be expected to endure if the beloved no longer loves in return. Wojtyla's thesis that love is strictly constant seems incompatible with his claims about reciprocity.

However, the doctrine that love is strictly constant is not incompatible with the doctrine that love is reciprocal. If love is strictly constant, x's love for y will continue even if y no longer loves x; hence (it seems) y's having the same emotion toward x is not, contrary to the doctrine of reciprocity, a necessary condition for x to love y. But if love is strictly constant, then we have no right to assume that y *no longer* loves x. According to strict constancy, if x's and y's emotions are really love, neither emotion will end. Hence, x's love is never faced with the test of enduring when y no longer reciprocates; the constancy of love prevents the situation from arising, in which x loves y but y does not love x, that would show that strict constancy is incompatible with reciprocity. Similarly, if x's or y's emotion does end, the emotion had not been love; but by the doctrine of reciprocity, if y's emotion had not been love, x's emotion, too, had not been love. Thus there had never been any love of x for y that might now be persisting even though not reciprocated by y; there is no love that fails to endure in the face of nonreciprocation. If love is by its nature reciprocal, it is conceptually impossible for x to stop loving y because y has stopped loving x.

Wojtyla gives another reason that love is by its nature reciprocal, implicitly acknowledging the notion that humans might love God in response to God's love for humans. When a person x loves a person y, x makes a gift of himself or herself to y. This gift is a "surrender of the innermost self"; the "magnitude of the gift" represents the value of the person as such. A person's love for another is reciprocated because the "realization of the value of the gift awakens the need to... reciprocate in ways which would match its value."[31] The beloved can match this value only by making a gift to the lover of himself or herself, that is, by loving in return. Notice three things about this argument. First, it presupposes that x's loving y and y's loving x begin nonsimultaneously, since y's loving x is a causal response to x's loving y. Love unilaterally generates its own reciprocity. Second, if x's loving y brings about y's loving x, it could not have been the case that y's loving x brought about x's loving y, for y's loving x occurs after x begins to love y. Hence, x's love for y must come about some other way than by y's loving x. Both loves involve a giving of the self but have a different basis; x's gift to and love for y could not have been a response to y's surrendering y's self to x. What is the basis, then, of x's love for y? Third, the argument is a conceptual and a psychological defense of reciprocity. Conceptually, the argument asserts that love involves the largest of gifts, a surrender of the self. (Recall the loss of autonomy in union-love; see Chapter Five.) Psychologically, it asserts that a gift of such magnitude has the power to induce love.

The Marxist psychoanalytic philosopher Erich Fromm (1900-1980) held a similar view:

> In giving he cannot help bringing something to life in the other person... ; in truly giving, he cannot help receiving that which is given back to him.... Love is a power which produces love; impotence is the inability to produce love."[32]

But the psychological component of these arguments, the claim that love begets love, is dubious. True, my loving you might show you what love is and invoke return love for me by setting an example, but not always. And perhaps a person cannot love anyone at all unless he or she has at some time been loved, has been shown thereby what love is.[33] But this provides no reason to think that my loving you will evoke your loving me in particular. Further, one person's giving a huge gift to another might evoke only gratitude or, oppositely, resentment. An already existing reciprocal love might be precisely the framework *within* which lavish giving can be welcomed as fitting rather than as threatening. And there are those (perhaps Stendhal and Woody Allen) who philosophize that my giving to you is a sure way to *prevent* you from loving me; you come to love me only if I withdraw from you or remain coolly detached. In a devious way this tactic might still involve love's begetting love. If a person x loves a person y and wants y to love x in return, x should hide the fact that x loves y; causally situated between x's loving y and eventually y's loving x is not Wojtyla's gift, but x's not giving. But if love does not always work to evoke love, neither does playing hard-to-get always work to evoke love. The person x who wants love from another person y must figure out in advance—by knowing y—whether showing or hiding his or her love will have the desired effect.

One more question should be addressed. If my love for you ends because your love for me has ended, is this reason for my love's ending an R_1 or an R_2 reason? That is, if a person x no longer loves a person y because y no longer loves x, does this bring into doubt x's love for y, or is it compatible with x's having loved y? Our intuition here might be to reach a decision about x's love independently of whether y's love itself ends for an R_1 or R_2 reason. If so, we might reason this way: x's no longer loving y because y no longer loves x is an R_1 reason for the end of x's love, since love conditional on reciprocity does not deserve the name; or this is an R_2 reason if x's love ends because x realizes that x's benevolent concern for y, x's desire to benefit y, can no longer bear fruit. But if we now take into account why y's love for x ended, matters quickly become complicated. Suppose y's love for x ends for an R_1 reason; for example, y was attached to x in virtue of x's wealth and this attachment dissipates when x's fortune evaporates. Here we want to say that if x no longer loves y because y no longer loves x, this is an R_2 reason (or at least not necessarily an R_1 reason) for the end of x's love. But if y's love ends for an R_2 reason (say, x reveals his or her abusive and deceitful side), then x's not loving y because y no longer loves x is an R_1 reason. But these are only examples, and whether any generalizations can be fashioned, given the multiplicity of reasons for the end of love and the difficulty of assigning reasons to the R_1 or the R_2 category, is doubtful.

CHAPTER SEVEN

SEX, LOVE, AND MARRIAGE

Wives, submit to your husbands as to the Lord. For the husband is the head of the wife as Christ is the head of the church, his body, of which he is the Savior. Now as the church submits to Christ, so also wives should submit to their husbands in everything.... In this same way, husbands ought to love their wives as their own bodies. He who loves his wife loves himself. After all, no one ever hated his own body, but feeds and cares for it, just as Christ does the church.... Each one of you... must love his wife as he loves himself, and the wife must respect her husband.

—St. Paul, Ephesians 5:22-33

his piece of Scripture seems to express a union view of marriage in Paul. At least, Aquinas reads Ephesians as "teaching that... the love a man has for himself is the motive for the love he has for the wife who is united to him."[1] But this must dampen our enthusiasm for a union model of marriage, as it dampened our enthusiasm for a union model of love, for a person's "benevolent" concern for a spouse is merely a species of his or her natural self-interest, the person's concern for himself. As argued earlier (see Chapter Five), union excludes Aristotelian, "robust" concern of both members of the union for the other. Further, despite protests from Christian spokesmen (Pat Robertson, for one), Paul's notion of marriage in Ephesians is patriarchal; wives are called on to "submit to" their husbands. This inegalitarian model of marriage seems not to fit well with 1 Corinthians, in which Paul insists on equal and mutual ownership of each other's body and sexual abilities:

7:4 The wife hath not power of her own body, but the husband: and likewise also the husband hath not power of his own body, but the wife.
7:5 Defraud ye not one the other, except it be with consent for a time, that ye may give yourselves to fasting and prayer; and come together again, that Satan tempt you not for your incontinency.

Marriage, for the author of this letter to the Corinthians, is *ad remedium concupiscentiae*: it exists for the purpose of providing mutual sexual satisfaction, lest the spouses be tempted into promiscuous fornication. Hence each spouse has toward the other the "marriage debt," the duty to supply sexual services on demand. But if we add to 1 Corinthians 7 the authoritarian hierarchy of Ephesians 5, we obtain part of the reason for how the marriage debt has come to be widely practiced: it is the man who has the unilateral right to demand sex from his wife, and she must "submit."

THE LINKS

It is curious that in Paul's account of marriage and marital sex in 1 Corinthians 7, no mention is made about two other purposes of heterosexual sexual acts: procreation and the expression or deepening of love between the spouses. These things are glaring by their absence. All four items—marriage, sexual activity, love, and procreation—have now been linked "inseparably" together for twentieth-century Catholicism by Pope Paul VI in his 1968 encyclical "Humanae Vitae."

Adrienne Rich senses a mystery in the linkage among these things, wondering "why species survival, the means of impregnation, and emotional/erotic relationships should have ever become so rigidly identified with each other."[2] How did the links among heterosexuality, love, marriage, and procreation ever become entrenched both in our social practices and in our personal thoughts, desires, and behaviors? To our consciousness and feelings, the links seem normal, natural, unexceptional, ordinary, not worth wondering about. The linkage is the kind of thing that the philosopher John McMurtry calls "an intractable given—dictated by the laws of God, Nature, Government, and Good Sense all at once."[3] Rich favors an acculturation answer; our society compels us into heterosexuality, marriage, and procreation (see Chapter Four). On this view, society wields enormous power over our personal lives. And recall Anthony Walsh's evolutionary thesis (Chapter Two), according to which it is nature, not society, that "compels" us to be the way we are. The links that feel natural are, in fact, natural: "Nature has emotionally enriched the human reproductive impulse through love, and in doing so she has immensely increased our enjoyment of both."[4] In one fell biological swoop, the perplexing question has been answered, how sex and love and reproduction have been welded together. Marriage does not figure into Walsh's evolutionary hypothesis; that, I guess, is a cultural artifact imposed on the linkage of the other three.

On Paul VI's view, God replaces Walsh's nature (although we could have it both ways). The

> inseparable connection [was] established by God, which man on his own initiative may not break, between the unitive significance and the procreative significance which are both inherent to the marriage act.[5]

The use of contraceptive devices by a married couple is wrong for Paul VI because it separates the inseparable (see Chapter Three). But if the "unitive significance" (the expression and deepening of spousal love) and the "procreative significance" of sexual activity in marriage are *inherent* to the "marriage act," then how could human beings, by their own devices, ever hope to separate that which God created inseparable? Some contraceptive sexual activity in marriage is meant to join the spouses more deeply together in their intimate bond, and can be unitively significant even if not procreatively significant. Further, some sexual activity in marriage, intended purely to achieve fertilization and not to express love, often occurs. That is, even when the spouses are concerned to employ sexual activity for its most important "inherent" purpose, procreation, the sexual act need not involve a deliberate attempt to express spousal love. Indeed, trying to express love *and* to fertilize at the same time might be more difficult (interfere with each other) than trying to procreate by itself or trying to express love by itself.[6]

Paul VI's speaking about what is "inherent" to sexual activity in marriage—the deepening of love and procreation—indicates that he has discounted other possible reasons to engage in sex. Human beings have a plurality of reasons to engage in sexual activity, a wide variety of purposes we try to fulfill, none of which seems to be more "inherent" than any other; we make of sex what we will. Thus the only meaning of "inherent" that makes sense in the context of Paul VI's encyclical is a *normative* meaning. Paul VI is saying that procreation and love ought to be joined together in the sexual marriage act, as its proper ends.[7] God designed nature so that it should be used in a certain way, by our acts of free will, not by our being compelled by nomic necessity. Paul VI, then, has dressed up his value judgments about the morally and religiously proper ends of sex so that they look like an ontological claim about what is "inherent" and "inseparable" in sex.

From a pluralist perspective, nothing much seems to be inherent to sex; nor does it seem to be inseparably joined to marriage, love, and procreation. The link between sexual activity and love is broken by loveless sex (any casual sexual relationship) and by the benevolent concern of love expressed by the performance of actions other than the sexual, which perhaps more reliably cement the bond between spouses. The link between love and marriage is broken by loveless marriages (say, arranged marriages or those grounded on economic, social, or reproductive considerations) and by loving relationships that exist outside the authority of the state and Church. The link between marriage and procreation is broken by the nonprocreative marriages of infertile, elderly, and "DINKS" couples (double income, no kids) and by the enormous amount of procreative sexual activity that has occurred throughout history, in all parts of the world, outside of marriage. The link between sex and procreation is broken by the many kinds of contraceptive devices as well as by the possibility of entirely artificial methods of human reproduction. The link between procreation and love is broken by any sexual activity intended to result in a child, if the biological parents are concerned neither about "being" in love at the time or expressing love during the sexual act, and by any relationship of love (heterosexual or homosexual) in which procreation does not figure into the shared goals of the partners. And, finally, the link between sex and marriage is broken by premarital, extramarital, and nonmarital sexual activity (all of which the world has long known) and by marriages in which the spouses do not engage in sex, either because they have no interest in doing so or they are busy accomplishing other things ("DINS," double income, no sex). To argue that we should, with Paul VI, condemn some of the ways this plurality of purposes and arrangements breaks the links among sex, love, marriage, and procreation is to make a value judgment that some uses or modes of sex and love are more respectable than others. That might be true, but whether we can rationally discern which ones are ideal and which are unsuitable, by investigating nature or scrutinizing the plan of an infinite and unfathomable God, is questionable.

SEX AND LOVE

The logical, psychological, and normative relationships between sexuality and love are among the most perplexing and controversial of human emotional phenomena.[8] On the one hand, there is the inseparable linkage among sex, love, marriage, and procreation asserted by Paul VI in his simple formula. But, on the other hand, breaking these links by acknowledging the plurality of human purposes and arrangements suggests that the territory is more complex than Paul VI would have us believe. Many people, at least in our culture, face the disconcerting psychological and moral problem of experiencing multiple loves and multiple sexual attractions: a person x loves another person y, but x might also feel love for yet a third person z; or x is fond of and sexually aroused in y's presence, yet experiences equally moving states of mind and body toward z. We do not always live by Paul VI's ideals. Still, there are some reasons, not necessarily conclusive, for thinking that multiplicity can be constrained.

Suppose, for example, that personal love conceptually ("inherently"?) included an element of sexual desire, or by human psychology love and sex were nomically or normally paired with each other. We might expect, then, love to be exclusive if sexual desire tended to be exclusive. In *The Passions of the Soul*, the French philosopher René Descartes (1596-1650) asserted that sexual desire was experienced as exclusive:

> Although we see many persons of the opposite sex, yet we do not desire many at one time.... But when we observe something in one of them which is more attractive than anything we observe at that moment in others, this determines our soul to feel towards that one alone all the inclination which nature gives it to pursue the good which it represents as the greatest we could possess.[9]

Sexual desire, on this view, is serially exclusive by its nature ("at that moment" we cannot conceive of desiring another); love, following suit, would also be serially exclusive. For Descartes, the phenomenon can be straightforwardly explained in terms of a "nature" that has "implanted certain impressions in the brain." Today, this type of explanation is offered by those biologists who try to provide an evolutionary account of serial sexual exclusivity among humans.[10] Descartes's explanation senses only a benign nature at work. Two hundred years later, Schopenhauer would claim that the feelings we have about "the good which [nature] represents as the greatest we could possess" are delusions (see Introduction)—nature is not so benign after all.

The exclusivity of sexual desire is often denied. Instead, sexuality is seen as an indiscriminate instinct, and so love, to the extent that it incorporates or is nomically tied with sexuality, will tend not to be exclusive. Go to the beach or a public swimming pool, sit down, and watch the people walk by: the next one is always even more attractive than the one that just went by, your heart leaps even higher in your chest, your limbs tremble, and you wonder what you ever saw in the first. "A lover has made a mistake, he has seen the beloved by artificial light... but her sister is the ideal."[11] We can and do desire more than one at a time, unless we understand Descartes's "at one time" narrowly and literally. As Diotima teaches the young Socrates,

> You must perceive that the beauty of one particular body
> is related to the beauty of another body.... Once you have
> understood this, you will become a lover of all beautiful
> bodies, but you'll despise your lust for the one and give it
> up, considering it petty.[12]

The possibility that sexuality is indiscriminate need not prompt such sober reflections. There is, by contrast, the humorous approach of James Thurber and E. B. White: "I am in love...but just the same I don't like the way I looked at Miriam last night.... And if she *is* my darling... what caused me to take such a long, critical look at the girl in the red-and-brown scarf this morning when I was breakfasting in the Brevoort?"[13]

Rather than the exclusivity of love depending on the exclusivity of sexuality, the relationship, if any exists, might be the other way around: the exclusivity of love makes the sexual impulse exclusive. The roving sexual eye of nondiscriminating sexual desire can be made to focus on one object by personal love. "Instinct tends to amplify indefinitely the number of objects which satisfy it," writes the Spanish philosopher José Ortega y Gasset (1883-1955), "whereas love tends toward exclusivism." Hence "nothing immunizes a male against other sexual attractions so well as amorous enthusiasm for a certain woman."[14] This optimism about the power of love to make exclusive a sexual drive that is not by its own nature exclusive has been, through the ages, applauded, but has also been the brunt of cynical realism. It has often been supplemented by the additional thesis that it is a woman's love for a man, and her stabilizing influence on him, that tames his animal nature and makes him a faithful husband and providing father:

> The sexual drive of men is much stronger than that of women. That is how the human race was designed in order that it might perpetuate itself. The other side of the coin is that it is easier for women to control their sexual appetites.... [A woman] can motivate him, inspire him, encourage him, teach him, restrain him, reward him, and have power over him that he can never achieve over her with all his muscle.[15]

One argument that love ought (morally) to be exclusive assumes that love includes a sexual element: the immorality of multiple sexual relations is transferred to multiple love, in the same way that we tried to transfer the phenomenal exclusivity of sexual desire to love. The argument depends on there being something morally wrong with multiple sexual relations independently of the fact that the person who engages in them might also love someone; otherwise the wrongness of multiple sexual relations could not explain why multiple loves are morally wrong. That is, the argument must be distinguished from the argument that because (or when) personal love or marriage involves a mutual promise of sexual fidelity, sexual relations outside the love or marriage are morally wrong. In this case, the moral obligation to love exclusively does not follow from the immorality of multiple sexual relations; the immorality of the sexual relations follows from a fact about some love or marital relationships—that they include promises—not from a truth about the logic of love. But if personal love does not necessarily include sexual desire as a component, or if multiple sexual relations are not always morally wrong, how could we continue to claim that one person ought to love one other person and no one else?[16]

Given the ubiquity of sexual impulses and fantasies, a person x's claim to love another person y (in or out of marriage) is not likely defeated by x's merely being sexually attracted to and wanting a third person z. This is a slightly sexually liberal view, since theologians often sermonize in the spirit of Matthew 5: 28, condemning sexual thoughts themselves as morally wrong, even in the absence of physical contact: x, who loves and/or is married to y, commits adultery as soon as x thinks lustful thoughts about z.[17] The slightly liberal view is that x's claim to love y is defeated not by sexual fantasies about z, but precisely by x's acting on x's desire for z, by pursuing or engaging in sexual activity with z. Perhaps we can reach this conclusion by arguing that, given the concept or nature of love, x's sexual activity must be exclusively restricted to y; carrying on multiple sexual relationships is the kind of behavior that is incompatible with love. Perhaps x's engaging in sexual activity with z destroys or undermines the intimacy between x and y; or x's unfaithfulness breaks an implicit promise to or agreement with y; or x's engaging in sex with z causes x's beloved y too much distress. But if one has desires, why not act on them? If, say, the spouses avoid deception and they deliberately refrain from making sexually binding promises, why take Augustine's advice to hold sexual desire in check?[18]

THE DEATH OF DESIRE

Sexual desire is often felt as exclusive. As Descartes, C.S. Lewis, Schopenhauer, and many others have claimed in their own ways, when one person x is sexually entranced by another person y, x's consciousness has no room for sexual desire directed toward anyone else; the x who is romantically head-over-heels in love with y feels that x's love and desire are exclusively fastened on y. This is often an illusion. Further, the wonderful feelings of romantic love set another trap that must be avoided: "the experience of falling in love [carries] the illusion that the experience will last forever."[19] Even as we know in our rational minds that love is not guaranteed to endure or to be exclusive, the immediate rush of love and its confluence with sexual desire causes some of us to feel, and hence believe, that our love for just this one person will last and last and last. Overwhelmingly blissful sexual satisfaction, too, generates illusions. The "I can't get enough of you" feeling that occurs early in a romantic sexual relationship registers to us as proof that the desire and satisfaction will never die. And powerful sexual desire is often taken to be love itself. But sooner or later we do "get enough." As Socrates lectures to Agathon, "one does not desire what one does not lack" (*Symposium* 200b).

One question we posed earlier was why a person wants the touch of another person instead of his or her own touch (see Chapter One). The answer we came up with was that a person wants to touch and be touched by another person because he or she seeks novel, sharp sensations. But if that is right, it could not be that he wants only the touch of that one other person; it must also be that he wants the touch of many others. If the source of the pleasure is the touch's novelty, then your touching and being touched by one other person will eventually provide less and less pleasure. Being touched by or smelling merely one other person becomes for a person as undistinguished as his or her touching or smelling himself or herself. Thus the romantic, passionate sexual desire that exists in abundance early in a love relationship or marriage slowly but surely dissipates as the partners' intimate bond grows older. The tendency for sexual desire to be multiple arises again, like the South.

While arguing in defense of the virtue of sexual abstinence in marriage, in part for religious reasons but also in part for family planning, Karol Wojtyla discovers a problem:

> Marital continence is so much more difficult than continence outside marriage, because the spouses grow accustomed to intercourse.... Once they begin to have sexual intercourse as a habit, and a constant inclination is created, a mutual need for intercourse comes into being.[20]

By "grow accustomed to intercourse," Wojtyla means that the spouses engage in sex, enjoy it, and as a result it becomes a regular part of their married life, difficult, on account of its pleasure, to do without. Abstinence becomes a chore. But Wojtyla misses, here at least, the problem we have been discussing, which assumes another meaning of "grow accustomed to intercourse": the spouses become *too* accustomed to it, so that they no longer derive much if any pleasure from it. Abstinence, in this case, is all too easy, made possible by the death of desire.

The romantic ideology of the trustworthiness of the feelings of exclusivity and constancy creates expectations that a marriage grounded in romantic love and passion will be satisfying. But hard reality—the attenuation or death of sexual passion between the spouses; the daily presentation of the physical, moral, and personality defects of each spouse to the other; the eventual recognition of differences between their domestic habits—intrudes, and exclusivity and constancy, which initially felt natural and spontaneous, become strenuous tasks that require a strong will to carry out. This is why we are encouraged not to take the feelings of passion too seriously, and not to base something as significant as marriage and procreation on these feelings.[21]

This is also why, perhaps, we should not place too much emphasis on sexual exclusivity. If a marriage can be sustained by shared values and common interests—the raising of children, the writing of books, traveling to foreign lands—the fact that one or both spouses enjoy sexual passion outside the marriage, when it has died in the marriage, would seem to be a viable option. Romance and marriage do not always, and perhaps not very often, go together. Both are or can be valuable parts of a whole life. Then why should not spouses—by utilizing the intimate, honest communication made possible by their bonds of love and marriage—agree that they will pursue, in a civilized way, romance outside their romance-dead marriage?

Recall, however, Aquinas's argument designed to show that one form of extramarital sex is unnatural and hence immoral:

> It is evident that the bringing up of a human child requires the care of a mother who nurses him, and much more the care of a father, under whose guidance and guardianship his earthly needs are supplied and his character developed. Therefore indiscriminate intercourse is against human nature. The union of one man with one woman is postulated, and with her he remains, not for a little while, but for a long period, or even for a whole lifetime.[22]

The natural purpose of sex is procreation, but that includes not merely fertilization, pregnancy, and birth, but also bringing the child into adulthood. According to this thick (or broad) sense of procreation, procreation has not been entirely accomplished unless and until the child matures; only this counts as the fulfillment of the "re-production" of the parents. Adultery by married persons who have children is unnatural, in Aquinas's argument, because it interferes with procreation in this broad sense; it diverts the father or mother away from caring adequately for their children, or it results in children outside the marriage that cannot be cared for. Does adultery really have these effects, or must it? Perhaps Aquinas's worries about neglected or abandoned children had a material and social justification in 1250, but in the economically and educationally developed parts of the world today, that spouses enjoy romantic affairs outside their marriage would not necessarily undermine their caring for their own children or the children created in their outside relationships.

Others deny that marriage and romantic passion are at odds with each other. The philosopher Irving Singer, for example, writes:

> Romantic love is part of a search for a long-term relationship such as marriage, and... married love not only completes the aspirations of romantic love but also permits some vestige of its continuance within the new context of marriage.[23]

Singer, that is, contests the "unwholesome dichotomy between romantic love and married love" (the view that the two do not go together), and Sigmund Freud's cynical view that "a woman loses her lover when she takes him as a husband."[24] Singer admits that the intensity of sexual passion does diminish with time in marriage.[25] Yet he insists that "a type" of passion remains in married love,[26] and he concludes that romantic love and married love are not incompatible:

> Far from precluding passionate love, [a couple's] companionate love will make them more thoroughly dependent on one another. That alone can *increase* their marital passion.[27]

Freud, I think, would not have been much impressed by this "vestige" of romanticism in marriage, and would have read Singer as confirming, rather than refuting, his "unwholesome" prognosis.

For yet other writers, the problem is how to transcend the loss of sexual passion in marriage. When love between the spouses deepens and matures, says Roger Scruton, "the trouble of desire" comes to "an end." Sexual passion, the bodily perturbations caused by the sexual impulse that Augustine admonished us to control, no longer bother us—toward our spouse.[28] "People who have lived together in domestic intimacy feel a particular revulsion at the thought of contact between them."[29] Scruton unflinchingly acknowledges the death of desire in even loving marriages. His solution is the old saw that "eventually desire is replaced by a love which is no longer erotic, but based in trust and companionship."[30] Kant, too, saw the problem with the constant bodily access that spouses have to each other: "too close a connection, too intimate an acquaintance produces sexual indifference and repugnance."[31] So perhaps *this* is the true reason married partners do not treat each other as sexual objects or merely as means to sexual satisfaction, and why they can now relax in the maturity of their relationship: not because mutual ownership of their bodies has united them ontologically into one person (see Chapter Three), but because they are no longer moved toward each other by sexual desire at all. Scruton mentions that even though the "trouble" of desire *between* the spouses is over when their love matures, the "trouble" of desire is, in another sense, just beginning: "how to prevent the calm love of nuptial union from being shattered by the turbulence of a new desire" that one spouse has for a third party—and perhaps the other, too, has for a fourth.[32]

A solution that neither Singer nor Scruton mention is for the married partners to vary their sexual activity, to try new positions, acts, and environments. And, further, why not invite the third or fourth into the dyad?[33] Perhaps the worry is that the reliance on sexual variety to produce pleasure becomes dangerous. Once the partners have satiated themselves in one area of unusual sexual activity, one or both will be eventually pushed by the need for sexual pleasure to try more bizarre sexual acts. Is marital celibacy better than the descent into perversion?[34]

Gilbert Meilaender, who characterizes *eros* as jealous and exclusive, in contrast to *philia*,[35] seems to hold out hope (unintentionally, I think) that a marriage can be maintained even with outside relationships:

> But when, for whatever reason, "passion is stilled," men and women may meet as individualities who care about the same things or seek the same truth.[36]

The shared activities of *philia*—raising the children, writing books, running a business, traveling, collecting antiques—and the companionship of friendship in marriage sustain their ongoing bond, while they candidly acknowledge that their erotic, passionate, or romantic needs are to be satisfied elsewhere. If their marriage is a companionate friendship, if it is trusting, intimate, and grounded in honesty and a commitment to the well-being of their children, then outside romantic attachments, which by their nature are, as we have seen, intense but short-lived, should be no threat to the marriage. This would seem to be true if their marital friendship consisted not of the self-interested attitude of a use-friendship but of genuine Aristotelian *philia*, in which the partners wished each other well for the other's own sake (which could include wishing each other well in their romantic affairs). There is some idealism (or naiveté) in this picture, of course. The background conditions of trust, open communication, and significant shared interests and values are not always sufficiently present to withstand the challenge of outside relationships, be they sexual or only friendly. But we do have models or paradigms of apparently successful marriages: John Stuart Mill and Harriet Taylor provide an example of married friends who based their love on joint projects, not children or sex. For such a *philia* union to exist, however, both men and women must be socially free:

> Mill's final prescription to end the subjection of women was not equal opportunity [to advance in worldly pursuits] but spousal friendship; equal opportunity was a means whereby such friendship could be encouraged.[37]

If men and women can be equals and genuine friends in marriage, engaging in romantic affairs outside of marriage may not be such a big deal—as long as women are as free as men to do so, and women are not psychologically and economically vulnerable (see Chapter Four).

We have spoken several times of sexual activity between

the spouses as being a way for them to deepen and express their love for each other, as if this assumption about the power of sexual activity were unproblematic. But if this claim is either overblown or false, we would have further reason to take less seriously the objections to engaging in romantic relationships outside one's marriage. According to Robert Solomon, the body language that constitutes sexual activity is

> essentially expressive, and its content is limited to inter-personal attitudes and feelings—shyness, domination, fear, submissiveness and dependence, love or hatred or indifference, lack of confidence and embarrassment, shame, jealousy, possessiveness.... Some attitudes, for example tenderness and trust, domination and passivity, are best expressed sexually. Love, it seems, is not best expressed sexually, for its sexual expression is indistinguishable from the expression of a number of other attitudes.[38]

Does Solomon mean that loving sexual activity is indistinguishable in its bodily movements from the physical expression of pure lust (that, as discussed in Chapter One, the polysemicity of the bodily action comes into full play here)? To be sure, the expression of love and lust may be constituted by the same bodily movements. But they need not be. As A. H. Lesser points out, the important distinction may not be that between love and lust, but between the bodily movements of care and concern and those of selfishness.[39] Sexual acts can be wholly giving or wholly taking, and many mixtures of these two exist. Maybe when sexual acts are mostly giving they are also loving, even if lustful, and can be recognized as such. But Solomon's general point, that love may not be well expressed sexually, seems to make sense when, in a love or marital relationship, mutual sexual desire has been attenuated and sexual activity is no longer ecstatic. If the excitement and pleasure of sexual activity becomes negligible, the sexual caress would seem to be able to express little or nothing at all.

(This is a more moderate thesis than Russell Vannoy's claim that sexual activity *cannot* express anything as different from itself as love.)[40]

For this reason, love might be expressed much better by doing the dishes, cleaning the attic or basement, or washing the car.[41] But even if sexual activity is not in general an especially effective way of expressing love, there are two other connections between sex and love that are worth mentioning. First, engaging in sexual activity could still be an expression of love in marriage, even when desire is dead, if the spouses do it to show that they are at least trying to please each other. Engaging in sexual caresses could still express love, exactly when executing the caress has all the character of doing the dishes, that is, when one person would prefer not to be caressing the other but does so anyway, out of duty or concern, for the latter's sake (and perhaps pretends to be enjoying what he or she is doing). In this case, it seems, the sexual interest in being touched by his or her spouse must still survive in one of the persons. Second, a person's *not* engaging in sexual activity outside the relationship can express his or her love for the spouse in a negative sense: not having sex outside the relationship, despite the strong need or temptation to do so, is for a person to abandon part of his or her own good for the sake of the good of the other and thereby shows the extent of the former's love for the latter. Richard Mohr says this about loving homosexual relationships, and then qualifies it:

> Gay men have realized that while sexual sacrifice may be part of the sacrifices that a couple choose to make in order to show their love for each other, it is not necessary for this purpose; there are many other ways to demonstrate mutual love.[42]

If doing the dishes can express love, and one does the dishes often and well enough (or engages frequently enough in dutiful sex for the sake of one's partner), there would seem to be no need to refrain from having sex outside the marriage in order to show one's love. It has already been shown, and having a romantic affair does not necessarily wipe out that achievement.

REASONS FOR MARRIAGE

Marriage need not be for sex (as in St. Paul), nor for procreation (as in Catholic theology), nor for love (as in romantic ideology). There are multiple reasons for getting married, as there are multiple reasons for engaging in sex. There are also multiple reasons or causes for our falling in love with and then loving someone. The fact that there are multiple reasons for these things suggests a disparity among sex, love, and marriage.

Before the twentieth-century, and even today in a large part of the world,[43] many people never had the chance to ask themselves, "Whom should I marry?" Marriages were often arranged for young people by matchmakers or by family members (fathers, in particular), and the choice of an appropriate mate was decided by religious, economic, status, political, and myriad other considerations. Nowadays, in the West at least, individuals have freedom in selecting their mates.[44] "Whom should I marry?" means, for us, "given that the purpose of marriage for me is M, that I want to be married, and that a person's having certain traits is required for my achieving M, which person has these traits?" Some of us answer this question by saying that marriage is a life-long relationship between two people who want to carry out certain shared projects (raising children, writing a history of Europe, avoiding loneliness). And we believe that a necessary condition for fulfilling this purpose is that both persons have the property "romantically loves the other person." In different times and places the important traits might have been "can contribute to our family's fortune, power, or status" or "will reliably milk the cows and collect the eggs every morning," either because marriage was given a different purpose or because it had roughly the same general purpose (carrying out shared projects), but different properties were essential for its fulfillment. In any event, marriage grounded in romantic love used to be a much less common phenomenon than it is now, at a time when the philosophy of Frank Sinatra's (or Sammy Cahn's) lyrics—"love and marriage go together like a horse and carriage"[45]—is nearly taken for granted. We sometimes hear about violations of this philosophy: "she only married him for his money," "he only married her [his trophy wife] to advance his career." The "only" is revealing, as if people never had a wide variety of reasons or purposes in marrying, as if marriage meant or should mean only one thing.[46] In 1800, would anyone have bothered to gossip, "he brought her in from St. Louis just to milk the cow"? In Europe just a few hundred years ago, did not "he actually married her for *love*" often speak of scandal?[47]

Love, I think, is rarely the only or major reason leading two people to get married; women have had, and still have, economic and social reasons to prefer the married state, and men like to have wives do for them the tasks that their mothers used to do. Craig Dean, in arguing for the legal right of gays and lesbians to get married, points not only to their love as a reason, but also to the same legal, social, economic, and personal privileges that attach to heterosexual marriage.[48] Shall we whisper, "he only married him for his medical insurance and inheritance rights"? In any event, the case for gay marriage is a strong one.[49] If friendship, or a desire to lead a shared life based on common interests and concerns, is an ingredient of love and marriage at their best, then both secularly and theologically the notion of marriage between persons of the same sex is coherent. Further, to the extent that romantic love and sexual passion is taken to be a decent reason for heterosexual pairs to marry, it is equally a decent reason for homosexuals to marry. The only argument that rules out gay or lesbian marriages is the one according to which "natural reproductive capability" is the basis or a *sine qua non* of marriage (see Chapter Two). But on that score, many healthy and happy marriages—that of John Stuart Mill and Harriet Taylor, for example—as well as marriages in which at least one partner is not fertile, could not be true marriages.

"Whom should I have sex with?" can be understood similarly: "given that the purpose of sexual activity for me, at this instant, is S" (to experience pleasure, to exercise, to conceive a child, etc.), "the ideal sex partner would have the traits required for fulfilling S (and, on top of it, must have a reason for wanting to have sex with me)." The traits presupposed for "marriage partner" and those presupposed for "sexual partner," given the wide variety of purposes we have in wanting to be married and in wanting to engage in sexual activity, are far from guaranteed to overlap significantly (unless one purpose of marriage is to have sexual access to another person). Reasons for engaging in sexual activity with a person are not necessarily (good) reasons for marrying that person; conversely, reasons for marrying a person are not necessarily (good) reasons for engaging in sexual activity with that person.

"Whom should I love?" resists, by contrast, the kind of analysis we applied to marriage and sexual activity. Love seems to have no purpose, either by its nature or by our assigning one to it, but is something whose point resides in itself. We do not fall in love with and then love someone as a means of attaining, or as a technique to produce, our happiness; the happiness seems intrinsic to love. That we should seek a love-partner with whom we can be happy is trite advice. If we cannot specify any purpose of love, that method of ascertaining the relevant traits of potential beloveds is not available. "Why do I want love?" unlike "Why do I want to marry?" and "Why do I want to engage in sexual activity?" has no clear answer that tells us what traits to look for. Or if we want love because we think that love contributes to a full life lived well, this reason is still not powerful enough to generate a list of specific relevant traits. We can comprehend, then, why some philosophers have claimed that there is no logical limit on what sort of person can be the object of one's love, on what counts as a "lovable" trait, or on what beliefs the lover must have about the beloved. But even if love has no purpose, this does not absolutely rule out an answer to the question "Whom should I love?" An activity or state's having a purpose is sufficient, but not necessary, for determining the traits relevant for its existence. "Why should I hate?" is as queer a question as "Why should I love?" Yet that fact does not make incomprehensible the questions "Should I hate the person y or someone else z?" and "Is my hate for y in virtue of y's having this trait (having done something nasty to me) justifiable?" If we want to maintain the analogy between love and hate, then, the question "Whom should I love?" must admit of answers, as well as the question "Is my love for y justifiable?" We can, of course, joke about this:

> Every man has entertained... the suspicion that if he waited twenty-four hours, or possibly less, he would likely find a lady even more ideally suited to his taste than his fianceé.... To deny the possibility of her existence would be, he felt, to do a grave injustice to her, to himself, and to his fianceé. Man's unflinching desire to give himself and everybody else a square deal was the cause of much of his disturbance.[50]

On the serious side, the point is that love's not having a specifiable purpose, while marriage and sexual relations do, must decrease our confidence that love is inherently or inseparably linked to the other two.

CHAPTER EIGHT

GENDER

The two sexes mutually corrupt and improve each other. This
I believe to be an indisputable truth.

—Mary Wollstonecraft,
A Vindication of the Rights of Women

What we did not discuss in the last chapter was the possibility of gender differences in the death of sexual desire
in monogamous love or marital relationships. In agreement with
Irving Singer, but going beyond him, Sidney Callahan thinks that

> The committed model [of sexual relations] can—happily—encompass and encourage romance, passion, and
> playfulness. In fact, within the security of long-term commitments, women may be more likely to experience
> sexual pleasure and fulfillment.[1]

Women, then, seem not to be vulnerable to habituation. Indeed,
exactly the opposite seems to be true; according to Callahan, in a
secure, monogamous relationship, women's sexuality blooms.
And the social psychologist Dolf Zillman claims that how to
maintain *male* potency is the problem in a long-term relationship: "After years of monogamy... it is not uncommon for men
to develop acute sexual disinterest—even secondary impotence."[2]
   It is a piece of folk wisdom that men experience habituation
sooner and more intensely in love and marital relationships than
women do. If so, it makes one wonder how heterosexual relationships could ever be successful; the habituation of male sexuality
is antagonistic to the monogamy that is apparently required for
female sexual "fulfillment." Perhaps, however, this folk wisdom

is not an accurate generalization about men and women, but only a stereotype or a normative claim disguised as factual. After all, the biologist Mary Jane Sherfey has claimed that women by their nature are sexually insatiable; were they left to their own devices unimpeded by the cultural imposition of norms of proper behavior (that is, if they were to exhibit their "authentic" sexuality), women would enjoy having multiple sexual partners probably even more than men do (or men think they would).[3] And the anthropologist Meredith Small thinks that neither men nor women are "naturally monogamous":

> Men and women initially agree to stay with each other and care for babies, but both sexes would really like an occasional fling if they could get away with it.... Men have more extramarital affairs than women, although the women are catching up.[4]

Given the disparity between the views of Callahan and Small (both women scholars), Zillman's warning is valuable: "systematic demonstrations of excitatory habituation to sexual stimulation in humans do not exist."[5] Are there in fact significant gender differences in love and sexuality, or are these tales mostly folk fiction? And if there are differences, are they natural in origin or largely the impact of culture? These controversial issues should be kept in mind as we proceed to expound generalizations about gender differences.

GENDERED SEX ACTS

Here is an excellent example of the problems that arise in doing research on gender differences in sexuality. Meredith Small, repeating a thought that occurs to many of us about the sexual behavior patterns of human males and females, says that "men have more sexual partners over a lifetime than women."[6] How could that be true, if for every goose, there must be a gander? Actually, there is some truth in what Small says, but it needs to be stated more carefully: men, when questioned in sexual behavior surveys, *report* having more sexual partners than women report having. One researcher relates that men report having over three times as many sexual partners in their lives than women report; as much as 60% of men's sexual contacts are therefore unaccounted for.[7] And in the massive survey of American sexual behavior conducted at the University of Chicago, Edward Laumann and his colleagues found that "over half the men but only about 30 percent of the women report having had five or more sex partners since turning eighteen"; and significantly fewer men than women report having had none or only one sexual partner.[8] Are men really having sex with more partners than women do? And if men are not having sex with more partners, why do surveys repeatedly find that men report that they do?

Laumann and his colleagues offered seven candidate explanations for the discrepancy found in their survey:[9]

1. In pondering how there could be a difference between the number of sexual partners for men and for women, we have assumed that men have sex only with women and women have sex only with men; if that were true, the average number of sexual partners for men and women should be the same. One possible explanation for the discrepancy, then, is that men are having sex with other men more so than women are having sex with other women. But there may not be enough homosexuals in the (survey) population to account for the difference; estimates range from two to ten percent of the population. Note that not all same-sex sexual activity should be classified as homosexual, for some same-sex sexual activity is carried out by heterosexuals opportunistically (see Chapter Two). Can the extent of opportunistic same-sex activity among men, compared with that for women, explain the large discrepancy? Would heterosexual men who engage in opportunistic same-sex activity even report that fact in a survey? Perhaps their self-esteem would not allow them to count such events as having had sex.

2. The women surveyed ranged in age from eighteen to fifty-nine. If men are having sexual relations with women below or above these ages, these sexual partners would inflate the men's totals but be absent from the women's. Do men seek sexual relations sufficiently with very young or older women to account for the difference between men and women? Are women younger than eighteen and older than fifty-nine sexually active enough for this explanation to work?

3. The persons surveyed lived in households in the United States. If men are having sex with women who do not live in households or who live outside the country, more frequently than women are having sex with men who do not live in households or who live outside the country, the number of men's partners would be larger than the women's. If men are having sex in foreign lands or with the homeless, more frequently than women are, would the amount of sexual activity this fact represents be large enough to account for the discrepancy?

4. There is a possibility that men and women are not using the same criterion when counting the number of people they have had sex with. Laumann and his colleagues give this example: "Men and women may differ in what they consider a sex partner—the men may consider a quick act of sex as counting, while women may not count a brief, inconsequential event." Hence, men and women might be having sexual contacts with roughly the same number of partners, but men count more of these events as sex than women do.

5. The study did not ask the subjects to report numbers of sexual partners that exceeded one hundred. Perhaps some women have had a large number of sexual partners, more than the limit; if these were counted, the discrepancy would disappear. The average number of sexual partners for men and women would really be the same, if a small number of women were having sex with a

large number of men. Note that the women who would have reported more than one hundred partners (and perhaps the women not surveyed because they do not live in households) might be prostitutes. Could men's sexual activity with prostitutes account for the whole discrepancy? Given the percent of the female population that engages in prostitution, the number of male sexual partners for each prostitute would have to be, on the average, enormous.[10] Further, would men's self-esteem allow them to count and report sex with a prostitute?

6. When questioned in surveys about their sexual behavior, men exaggerate the numbers of women they have had sex with and (or) women understate the number of men they have had sex with. The subjects are not telling the truth, consciously or unconsciously making their reported numbers suit their own tastes.

7. There are more women than men in the United States; this fact would tend to lower the average number of partners for women as compared with men's.

Laumann and his colleagues, after laying out these possibilities, state: "we conjecture that the largest portion of the discrepancy rests with explanation 6."[11] I am not convinced. In trying to arrive at other explanations, let's assume two things: that the subjects were not consciously or unconsciously fudging their numbers, and that in determining, for the sake of answering the survey question, how many sexual partners they have had, both men and women sincerely applied the definition of "sexual activity" supplied to them in the survey itself. According to this definition, sexual activity is

> mutually voluntary activity with another person that involves genital contact and sexual excitement or arousal, that is, feeling really turned on, even if intercourse or orgasm did not occur.[12]

This definition of sexual activity is not a good one; recognizing where it goes wrong might help us partially explain the difference between the number of partners reported by men and by women. The fact that the definition requires that a person be "really turned on" for an event to *be* sexual means that the definition is not of sexual activity *per se* but, instead, of *good* sexual activity, in the nonmoral sense, that is, pleasurable (see Chapter One). At this point, we could mention that "more men than women report having regular orgasms."[13] If so, we can suggest that when the men report that they have more sexual partners, what they are really reporting is that they have more partners with whom they achieve orgasm. That would explain the discrepancy found in this study. But the survey's definition of a sexual act does not require orgasm for an act to be sexual, but only that a person be "really turned on." We can propose, instead, that because men are more easily aroused than women, what men are really reporting when they report having had more sexual partners is that they have had more sexual partners with whom they had a pleasurable (erection-producing?) experience. For any given sexual contact, men rate it better than women rate it; or men rate much sexual activity as "good" that women would not rate that way. Women do not count "brief" sexual events (as Laumann and his colleagues proposed in their fourth explanation) not because these events are brief *per se* or "inconsequential," but because they haven't had time to get "really turned on."[14]

Again we are led to wonder how heterosexual relationships could be successful. Not only may there be a gender difference in habituation, but also a difference in the sexual arousal patterns of men and women.

FAILURE

What does the man mean (see Joseph Farris's cartoon in figure 4) when he says, "if there is not going to be any sex between us, there won't be any love—from me"? Maybe he's revealing that the woman's willingness to engage in sex with him is the reassurance he needs to allow him to enter an intimate relationship; that he would be more confident about himself, and hence more comfortable loving her, after she agrees to engage in sexual activity with him; or, being egoists, men do not want to commit themselves to a relationship until they get what they primarily want first. In any event, it appears that the man places more value on sex than the woman does. For her part, the slogan on the woman's sign could mean that a man's willingness to wait is, for her, in agreement with Pausanias in Plato's *Symposium*, a test or sign of his love; that she would be more comfortable engaging in sex with him, and enjoy it more, after they have established a loving relationship; or even that women are egoists in their own way, not wanting to give what the man desires until they get what they primarily want. Love seems more important to the woman than to the man. Or the man and the woman are expressing different causal links between sex and love: for the man, good sex will lead him into love; for the woman, love will lead her into good sex. This is one of the standard disagreements in the folklore of heterosexuality. But the "battle of the sexes" is no joke.

If we take the slogans on the two signs literally, there could not be, as a matter merely of logic, any heterosexual relationships at all; they could never get started. There could be only homosexual relationships. But we know that there are heterosexual relationships, even if they are not always successful. Does each person give in a little? What would such a compromise consist of? Perhaps he first provides a little bit of love, and she responds with a little sex. Or she first provides a little sex, in a strategy designed to win his heart, and he responds with some love. Or he only pretends to provide love, in his own secret strategy designed to induce her to provide sex. Heterosexual relationships are starting to look like Aristotelian use-friendships, in which sex and love are exchanged. This bargaining and duplicity must create tension in their relationship from its beginning, if not also resentment and loss of face.[15]

Figure 4: Failure

If each person sticks to his and her respective principle, they will sit in their chairs forever, as dead as couch potatoes. Given the expressions on their faces, both seem stubbornly intent on going to their fates alone, never touching physically or emotionally.

Instead of this see-saw compromise, one person might give in right away, abandoning his or her slogan. Who gives in? The woman, usually, nowadays.[16] Her economic and social disadvantage and the pressure of compulsory heterosexuality and compulsory marriage; her incorporation of the social norm that demands of women that they not insist on satisfying their own needs and preferences at the expense of the needs of other persons; the social ingredients of a sexually free culture that operate against her sense that sex is properly and pragmatically best kept to a loving, monogamous context; her hope beyond hope that the man will make good on his implicit promise to return her gift of sex with his gift of love—all these things, to varying degrees, influence her to occupy the bed before she is ready to be there.

We are reminded here of the lovers' quarrel: in reply to one person's saying "if you loved me, you would do A," the other person says "if you loved me, you wouldn't ask me to do A." Replace "A" with "engage in sex," and we have a version of Farris's cartoon. Another reason emerges for wondering how heterosexual relationships could ever be successful: not only habituation, and not only different arousal patterns, but also different connections between sex and love. It would seem, then, that the ideal relationship would be between people who experienced habituation to the same degree, had similar sexual natures, linked sex and love in the same way, and agreed about what behaviors were entailed by love. Further, they would have similar economic resources and social and political power, if the relationship is not to be undermined by one person's vulnerability. The ironic implication is that homosexual relationships might be the best. "Vive la différence" is not the principle to follow if we want sturdy relationships, but "birds of a feather fly together," as in the homoeroticism or friendship praised by, among others, Plato, Aristotle, Montaigne, and Adrienne Rich.[17]

Callahan proposes that men should be encouraged to be more like women, since it is the social affirmation and encouragement of the features of men's sexuality that is the root cause of the problem.[18] The male "sexual orientation," which undoes the links among sex, love, marriage, and procreation, "has been harmful to women and children. It has helped bring us epidemics of venereal disease, infertility, pornography, sexual abuse, adolescent pregnancy, divorce, displaced older women, and abortion."[19] Hence,

> Women will only flourish when there is a feminization of sexuality, very different from the current cultural trend toward masculinizing female sexuality. Women can never

have the self-confidence and self-esteem they need to
achieve feminist goals in society until a more holistic,
feminine model of sexuality becomes the dominant cultural ethos.[20]

Callahan, too, supposes that a principle of similarity, not one of
difference, is the solution. Women have been adopting the sexual
style of men, but men should, instead, adopt the sexual style of
women. Were both men and women to abide by the woman's
slogan in figure 4, human relationships (heterosexual) would blos-
som, and perhaps even society itself would be better off.

GENDERED SEXUALITY

The gender differences mentioned so far may be only the tip of
the iceberg. Consider, as well, that men are interested, more so
than women, in having sex with prostitutes, looking at and getting aroused by pornography, engaging in perverted sexuality (in
some Thomistic sense), and drinking beer in bars where women
dance in the nude (or eating at "Hooters"). Fifty-four percent of
men report that they think about sex once or more a day; only
nineteen percent of women report that they think about sex as
frequently as that.[21] It is commonly said, as a result, that men are
more interested than women are in sex for its own sake, sexual
activity just for the pleasure of it, or sex deliberately devoid of
the emotional, economic, and social entanglements of love, marriage, commitment, and procreation.

There is reason to take this suggestion seriously. Women
remain identified with the mother, so it is easier for them to form
and prefer intimate bonds, but they have difficulty with autonomy;
men, as young boys, are forced to separate from the mother, so
they are more at home with autonomy and find intimacy a threat
to their identities. Men tend to prefer maintaining their autonomy
and independence at the cost of reducing or threatening the intimacy of their love relationships (this manifests itself in the sexu-

ally wandering eye of the man), while women tend to prefer to maximize the closeness of the love bond even at the cost of their autonomy (and so prefer monogamous relationships). Thus there is a gender difference in how the tension in love between autonomy and intimacy is approached.[22] For men, the psychic threat is an engulfing intimacy at the expense of their individuality, while for women the threat is an empty separateness at the expense of intimate union. A man's reluctance to probe and express his emotions, and the lack of significance he places on that aspect of his life, threatens the depth and stability of relationships. A woman's fear of becoming separate, and what appears to a man as her indulgence of the emotions, contributes to this instability. This disparity between a man and a woman has profound implications for their sexualities and for their relationship.[23] The man who has sex with a prostitute or has an affair with a co-worker is, in part, attempting to maintain his separateness from a marital bond that threatens his identity. The woman who prefers monogamy does so for the same reason; her identity is wrapped up in the relationship.

Not everyone agrees with this analysis, of course. For example, the sociologist Steven Seidman thinks that claims of gender differences in sexuality are overblown, and he offers this sobering observation:

> Although girls continue to insist more than boys that sex be tied to romance or love... girls often use the word "love" in a way that lacks its traditional connotation of a long-term relationship.... Love indicates little more than feelings of attraction.... Some girls have sex for reasons of... pleasure but to avoid guilt and disapproval frame sex in the culturally approved language and symbolism of romantic love.[24]

Seidman is talking about teenagers. But if this is true for young girls, why would it not also be at least somewhat true for the women the girls become? On this view, the woman in Farris's cartoon never meant her slogan seriously in the first place, so when she "abandons" her principle to accommodate the man, she is not compromising herself. She held up her sign to save face; after all, there is the bit of cultural ideology according to which women are (expected to be) superior to men, or more Christian, since they are (or should be) more concerned with love than with sex.

Nevertheless, some clear gender differences in sexual behavior exist, even if the meaning of these facts is debatable. Pornography appeals to more men than it does to women; while many men find the depictions of nudity or raw sex in pornography arousing, women find the steady stream of bodies and their organs disgusting—or laughable. Women, for their part, have a much more extensive interest in romance novels, which, even when they deal explicitly with sex, situate the eroticism in the context of a whole relationship or link it with the emotional life of human beings. Men find romances either utterly boring—or laughable. How could two sexes with such different tastes in erotic literature and depictions, not to mention Hollywood movies, ever get together? Perhaps Atkinson and Rich are right: that without the institution of compulsory heterosexuality, they wouldn't.

The sexual perversions represent another clear gender difference. Most men do not enjoy or prefer the more unusual Thomistic perversions—fetishes, urolagnia, voyeurism and exhibitionism, masochism—but the men who do engage in sexual perversions or entertain perverted sexual fantasies far outnumber the women who do so (I do not include oral sex here).[25] Dolf Zillman discusses one psychological conditioning theory of the genesis of sexual perversion in men:

> Common to all deviation... is that elements of the climactic experience of ejaculation are conditioned to some aggregate of overt and covert stimuli that preceded the climactic experience.... Men masturbate to climax very liberally... , making them particularly susceptible—in contrast to women—to developing deviations in [a] piecemeal fashion.[26]

Men, being more interested in sex for its own sake, masturbate more than women do. This masturbation occurs with ever more intricate fantasies and in conjunction with any material hint a man can get of a woman: pornographic pictures, pieces of clothing, a woman's hair. Further, if the desire for sexual novelty is more a feature of male than female sexuality (see Callahan), the quest for sexual stimulation and pleasure in new and different ways might eventually lead men into the perversions. All this is conjecture, of course. Women masturbate, even if not as frequently as men do. And scholars like Small and Sherfey are always available to defend the claim that women, too, are drawn to sexual novelty. As Camille Paglia rhetorically asks:

> If gay men go down to bars and... have their asses whipped, how come we can't allow that a lot of wives like the kind of sex they are getting in... battered-wife relationships? We can't consider that women might have kinky tastes, can we? No, because women are naturally benevolent and nurturing, aren't they?[27]

The psychologist Louise Kaplan has devised a theory according to which women, too, display sexual perversion. Perversions, for Kaplan, are "pathologies of gender role identity."[28] In contrast to male perversion, however, "sexual excitement and genital arousal will not always or usually be at the forefront of female perversion."[29] In women, a perversion is "a masquerade that disguises the woman's forbidden masculine wishes.... Nearly every female perversion disguises vengeful sadistic aims beneath a cloak of feminine masochism."[30] But if sexual arousal is not part of the female perversions, is it right to speak of them as *sexual* perversions (see Chapter One)?

One more indisputable gender difference in sexual behavior is worth mentioning. It is, by and large, only men, and a fair number of them, who have promiscuous sex with prostitutes. Gay men have more of a reputation (but nowadays only that) for promiscuity than do straight men. Michael Levin pounces on this purported fact, conceiving of male homosexual promiscuity as a psychological abnormality. On his view, anyone who is promiscuous, having had sexual relations with one hundred to five hundred partners—but he means gays in particular—shows "maladjustment and compulsivity, a chronic inability to find anyone satisfactory."[31] This may not be quite right; the promiscuous person seems to find almost everyone satisfactory. At any rate, the promiscuous gay person need not be judged any more "maladjusted" than a promiscuous heterosexual or any straight male who wished he could be promiscuous, if only women would accommodate. Paglia senses, in this regard, the similarity between the homosexual man and the heterosexual man:

> Gay men [in their promiscuity] are guardians of the masculine impulse. To have anonymous sex in a dark alleyway is to pay homage to the dream of male sexual freedom.... Similarly, straights who visit prostitutes are valiantly striving to keep sex free from emotion, duty, family—in other words, from society, religion, and procreative Mother Nature.[32]

Male homosexual sexual patterns and desires—yearning for or seeking promiscuous sex for its own sake—display male sexuality in its pure form, relieved of the necessity in either action or fantasy of conforming to or compromising with the sexual style of women.[33] This is why "homosexuals are the acid test for hypotheses about sex differences in sexuality."[34]

But even if heterosexual men are not appreciably more promiscuous than heterosexual women, the cultural ideology of the "double standard" judges promiscuous male and female sexual behavior differently.[35] Promiscuous men are "studs," which is not derogatory, while promiscuous women are "sluts," "whores," or "tramps," which are terms of severe disparagement. One can insult a woman by calling her a "slut," even if she is not promiscuous; calling a man a "stud," by contrast, does not work as an insult (unless it is said with sarcasm). A man can try to be a "stud" and be pleased at his success; this achievement provides him with something to brag about. But a woman cannot try to be, and succeed at being, a slut (except Kelly Bundy); her promiscuity does not count as an *accomplishment*.

GENDERED LOVE STYLES

The ancient Greek poet Sappho[36] began one of her compositions with these lines:

> There are those who say an array of horsemen, and others of marching men, and others of ships, is the mostbeautiful thing on the dark earth. But I say it is whatever one loves.[37]

Sappho might mean that love has the highest value and is more important than other things (military and commercial success). Or Sappho is referring to the importance of love in the lives of women, something scoffed at by George Byron in *Don Juan* (I, 194):

> Man's love is of man's life a thing apart,
>   'Tis woman's whole existence.

and lamented by the feminist writer Shulamith Firestone,

> Her whole identity hangs in the balance of her love life.[38]

Love is a much more important thing than men's worldly pursuits (which men might use to flee from the trials of love); women are the guardians and promoters of a superior way of life that is constituted by love and harmony.

Sappho might be asserting, instead, that what makes a beloved attractive for the typical Greek man (military prowess, political power, and physical beauty) is not what makes beloveds attractive for women. Men's *eros* involves shallow evaluations of beloveds, while women's *eros* involves the "whole" person, body and character (see Chapter Five). She might, then, be insisting on the nonutilitarian value of women in opposition to a culture that found no value in women other than domestic. Finally, and perhaps most convincingly, Sappho might be praising the a-type relationship between love and the lover's evaluation of the beloved, thereby making a more radical break with Greek *eros*. To say that "the most beautiful thing... is whatever one loves" is similar to saying that if a person x loves another person y, x as a result of this love perceives or judges y to be beautiful. In this case, Sappho inaugurates a women's (and, later, Christian) love tradition that incorporates the a-type, rather than the e-type, relationship between love and value.

Whatever Sappho meant, these lines have suggested some possible differences in love between men and women and, hence, more reasons for wondering how heterosexual relationships could ever be successful. Men's love is often conceived of as e-type, women's love as a-type. Men love on the basis of physical beauty, they love egocentrically or even selfishly (demanding the continual satisfaction of their desires), and they are notoriously inconstant and nonexclusive in their love. Women, by contrast, are said to love unconditionally (and it is a good thing, since men are so unlovable), despite the nasty properties of those they choose to care about; they value love for its own sake rather than instrumentally; they give more in a relationship than they take or get from it; and their love tends to be constant and exclusive. "Women often define themselves as both persons and moral agents in terms of their capacity to care," writes Nel Noddings.[39] It has often been said that women think, in their relationships with others, more in terms of "care" than men do.[40] Women try to treat their intimates with unselfish and selfless concern and giving. But they need to be encouraged to think in terms of themselves as well.[41] Women tend to stay with men too long, to the detriment of themselves and others, for the sake of the intimate union itself and to safeguard their identity as defined in and by it.

It makes sense, then, as Erich Fromm has claimed, that a woman's mother love for her children is an a-type love, whereas a man's father love for his children is an e-type love (or that the concept of mother love fits into the *agape* tradition, and the concept of father love into the *eros* tradition).[42] In mother love the child is loved unconditionally, just because it exists; in father love, the child is loved when or because it fulfills the father's expectations, obeys his moral demands, and achieves worldly success. In mother love, the child's merit is irrelevant; in father love, merit is central. (Fromm also claims that the Old Testament God, Yahweh, is a projection of this concept of father love, and the New Testament God is a projection of the concept of mother love. The theory of human parental love is not derived from the idea of God's love for humans, but the human idea of God's love is modeled after recognizable features of human parental love.) Of course, Fromm is painting in broad strokes. We can easily challenge the claim that styles of parental love are gender-linked, by pointing out that some fathers love their children unconditionally and some mothers love them conditionally. But Fromm's line of reasoning still has some validity. Mothers, by and large, are the loving caregivers, while fathers are the family authorities, expecting respect and obedience and having less patience for childish antics. Indeed, although fathers commonly work and provide for the family, they spend much less time attending directly to a child's needs than does the mother.[43] If we measure love in terms of providing direct and unselfish care for the child, mothers show more love than fathers, even if mom's and dad's subjective experiences of the feeling of love for their child are the same.

What complicates this picture of the different love styles of men and women is a consideration of their respective bases for love and marriage. Men, more than women, prefer their lovers and mates to be physically attractive. Even though for both men and women being physically attractive is not the most important selection criterion (kindness is frequently mentioned as being more important; but beware of people only paying lip service to that ideal), and even though women also think that physical attractiveness is important, beauty and sex appeal are regularly found to be more significant for men than women.[44] Men are roughly divisible (among themselves, or in their own minds) into "tit-men," "leg-men," and "ass-men"; there is no corresponding cultural categorization of women. Men have attributes other than their physical features that heterosexual women are concerned with. On one view, women are more concerned with the character or mental beauty of men; in this case, men's love for women contains a large element of vulgar *eros*, while women's love for men contains heavenly *eros*. On another view, behind a woman's search for a mate with the appropriate character traits lies her search for other things that are often, but not always, tied to character; women pick men on the basis of their material resources, wealth, power, prestige, industriousness, reliability, and intelligence. Women, on this view, barter their sex appeal and physical beauty in exchange for the material support men can provide in marriage. Women apparently focus on the reproductive effect of sexual activity and hence think pragmatically about their subsequent needs. We know that men often pay women to engage in sexual relations with them (odd is a woman's paying a man to engage in sex with her). But on this tit-for-tat view of heterosexual relations, men pay for sex (or use their money to extract it) no matter what; sex in marriage is a service that the wife provides to the husband in exchange for his resources.[45] Little room exists in this arrangement for the selfless giving that is supposed to be women's endowment.

Scholars have endlessly debated the cause of this apparent gender difference in sexuality, some theorists favoring evolutionary mechanisms, others emphasizing culture.[46] The evolutionary hypothesis is that the pattern is natural, even if modified and elaborated in various ways by different cultures. Men are attracted to and prefer women on the basis of their procreative capacity, for their healthiness, as signaled by their youth and beauty; women are attracted to and prefer men on the basis of their resource acquisition ability. Both sexes employ a strategy designed to maximize their own reproductive success.

On a socialization hypothesis, women are "taught from their infancy that beauty is woman's sceptre, the mind shapes itself to the body, and roaming around its gilt cage, only seeks to adore its prison."[47] Men, compelled into the aggressive or macho sexuality promoted by sexist institutions, devalue the character, intelligence, and varied talents of women, coming to value women primarily for their sexuality, their ability to provide sexual pleasure and bear children. Hence men focus on beauty, becoming connoisseurs of perfectly-shaped breasts or buttocks. Women, in turn, are socialized to apply these standards to themselves, to make themselves beautiful for the sake of catching the eyes of men. But women nowadays make themselves beautiful not only for marriage, but also to get and keep a job. In addition to the skills required for the efficient performance of a job, women must also have what it takes to meet an unstated, informal job requirement, the "beauty qualification."[48] If men pay for sex with money in or out of marriage (prostitution), women pay for resources (or extract them) with sex, in or out of marriage (on the job). If this is right, and if money-power dominates sex-power, we can comprehend that

> to the extent that men control more power and resources than do women... men can afford the luxury of picking partners on the basis of their physical appearance. For women of lower power or fewer resources, choices may need a more pragmatic base.[49]

If women were not economically dependent on men, if women had their own plentiful resources equal to those of men, the gender difference in mate selection criteria might disappear, since women, too, would have the luxury of focusing on physical beauty, and men would have more reason to take a pragmatic interest in the incomes of women.[50] As women gain their own political power and economic resources, they will be free, unhindered by constraints that limit them now, to marry and divorce, form and dissolve relationships, as they see fit, according to their own tastes. Would this mean that men and women would replace their Aristotelian use-friendships, in which they exchange sex for material resources, by pleasure-friendships, in which they appreciate each other's company, sexual or otherwise, simply for the joy of it? But equal rights and opportunities for men and women might not lead to a convergence of male and female sexual behavior patterns. If men and women are different by their very natures, equal rights and opportunities for women could show us, instead, that women have been reinforced or encouraged to do by socialization what they would have done anyway by their nature.[51]

NOTES

INTRODUCTION

1. Here are five of the "Top 10 Signs Your Spouse is Having an Affair By Computer" (from the David Letterman show, early 1996): lately she sits at the computer naked; after logging off, he always has a cigarette; he's gotten amazingly good at typing with one hand; there's lipstick on the mouse; she makes sarcastic comments about your "software."
2. W. Speers, "Newsmakers."
3. "Pornography and Rape: Theory and Practice," in *Going Too Far*, 163-9.
4. *Marriage and the Love of God*, 73.
5. See Sigmund Freud, "Character and Anal Erotism," *Standard Edition*, vol. 9, 175; "Notes Upon a Case of Obsessional Neurosis," *SE*, vol. 10, 241 ("a man's attitude in sexual things has the force of a model to which the rest of his reactions tend to conform"); "Contributions to a Discussion on Masturbation," *SE*, vol. 12, 251-2; and "'Civilized' Sexual Morality and Modern Nervous Illness," *SE*, vol. 9, 198-200.
6. *On Marriage and Concupiscence*, bk. 1, ch. 9. See W. Alexander, "Sex and Philosophy in Augustine."
7. The Lord did some slaying himself. "Judah got a wife for Er, his firstborn, and her name was Tamar. But Er... was wicked in the Lord's sight; so the Lord put him to death. Then Judah said to Onan, 'Lie with your brother's wife [Tamar] and fulfill your duty to her as a brother-in-law to produce offspring for your brother'. But Onan knew that the offspring would not be his; so whenever he lay with his brother's wife, he spilled his semen on the ground to keep from producing offspring for his brother. What he did was wicked in the Lord's sight; so he put him to death also" (Genesis 38:6-10).
8. *Lectures on Ethics*, 163.
9. See Barbara Herman, "Could It Be Worth Thinking About Kant on Sex and Marriage?" and Jeanne Schroeder, "Feminism Historicized: Medieval Misogynist Stereotypes in Contemporary Feminist Jurisprudence."

10. For a comprehensive presentation of this view, see Russell Vannoy, *Sex Without Love*.

11. *The Limits of Love*, 47.

12. See Robert Mapplethorpe's 1978 photograph "Helmut and Brooks" (reproduced in Richard Mohr, *Gay Ideas*, 189).

13. "Sexuality," *The Examined Life*, 67.

14. *Love and Will*, 75.

15. "Homosex/Ethics," 10.

16. "Sexual Behavior," in A. Soble, ed., *Philosophy of Sex*, 2nd ed., 70.

17. "Sexuality," *The Examined Life*, 61.

18. Hesiod, *Theogony*, lines 120-22.

19. Roger Scruton, *Sexual Desire*, 337.

20. *Confessions*, bk. 3, par. 1.

21. *The World as Will and Representation*, vol. 2, 538, 540.

22. *Amazon Odyssey*, 13.

23. Andrea Dworkin claims that heterosexual coitus is also constructed to be the subordination of women. In intercourse, "female is bottom, stigmatized." Sexual intercourse makes "a woman inferior: communicating to her cell by cell her own inferior status, impressing it on her, burning it into her by shoving it into her, over and over, pushing and thrusting until she gives in." Sexual intercourse "is the pure, sterile, formal expression of men's contempt for women" (*Intercourse*, 137, 138).

24. *Amazon Odyssey*, 20.

25. "Personal Rights and Public Space," 100.

26. See *Civilization and Its Discontents* and *The Future of an Illusion*, both in *Standard Edition*, vol. 21.

27. *Three Essays on the Theory of Sexuality*, in *Standard Edition*, vol. 7.

28. John McHugh and Charles Callan, *Moral Theology*, vol. 2, point 2492; quoted by Peter Gardella, *Innocent Ecstasy*, 38, 167.

29. *The World as Will and Representation*, vol. 2, 539.

30. "The Beautiful Decadence of Robert Mapplethorpe," in *Sex, Art, and American Culture*, 43, 44, 45.

31. Another advocate of this view is the French existentialist philosopher, Jean-Paul Sartre; see *Being and Nothingness*, pt. 3, ch. 3, sec. 2.

32. *Refusing To Be a Man*, 112. There would also be no hope for

Sheila Jeffrey's goal of making equality "exciting" (*Anticlimax*, 4, 300).
33. "Crazy Jane Talks With the Bishop," *Collected Poems*, 259-60.
34. "Beyond Bisexual," 511.
35. "Homosex/Ethics," 12. See also Russell Vannoy's list in *Sex Without Love*, 97-8.
36. "The Irrelevance of Theology for Sexual Ethics," 249.
37. Ibid., 251ff.

CHAPTER ONE: SEXUAL CONCEPTS

1. "Prostitution," in A. Soble, ed.,*Philosophy of Sex*, 2nd ed., 275.
2. Some Victorian lesbian lovers who engaged in cunnilingus "felt themselves perfectly innocent" of the accusation that they were sexual partners, and hence could think of themselves as not lesbians at all, because they (and their patriarchal society) defined sex in terms of the penetration of the penis into the vagina (Karla Jay, "School for Scandal," 9). Contemporary feminists avoid such obfuscation, proclaiming that lesbian sexuality is the genuine article and not something that women should be ashamed of doing.
3. A humorous presentation of the difficulties in defining "sexual act" can be found in Greta Christina, "Are We Having Sex Now Or What?"
4. Dolf Zillman counts homosexual activity as sexual on the grounds that it is an "emulation" of heterosexual activity (*Connections Between Sex and Aggression*, 19).
5. "Sex and Sexual Perversion," in A. Soble, ed., *Philosophy of Sex*, 1st ed., 163.
6. "Toward a New Model of Sexuality," in A. Soble, ed, *Sex, Love, and Friendship*.
7. "Freud and Perversion," 207-8. But how do we distinguish the surgeon who is only a surgeon from the surgeon who is *also* obsessed?
8. Susan Estrich, *Real Rape*, 83.
9. Gray, "Sex and Sexual Perversion," 162.
10. "Plain Sex," in A. Soble, ed., *Philosophy of Sex*, 2nd ed., 74.
11. "A Theory of Love and Sexual Desire," 353.
12. Giles acknowledges that fetishism (a sexual interest in shoes but not the body that wears them) presents a problem for his

definition of sexual desire. To make room for fetishism as sexual, Giles views the fetish object as a "fantasized body" or a body "extension."

13. "Sexual Desire," 186-7.
14. Rockney Jacobsen ("Arousal and the Ends of Desire," 630) says, about his own analysis of sexual desire—but his point applies as well to Shaffer's account—that it

> makes our concept of sexual desire, and our concept of sex generally, dependent on a notion of sexual arousal. But... the issue is tractable.... Sexual arousal is primarily arousal...of the sexual organs and those are, of course, the reproductive organs.... Flushed faces or tingling earlobes borrow their status as *sexual* arousal from their well-known but contingent associations with the arousal of the reproductive parts.

But the fact that the connection between sexual desire and sexual arousal is only contingent means that Jacobsen has not adequately analyzed the notion of the sexual.

15. "Plain Sex," 75-6.
16. See all the volumes of his *The History of Sexuality*, which is often cited as the seminal and most provocative, even if not the first (or final), statement of social constructionism (Hilary Rose, "Gay Brains, Gay Genes, and Feminist Science Theory"). Among those who have defended or explicated social constructionism (especially regarding homosexuality) are David Halperin, *One Hundred Years of Homosexuality* and *Saint Foucault*; Ned Katz, *The Invention of Heterosexuality*; Timothy Murphy, "Homosex/Ethics," 10-12; and the essays collected in D. Halperin, J. Winkler, and F. Zeitlin, eds.,*Before Sexuality*. Among those who have argued against social constructionism are John Boswell, *Christianity, Social Tolerance, and Homosexuality*, chs. 1 and 2; Richard Mohr, *Gay Ideas*, 221-42; Camille Paglia, *Sex, Art, and American Culture*, 170-248; Richard Posner, *Sex and Reason*, 23-30; Alice Rossi, "Eros and Caritas," 5-9; and Alan Soble, *Sexual Investigations*, 122-7. Edward Stein's anthology,*Forms of Desire*, usefully brings together essays pro and con the social constructionist position.
17. See H. Tristram Engelhardt, "The Disease of Masturbation: Values and the Concept of Disease"; Peter Gay, *The Bourgeois*

Experience, vol. 1, *Education of the Senses*, 294-318.

18. The examples are taken from Edward Stein's concluding essay in his anthology *Forms of Desire*.

19. See Foucault, *History of Sexuality*, vol. 1, 118; Arnold Davidson, "Sex and the Emergence of Sexuality"; Susan Edwards, *Female Sexuality and the Law*, 80-1.

20. On Benkert, see Peter Gay, *The Bourgeois Experience*, vol. 2, *The Tender Passion*, 224.

21. Robert Padgug, "Sexual Matters," in E. Stein, ed., *Forms of Desire*, 54 (italics added).

22. *Money, Sex and Power*, 156.

23. See Anne Fausto-Sterling, "The Five Sexes" and "How Many Sexes Are There?"

24. For an introduction to the topic, see Magnus Hirschfeld, *Transvestites*, and Gilbert Herdt, ed., *Third Sex. Third Gender*.

25. *Making Sex*, 8, 134.

26. Ibid., 63.

27. Ibid., 67-9, 148-50.

28. See Thomas Kuhn, *The Copernican Revolution*.

29. On parthenogenesis, see David Concar, "Sisters Are Doing It for Themselves."

30. *Making Sex*, viii.

31. If the sexual radically varies from culture to culture, if no universal feature connects the sexual acts of one culture with those of another, there could be no way to *identify* acts in different cultures as all of them sexual and, hence, no way to *discover* that sexuality has no transcultural essence (Joseph Diorio, "Feminist-Constructionist Theories of Sexuality," 25).

32. Nadine Strossen, *Defending Pornography*, 162 (quoting the lawyer Nan Hunter).

33. "Pornography and the Erotics of Domination," 146-7.

34. Avedon Carol, "Snuff: Believing the Worst," 126-7.

35. Susan Barrowclough, "Not a Love Story," 29.

36. Goldman's analysis seems to entail that solitary masturbation is not a sexual act; for discussion, see my *Sexual Investigations*, 67-71.

37. "Sexual Paradigms," in A. Soble, ed., *Philosophy of Sex*, 2nd ed., 53-62; "Sex and Perversion," in R. Baker and F. Elliston, eds., *Philosophy and Sex*, 1st ed., 268-87.

38. "Philosophy and Sex," 448.
39. *Amazon Odyssey*, 20.
40. Ibid., 21.
41. Ibid., 22.
42. Ibid., 23.
43. Janice Moulton made this point against Solomon's communication model of sexuality; see her "Sexual Behavior: Another Position," in A. Soble, ed., *Philosophy of Sex*, 2nd ed., 63-71.
44. Ibid., 67, 71.
45. *Sex Without Love*, 32.
46. Genesis 29:20-25. Jacob loved Rachel dearly, not Leah, and knew her for many years. Yet Jacob was fooled into thinking that the woman in his arms that night was Rachel. Didn't Leah once open her mouth; or did she deliberately contribute to Laban's deception? Perhaps Jacob was drunk and Leah fully clothed and veiled. (Thanks to Amy Bordelon for help with this.)
47. *Matthews v. Superior Court* (1981). For discussion, see Stephen Schulhofer, "The Gender Question in Criminal Law," 308-9.

CHAPTER TWO: SEXUAL PERVERSION

1. For a recent defense of the Judaic analogue, see Dennis Prager, "Homosexuality, the Bible, and Us." See also Leviticus, quoted in the Introduction.
2. This information was supplied by the National Headquarters of the Lambda Legal Defense and Education Fund, New York City.
3. 106 S. Ct. 2841 (1986); 487 U.S. 186 (1986).
4. For a recent scholarly debate about whether, and to what extent, the ancient Greeks, including Plato, objected to homosexual acts, see John Finnis, "Law, Morality, and 'Sexual Orientation'" and Martha Nussbaum, "Platonic Love and Colorado Law." An extremely short version of their conflicting views is presented in their joint essay "Is Homosexual Conduct Wrong? A Philosophical Exchange."
5. "That Not All Sexual Intercourse Is Sinful," *Summa Contra Gentiles*, bk. 3, pt. 2, ch. 126.
6. *Summa Theologiae*, 2a2ae, q. 154, a. 1.
7. Ibid., a. 11.
8. Note that Aquinas does not object to incest on the grounds that

it is an unnatural sexual act: it might involve heterosexual intercourse, i.e., be procreative in form. For an interesting philosophical account of incest that emphasizes, as Aquinas does, "who people are in relation to each other," see Jerome Neu, "What Is Wrong with Incest?"

9. *Summa Theologiae*, 2a2ae, q. 154, a. 12.

10. In endnote 22 of Karol Wojtyla's [Pope John Paul II] *Love and Responsibility* (296), we find this modification:

> It must always be kept in mind that 'nature'... does not mean 'biological nature'. Rather, we must investigate "the nature of man in the deeper sense, which... gives pride of place to... those elements which... cannot be embraced by a physical... conception of man."

This makes the determination of human nature even more difficult, since the sciences can tell us nothing about this "deeper" nature. The sciences are methodologically limited, in any event; observations of the sexual behavior of higher mammals, infants and young children, and of the peoples of "primitive" tribes are not likely to yield much that is illuminating about natural human sexuality.

11. C. and W. Whiteleys's Chapter Five in *Sex and Morals* (79-100) is an elegant explication, a thorough discussion, and a fair criticism of Natural Law ethics, especially as applied to sexuality. See also Timothy Murphy, "Homosexuality and Nature: Happiness and the Law at Stake"; Christine Pierce, "Natural Law Language and Women"; Burton Leiser, *Liberty, Justice, and Morals*; Michael Ruse, *Homosexuality: A Philosophical Inquiry*, and Robert and Katherine Baird, eds., *Homosexuality: Debating the Issues*.

12. *Heterosexism*, 23. See also Edward Vacek, "A Christian Homosexuality?"

13. *Body, Sex, and Pleasure*, 65.

14. "Why Homosexuality is Abnormal," 253.

15. See Ruse, *Homosexuality*, 190-1; and, specifically on Levin, Murphy, "Homosexuality and Nature."

16. Christopher Boorse, "On the Distinction Between Disease and Illness," 62.

17. Richard Taylor, *Having Love Affairs*, 72-3.

18. See Simon LeVay, *The Sexual Brain* and *Queer Science*; Dean

Hamer and Peter Copeland, *The Science of Desire*; Simon LeVay and Dean Hamer, "Evidence for a Biological Influence in Male Homosexuality"; Chandler Burr, "Homosexuality and Biology"; and David Nimmons, "Sex and the Brain." For criticism of biological explanations of homosexuality, see William Byne and Bruce Parsons, "Human Sexual Orientation"; William Byne, "The Biological Evidence Challenged"; Bonnie Spanier, "Biological Determinism and Homosexuality"; and Hilary Rose, "Gay Brains, Gay Genes, and Feminist Science Theory." In "Are There Gay Genes?" Michael Ruse outlines possible sociobiological mechanisms for the existence of gay genes; see his *Homosexuality*, 203-35 (reprinted in A. Soble, ed., *Sex, Love, and Friendship*). On Ruse, see Lee Rice and Steven Barbone, "Hatching Your Genes Before They're Counted," also in Soble, *Sex, Love, and Friendship*.

19. See Thomas Kuhn, *The Structure of Scientific Revolutions*.
20. See Edward Stein, "The Relevance of Scientific Research About Sexual Orientation to Lesbian and Gay Rights."
21. See K. Ernulf et al., "Biological Explanation, Psychological Explanation, and Tolerance of Homosexuals: A Cross-National Analysis of Beliefs and Attitudes."
22. Because there are different types of adultery, Aquinas does not contradict himself (as claimed by John Boswell in *Christianity, Social Tolerance, and Homosexuality*, 324) when he says, on the one hand, that sexually monogamous marriage is part of the natural design (and hence adulterous fornication is unnatural and a mortal sin) and, on the other, that adultery consisting of heterosexual coitus is only a violation of proper relations among men (if a natural sexual act has been performed, the adultery is only a venial sin). For Aquinas, there is a difference between a married man's committing adultery *before* he has children with his wife and *after* he has children with her.
23. *Summa Theologiae*, 2a2ae, q. 154, a. 2; see *Summa Contra Gentiles*, bk. 3, pt. 2, ch. 122.
24. "Love and Sex," 370-1.
25. A similar idea appears in Alice Rossi, "Eros and Caritas: A Biopsychological Approach to Human Sexuality and Reproduction." *Eros* (sexual desire based on physical beauty) is required

for mate choice and reproduction; *caritas* (love as an enduring concern for the beloved's well-being) is required for the raising of children (3-4). See Chapter Five.

26. "Love and Sex," 371.
27. *Sex Without Love.*
28. *Gays/Justice*, 113. See also the "intense... ecstasy" mentioned in the passage from Thomas Nagel's "Personal Rights and Public Space," quoted in the Introduction.
29. "Sexual Perversion," in A. Soble, ed., *Philosophy of Sex*, 2nd ed., 39-51.
30. Another contemporary philosopher, Sara Ruddick, in agreement with Aquinas, views human sexual perversion biologically (as nonprocreative sex), emphasizing for the purposes of *this* evaluation the continuity between the human and the animal. But she departs from Aquinas by denying that the unnaturalness alone of a sexual activity makes it immoral. See "Better Sex," in R.Baker and F. Elliston, eds., *Philosophy and Sex*, 2nd ed., 280-99.
31. "Sexual Perversion," 49.
32. Ibid., 39.
33. On the definition of "homosexual(ity)," see Frederick Suppe, "The Diagnostic and Statistical Manual of the American Psychiatric Association," "Curing Homosexuality," and "Explaining Homosexuality"; and Eli Coleman, "Bisexuality: Challenging Our Understanding of Human Sexuality and Sexual Orientation." See also the social constructionist material referred to in note 16, Chapter One.
34. "Sexual Perversion," 49-50.
35. *Homosexuality*, 201.

CHAPTER THREE: SEXUAL ETHICS

1. 85 S. Ct. 1678 (1965).
2. 85 S. Ct. 1689, 1693.
3. It is intellectually challenging to comprehend the Court's ruling in *Bowers v. Hardwick* (106 S. Ct. 2841 [1986]), in which it was decided that the state of Georgia did not violate the U. S. Constitution in prohibiting consensual homosexual sexual acts done in private, when the Court had earlier ruled on privacy considerations (among others) that Connecticut may not prohibit the

use of contraception, that a person has a constitutional right to possess obscene literature in the privacy of his own home (*Stanley v. Georgia*, 89 S. Ct. 1243 [1969]), and that a woman's decision to secure an abortion during her first trimester is her own private affair, a matter to be worked out in consultation with her doctor (*Roe v. Wade*, 93 S. Ct. 705 [1973]).

4. *Summa Theologiae*, 2a2ae, q. 154, a. 1.
5. Not hormonal pills in those days, but olive oil, acacia gum, a sponge soaked in vinegar (Vern and Bonnie Bullough, *Sexual Attitudes*, 128).
6. *Summa Contra Gentiles*, bk. 3, pt. 2, ch. 122.
7. *Abortion and the Roman Catholic Church*, 8-9.
8. "Sexual Ethics," 1580. John Noonan, in agreement with Farley, relies on the *Summa Contra Gentiles* passage quoted in the text above to argue that, for Aquinas, contraceptive sex was contrary to nature (*Contraception*, 242).
9. "Theological Approaches to Sexuality," 202.
10. "Humanae Vitae," in R. Baker and F. Elliston, eds., *Philosophy and Sex*, 2nd ed., §11.
11. Ibid., §14.
12. Ibid., §17.
13. *Love and Responsibility*, 239; see 228, 235-6.
14. "I would define contraception as the use of the human faculty for sexual expression of human personal love in marriage in such a way as to make this expression effectively an absolute value, closed to the intervention of God's invitation to sacrifice, whether that sacrifice take the form of the responsibility for children or the abstaining from sexual intercourse" (George Wilson, "Christian Conjugal Morality and Contraception," 108).
15. "Humanae Vitae," §16. Pope Pius XI had voiced this idea in his 1930 encyclical "Casti Connubii" (see "On Christian Marriage," 37, 39).
16. "Evangelium Vitae," 722.
17. "Humanae Vitae," §16. For critical discussion, see my *Sexual Investigations*, 13-15, and Carl Cohen, "Sex, Birth Control, and Human Life," 194-5. For a reply to Cohen, see E. D. Watt, "Professor Cohen's Encyclical." See also G. E. M. Anscombe, "Contraception and Chastity" and "You Can Have Sex Without Children."

18. *Summa Theologiae*, 2a2ae, q. 154, a. 12.
19. *Lectures on Ethics*, 167.
20. *Love and Responsibility*, 30.
21. See J. F. M. Hunter, *Thinking About Sex and Love*, 28, 111-12.
22. *Groundwork of the Metaphysic of Morals*, 96.
23. *Lectures*, 163. Also see his *Metaphysical Principles of Virtue*: "the allowed bodily union... of the two sexes in marriage" is "in itself... only animal union" (86).
24. John Stoltenberg, *Refusing To Be a Man*, 37.
25. Robert Nozick asks this Kant-inspired question in *Anarchy, State, and Utopia* (32): "In getting pleasure from seeing an attractive person go by, does one use the other solely as a means? Does someone so use an object of sexual fantasies?" There are, obviously, difficulties in applying Kant's maxim. Three essays on Kantian (sexual) ethics that are worth reading are Thomas A. Mappes, "Sexual Morality and the Concept of Using Another Person"; Larry Blum, "Deceiving, Hurting, and Using"; and Joel Rudinow, "Manipulation."
26. Irving Singer, *The Nature of Love*, vol. 2: *Courtly and Romantic*, 382.
27. *Lectures*, 166-7. See *Metaphysical Principles of Virtue*, 85.
28. "Sexual Ethics," 11. See also Margaret Farley, "Sexual Ethics," 1584.
29. "If a fusion of one and the other truly exists... the very possibility of using an *other* as a means no longer exists" (Robert Baker and Frederick Elliston, *Philosophy and Sex*, 1st ed., 18; 2nd ed., 26-7).
30. "Philosophy and Sex," 445.
31. Irving Singer thinks that in a Kantian marriage "love and sex can be harmonized" (*The Nature of Love*, vol. 2, 377), and that showing this was one of Kant's philosophical goals. Yet Singer's illuminating and eminently clear exposition (379-81) of Kant's solution to the puzzle in the *Lectures* makes no mention of love. It is true that before Kant lays out his solution, he says that sexuality by itself excludes genuine love (*Lectures*, 163); but Kant never says that sex in marriage, or marriage itself, either creates love or presupposes it. And it is a *non sequitur* to argue that if sex without marriage excludes love, sex within marriage must include it. What Vannoy and Singer overlook is that, given the

social context in which Kant thought and wrote, there was little reason for him to inject love into marriage. The Church had not yet officially embraced the expression or deepening of love as one of the purposes of marital sex. And marriage in the West was still a familial, social, and economic arrangement, not yet an affair of love (either genuine, in Kant's sense, or romantic) between two individuals. See Chapter Seven.

32. Barbara Herman, "Could It Be Worth Thinking About Kant on Sex and Marriage?" 66 n. 22.

33. This is why Gardell's reading of Kant, already mentioned, that "marriage transforms an otherwise manipulative masturbatory relationship into one that is essentially altruistic in character," is doubly wrong. I would have put it: marriage eliminates use by changing a mutually manipulative relationship into one that is essentially masturbatory (and hence use-free) in character.

34. *Lectures on Ethics*, 170.

35. *Sex and Reason*, 227.

36. Here's another view: "Masturbation isn't really a sign of heightened male sexuality, sexual interest, or desire, but a strategy selected over time [by evolutionary processes] to keep sperm supplies fresh in a species that isn't very sexual" (Meredith Small, *What's Love Got To Do With It?*, 119).

37. Hegel claims that a genuine union of two persons, x and y, occurs when they have produced a child together ("On Love," 307-8). This chestnut is repeated for the twentieth century by Nozick: "the couple's first child is [also] their union" ("Love's Bond," 85).

38. Hegel wrote that no "true union" occurs "if part of the individual is severed and held back" ("On Love," 304, 306). See Chapter Five.

39. See Bernard Baumrin's happy concession to Kant that all sexual interaction *is* manipulative, and his moral defense of sexual activity on the basis of consent ("Sexual Immorality Delineated").

40. See Raymond Belliotti, "A Philosophical Analysis of Sexual Ethics" and *Good Sex*, chs. 4 and 7.

41. John Finnis and Martha Nussbaum, "Is Homosexual Conduct Wrong? A Philosophical Exchange," 12-13, at 12. See also Finnis, "Law, Morality, and 'Sexual Orientation,'" and Germain Grisez, *The Way of the Lord Jesus*, vol. 2, 649-54.

42. *On Liberty*, 54.
43. Ibid., 79.
44. See Ronald Atkinson, *Sexual Morality*, a utilitarian treatise on sexuality.
45. For example, definitions of the various sexual pathologies listed in the *Diagnostic and Statistical Manual* of the American Psychiatric Association (4th ed.) often include "harm" done to other persons as a *diagnostic* (i.e., medical) criterion.
46. See Stephens's critique of Mill in *Liberty, Equality, Fraternity*.
47. Devlin, *The Enforcement of Morality*; Hart, *Law, Liberty, and Morality*. See also Richard Wasserstrom, ed., *Morality and the Law*.
48. Consider Richard Mohr's claim that because sex makes "a necessary and positive contribution" to love, the state, "in blocking gays from having sex," as in the U. S. Supreme Court decision in *Bowers v. Hardwick*, "would also deny them love" (*Gays/Justice*, 113).
49. *Summa Theologiae*, 2a2ae, q. 154, a. 11.
50. *Volenti non fit injuria* is the Latin legal expression.
51. Hilda Hein claims that degradation is wrong even if consented to ("Sadomasochism and the Liberal Tradition," 87):

    To degrade someone, even with that person's... consent, is to *endorse* the degradation of persons. It is to affirm that the abuse of persons is *acceptable*. For if some people may be humiliated,... all may be.... To voluntarily make a victim of oneself is to endorse the state of victimization implicitly for others.

52. Susan Farr, "The Art of Discipline," 184.
53. Diane Vera, "Temporary Consensual 'Slave Contract'," 76.
54. *Love and Responsibility*, 126, 129.
55. Mary Katzenstein and David Laitin, "Politics, Feminism, and the Ethics of Caring," 274.
56. Compare Ruth Linden et al., eds., *Against Sadomasochism*, with Samois, ed., *Coming to Power*. See also Patrick Hopkins, "Rethinking Sadomasochism: Feminism, Interpretation, and Simulation"; and Thomas Weinberg, ed., *S&M: Studies in Dominance & Submission*.
57. Compare the anti-pornography writings of Catharine MacKinnon (*Feminism Unmodified, Only Words, Toward a Feminist Theory of the State*) and Andrea Dworkin (*Pornography*) with Nadine

Strossen, *Defending Pornography*.
58. *Lesbian Choices*, 221.
59. Alan Goldman, "Plain Sex," in A. Soble, ed.,*Philosophy of Sex*, 2nd ed., 87.
60. *Homosexuality*, 185.
61. Craig Dean, "Fighting For Same Sex Marriage," 276.

CHAPTER FOUR: SEXUAL POLITICS

1. See Gilbert Herdt, *Guardians of the Flute* and, for discussion, A. Soble, *Sexual Investigations*, 153-5.
2. Pat Califia, "A Thorny Issue Splits a Movement," 20. See also Robert Ehman, "Adult-Child Sex," in R. Baker and F. Elliston, eds., *Philosophy and Sex*, 2nd ed., 431-46; Marilyn Frye, "Critique" [of Ehman], in *Philosophy and Sex*, 447-55 (and the revised version, "Not-Knowing About Sex and Power," in her *Willful Virgin*); Jeffrey Weeks, *Sexuality and Its Discontents*, 223-31; Steven Seidman, *Embattled Eros*, 198-203; and (on Seidman) Laurie Shrage, *Moral Dilemmas of Feminism*, 52-4.
3. "Feminism, Sexuality, and Authenticity," 136.
4. *On Liberty*, 57.
5. Ellen Willis, *Beginning To See the Light*, 209.
6. The organization (business association) of prostitutes COYOTE (Call Off Your Old Tired Ethics) has issued a "Code of Ethics for Prostitutes" that in many respects (clauses about confidentiality, stealing clients, and fees for consultation) resembles the codes of ethics of the American Medical Association and other professional groups.
7. On prostitution, see Karen Green, "Prostitution, Exploitation, and Taboo"; Lars Ericsson, "Charges Against Prostitution: An Attempt at a Philosophical Assessment"; Alison Jaggar, "Prostitution," in A. Soble, ed., *Philosophy of Sex*, 2nd ed., 259-80; Carole Pateman, "Defending Prostitution: Charges Against Ericsson" and *The Sexual Contract*; Laurie Shrage, "Is Sexual Desire Raced? The Social Meaning of Interracial Prostitution," "Should Feminists Oppose Prostitution?" and *Moral Dilemmas of Feminism*; and, on Shrage, both Robert Stewart, "Moral Criticism and the Social Meaning of Prostitution," and Igor Primoratz, "What's Wrong with Prostitution?"

8. *Marriage and Morals*, 121.
9. Ibid., 122.
10. "What's Wrong With Prostitution?" 173.
11. Ibid., 174.
12. *Marriage and Morals*, 122.
13. *The Origin of the Family, Private Property, and the State*, 144.
14. See Jeffrey Weeks, *Sexuality and Its Discontents*, 27.
15. Russell was optimistic (*Marriage and Morals*, 118):

> prostitution... appears to be on the decline, partly... owing to the fact that other means of livelihood are more available to women than they used to be, and partly also to the fact that many more women than used to be the case are now willing to have extra-marital relations with men, from inclination and not from commercial motives.

16. "Prostitution and Male Supremacy."
17. See Julia Davidson, "Prostitution and the Contours of Control."
18. *Going Too Far*, 165-6; italics omitted. Victoria Woodhull had made a point similar to Morgan's about marital sex a century earlier ("Tried As By Fire," 8 [1874]):

> Night after night... millions of poor, heart-broken, suffering wives are compelled to minister to the lechery of insatiable husbands, when every instinct of body and sentiment of soul revolts in loathing and disgust.

(Why "insatiable"? Were these men immune to habituation? See Chapter Seven.) Andrea Dworkin also attributes Morgan's *definition of rape* to Woodhull (*Right-wing Women*, 60). A close reading of Woodhull, however, reveals that her nineteenth-century feminism was a hundred years more conservative than contemporary second- or third-wave feminism. According to Woodhull, men and women should marry and have sex only when they love each other, the reason being that this arrangement is biologically best for any child that results from their sexual congress. And only in such a marriage, for Woodhull, can women fulfill their natures in "motherhood." None of this is mentioned by Dworkin in her interpretation of Woodhull as a feminist sexual radical (*Intercourse*, 135-8).

19. *Sex and Reason*, 389.
20. *Whose Science? Whose Knowledge?* 126. This is why Catharine MacKinnon claims that the distinction between rape and consen-

sual intercourse in our society is "difficult to sustain" (*Toward a Feminist Theory of the State*, 146). In a footnote, MacKinnon approvingly quotes Carole Pateman, whose thesis is that in contemporary patriarchy, we cannot speak meaningfully of the consent of women to sex (*Toward*, 298 n. 25).

21. "The Harms of Consensual Sex," 53.
22. "Compulsory Heterosexuality and Lesbian Existence," 35.
23. "From the point of view of psycho-analysis the exclusive sexual interest felt by men for women is also a problem that needs elucidating and is not a self-evident fact based upon an attraction that is ultimately of a chemical nature" (Sigmund Freud, *Three Essays on the Theory of Sexuality*, in *Standard Edition*, vol. 7, 146).
24. "Compulsory Heterosexuality and Lesbian Existence," 34, 57, 49. See also Sheila Jeffreys, *Anticlimax*, 3-4 and ch. 6.
25. *Intercourse*, 63.
26. "Heterosexuality and Feminist Theory," 10.
27. *Amazon Odyssey*, 19-20.
28. *The Dialectic of Sex*, 8-12, 225-8, 233-4.
29. *Intercourse*, 138.
30. *The Limits of Love*, 47.
31. "Nonviolent Sexual Coercion," 115; see also Charlene Muehlenhard et al., "Definitions of Rape: Scientific and Political Implications."
32. About the woman who accused William Kennedy Smith of rape, Camille Paglia says that she was "trying to *glom* onto the Kennedy *glamour*.... You go back to the Kennedy compound late at night and you're surprised at what happens? She's the one who should be charged—with ignorance. Because everyone knows that Kennedy is spelled S-E-X.... This is not a rape. And it's going to erode the real outrage that we should feel about actual rape" (*Sex, Art, and American Culture*, 73, 58).
33. Mary Koss and Kenneth Leonard, "Sexually Aggressive Men," 216.
34. See Alan Wertheimer, "Consent and Sexual Relations."
35. Jeffrie Murphy, "Some Ruminations on Women, Violence, and the Criminal Law," 218.
36. On the partial responsibility of a woman for date rape, see Camille Paglia, *Sex, Art, and American Culture*, 56-61, 72-4. On this issue more generally, see Katha Pollitt, "Not Just Bad

Sex," in *Reasonable Creatures*, 157-68; Adele Stan, ed., *Debating Sexual Correctness*; Andrea Parrot and Laurie Bechhofer, eds., *Acquaintance Rape*; and Peggy Reeves Sanday, *A Woman Scorned*.

37. *Going Too Far*, 168. See also Diana E. H. Russell, "Pornography and Rape: A Causal Model."

38. "Pornography and Violence: What Does the New Research Say?" in Laura Lederer, ed., *Take Back the Night*, 224.

39. When Dolf Zillman and Jennings Bryant ("Pornography, Sexual Callousness, and the Trivialization of Rape") write about Russell's data that "men were *found* to have made women comply with their requests to try what they had seen" (12, italics added; see also 19-20), they forget that Russell recorded only women's *beliefs* that the men were inspired by pornography.

40. Lillian Rubin, *Worlds of Pain*, 140; Catharine MacKinnon, *Toward a Feminist Theory of the State*, 177-8.

41. *Only Words*, 15.

42. "Symposium on Pornography. Appendix," 760. Dworkin and MacKinnon composed their Model Law in the early 1980s; it was subsequently legislatively enacted in Minneapolis and Indianapolis. In Minneapolis, the law was vetoed by the mayor; a federal judge struck down the Indianapolis version.

43. *Feminism Unmodified*, 180.

44. Nan Hunter and Sylvia Law, "Brief *Amici Curiae*," 475.

45. "Date Rape," 224, 233, 243.

46. "Misguided, Dangerous, and Wrong," 32. See also Barry Lynn, "'Civil Rights' Ordinances and the Attorney General's Commission," 100, and Donna Turley, "The Feminist Debate on Pornography," 90.

47. *Feminism Unmodified*, 180. See also this chapter's epigraph, above (*Feminism Unmodified*, 136).

48. Ibid., 180.

49. "Sex and Power," 406.

50. MacKinnon claims that "pornography is made... overwhelmingly by poor, desperate, homeless, pimped women who were sexually abused as children" (*Only Words*, 20). But MacKinnon provides no evidence for her claim. At any rate, it is logically irrelevant to the thesis that even if a woman has other opportunities for a livelihood, she is coerced to make pornography by the lure of better money.

51. In "How Bad Is Rape?" H. E. Baber compares the harms caused by rape and by work and arrives at some surprising conclusions.
52. *Only Words*, 27.
53. *Feminism Unmodified*, 11.

CHAPTER FIVE: VARIETIES OF LOVE

1. "Love" and "art," like "justice" and "democracy," are essentially contested (even contestable) concepts. See W. B. Gallie, "Essentially Contested Concepts."
2. A good summary of the varieties of love (*eros, agape, philia,* Kantian respect, and utilitarian beneficence) is presented by Gene Outka, "Love."
3. *Love*, 96.
4. This dilemma is analogous to the one Plato outlined in his dialogue *Euthyphro* (9d-11c): is an act A the right act to perform because the doing of A has been commanded by God, or has the doing of A been commanded by God because A is the right act?
5. "Great folly" is Hamilton's translation. Others are: "great mindlessness" (Martha Nussbaum, *The Fragility of Goodness*, 179); "utterly senseless" (Suzy Groden); and "altogether mindless" (Stanley Rosen, *Plato's Symposium*, 2nd ed., 265).
6. *Analyzing Love*, 24.
7. Kraut, "Love *De Re*," 423. Consistently, Kraut also claims "it is hardly clear that emotions like love are based upon reasons" (417).
8. Ibid., 416.
9. "Respect for Persons as a Moral Principle—I," 205.
10. Anders Nygren, *Agape and Eros*, 78.
11. Douglas Morgan, *Love: Plato, the Bible, and Freud*, 74.
12. Nygren, *Agape and Eros*, 75.
13. See 1Corinthians 13 and Romans 12:9-21.
14. *Works of Love*, 158; italics deleted.
15. Ibid., 343.
16. Ibid., 342.
17. See Outka, *Agape*, 158-60.
18. See Nygren, *Agape and Eros*, 96-8, and Morgan, *Love*, 123 n. 74.
19. See Shirley Robin Letwin, "Romantic Love and Christianity," 133.

20. *Relationship Morality*, 103-4.
21. Paul Tillich, for example, claims that the human love for God is *eros*, the drive of the human to be united with God in virtue of His perfection (*Love, Power, and Justice*, 31).
22. See also C. S. Lewis: "By a high paradox, God enables men to have a Gift-love towards Himself." We can "withhold," or lovingly not withhold, "our wills and hearts" from Him (*The Four Loves*, 177).
23. Irving Singer, *The Nature of Love*, vol. 2, 49.
24. Brentlinger, "The Nature of Love," 124.
25. Ibid., 127.
26. Ibid., 117.
27. Karol Wojtyla, *Love and Responsibility*, 91-2, 117, 123, 134-5, 185; and M. Scott Peck, *The Road Less Traveled*: "commitment is inherent in any genuinely loving relationship" (140-1; see also 81, 119).
28. See William Shakespeare's *Sonnet 116*, line 5.
29. A more detailed account of the various ways in which love can be irrational is provided by Gabrielle Taylor in "Love."
30. "A Conceptual Investigation of Love," 125.
31. Amelie Rorty in effect replies to Newton-Smith in the title of her essay, "The Historicity of Psychological Attitudes: Love is Not Love Which Alters Not When It Alteration Finds." Rorty, that is, denies Shakespeare's famous assertion from *Sonnet 116*: "love is not love which alters when it alteration finds" (lines 3-4).
32. "The Individual As an Object of Love in Plato," 31.
33. *Nicomachean Ethics*, bks. 8 and 9. See John M. Cooper, "Aristotle on Friendship," and A. W. Price, *Love and Friendship in Plato and Aristotle*.
34. For discussion, see Elijah Millgram, "Aristotle on Making Other Selves," and Neera Badhwar, "Friends As Ends in Themselves."
35. It is surprising, then, to find Edward Vacek claiming that *philia* "is the love that constitutes our 'friendship with God'." We have already seen that the human love for God is more easily characterized as a type of *eros* than as a type of *agape*. Vacek proposes that we think of the mutual love between human beings and God as *philia*. "Philia is distinguished from agape and eros by the *mutuality* of the relation it creates. In philia, as in all love, we love our beloveds. But in philia we love them not for their

own sake, as separate individuals, nor for our sake..., but for the sake of the mutual relationship we share with them" (*Love, Human and Divine: The Heart of Christian Ethics*, 281). Vacek departs from Aristotle. Why call it *philia*, if the love is not for our friend for our friend's own sake? And how can there be genuine mutuality between humans and God, given their vast differences? To say that in *philia* we love the other precisely for the sake of our relationship with him or her is similar to the view that we should stay married not for the other's sake, nor for the sake of the children, but for the marriage itself.

36. Irving Singer, in his trilogy *The Nature of Love*, claims—on my reading of his enormous text—that the bestowal of value (on persons and on things) is the fine gold thread of love. He runs into trouble, however, in explaining the human love for God; for discussion, see my *The Structure of Love*, 23-30. (This section of *Structure* is reprinted in Robert Stewart, ed.,*Philosophical Perspectives on Sex and Love*, 227-30.)

37. See Søren Kierkegaard, *Works of Love*.

38. "Maintaining Loving Relationships," 303.

39. "The Phenomena of Love and Hate," 13. Hamlyn's argument depends on the claim that love is an a-type emotion to begin with.

40. *Analyzing Love*, 30.

41. "On Affectionate Relationships," 215. See, on Montaigne, Allan Bloom, *Love and Friendship*, 410-28.

42. "On Love," 306.

43. Tillich, *Love, Power, and Justice*; Wojtyla,*Love and Responsibility*; Fromm, *The Art of Loving*; Gaylin, *Rediscovering Love*; Hunter, *Thinking About Sex and Love*; Fisher, *Personal Love*; and Nozick, "Love's Bond." Here is Tillich, sounding much like Aristophanes: "Love in all its forms is the drive towards the reunion of the separated" (28).

Kierkegaard found union views not benign and beautiful but pernicious: "All pleasure is selfish. The pleasure of the lover... is not selfish with respect to the loved one, but in union they are both absolutely selfish, inasmuch as in union and in love they constitute one self" (spoken by the Young Man in "The Banquet," *Stages on Life's Way*, 56). He continues, in the manner of Schopenhauer: "And yet they are deceived, for at the same instant the genus triumphs over the individual, the genus is victorious whereas the individuals are reduced to the position of being in its service. This I find is more ridiculous than what Aristophanes found so ridiculous."

44. "On Love," 304.
45. Ibid., 305.
46. Ibid., 305; italics added.
47. Ibid., 307; italics added.
48. *Love and Responsibility*, 84.
49. "On Love," 305.
50. Wojtyla expects Christian married couples to introduce "love into love," that is, to infuse *agape* into their sexual love relationship or even change sexual love into *agape* (*Love and Responsibility*, 17). But doing so would seem impossible, if the married lovers have become a unity that excludes robust concern.
51. Fromm, *The Art of Loving*, 6-8.
52. See Lillian Rubin, *Intimate Strangers*.
53. *The Second Sex*, 613-14.

CHAPTER SIX: FEATURES OF LOVE

1. *Works of Love*, 74.
2. *Analyzing Love*, 33.
3. "Personal Love," 119.
4. "A Conceptual Investigation of Love," 134-5 (italics added).
5. *The Four Loves*, 135.
6. *The Dialectic of Sex*, in A. Soble, ed., *Eros, Agape, and Philia*, 38.
7. "Self-Deceptive Emotions," 694-5. Sigmund Freud ("A Special Type of Choice of Object Made by Men," in *Standard Edition*, vol. 21, 169) gave a psychoanalytic account of a man's belief in the irreplaceability of his beloved:

    The trait of overvaluing the loved one, and regarding her as unique and irreplaceable, can be seen to fall... into the context of the child's experience, for no one possesses more than one mother, and the relation to her is based on an event that is not open to any doubt and cannot be repeated.

8. "Sexual Perversion," in A. Soble, ed., *Philosophy of Sex*, 2nd ed., 43.
9. *Sexual Desire*, 78 (first italics added).

10. Ibid., 78-9.
11. Recall the story from Genesis about Jacob, Leah, and Rachel (see Chapter One).
12. *Sexual Desire*, 163.
13. Ibid., 76; see also 103. I guess we are to imagine John pining away after Mary, singing to himself in falsetto the 1977 Yvonne Elliman recording, written by the Gibbs brothers: "if I can't have you, I don't want nobody, baby."
14. *Sexual Desire*, 95.
15. Ibid., 136-7. Our loves "contain a vast metaphysical flaw" (391).
16. Ibid., 130.
17. Ibid., 136; see also 104-5.
18. *Love and Responsibility*, 134.
19. Ibid., 17.
20. Ibid., 135.
21. Ibid., 42, 79, 121, 133.
22. Ibid., 211.
23. Ibid., 212.
24. *Works of Love*, 320-2.
25. *Analyzing Love*, 21.
26. *Kierkegaard*, 264-5.
27. "Personal Love," 123.
28. Ibid., 136.
29. *Love and Responsibility*, 85; see also 86.
30. Ibid., 84.
31. Ibid., 129.
32. *The Art of Loving*, 21. M. Scott Peck agrees: "Love... is invariably... a reciprocal phenomenon.... Value creates value. Love begets love" (*The Road Less Traveled*, 123, 126).
33. Consider further the hypothesis that in order for a person to be able to love another, he or she must have been loved by someone else. The point is, for example, that parents must love their children if their children are to be able to love other persons later. But how were the parents able to love their children? By our hypothesis, by being loved by someone else, say, *their* parents; and why were they able to love? We have here a version of the causal stream paradox. Perhaps at one point, way back, there was someone who was able to love in the absence of himself or herself being loved. This original unloved lover started things

going. But then our hypothesis is false. Or perhaps God loved that person, who was not loved by any other person, in which case we can get the stream of love going without violating our hypothesis. But now we have to say that God, at least, can love without being loved. But if God loved that humanly-unloved person so that that person would be able to love other persons and get the love-stream going, then there is no reason to assert our hypothesis. For any humanly-unloved person today will be able to love others as long as God loves him or her. Given the characterization of God as all-loving, we are all loved by God and hence will be able to love others in spite of the fact that we are not loved by other humans. Perhaps we should assert only that, *ceteris paribus*, a person is less likely to be able to love others if he or she has not been loved. This more reasonable claim might be true, but might also be a truism. Without a precise statement of the other conditions that are necessary and of the relationship between these and the loving-beloved chain, the psychology of love becomes a guessing game.

CHAPTER SEVEN: SEX, LOVE, AND MARRIAGE

1. *Summa Theologiae* 2a2ae, q. 26, a. 11, r. 2.
2. "Compulsory Heterosexuality," 35.
3. "Monogamy: A Critique," 107.
4. "Love and Sex," 371.
5. "Humanae Vitae," §12.
6. See Carl Cohen, "Sex, Birth Control, and Human Life," 192.
7. See "Humanae Vitae," §10.
8. On sex and love, see Robert Brown, *Analyzing Love*, ch. 2; Paul Gilbert, *Human Relationships*, ch. 2; J. F. M. Hunter, *Thinking About Sex and Love*; Richard Taylor, *Having Love Affairs*; Russell Vannoy, *Sex Without Love*; J. Martin Stafford, "On Distinguishing Between Love and Lust"; A. H. Lesser, "Love and Lust"; Joseph Diorio, "Sex, Love, and Justice"; Alan Goldman, "Plain Sex"; Paul Gregory, "Eroticism and Love"; John McMurtry, "Sex, Love, and Friendship" and "Monogamy: A Critique"; and Thomas Gregor, "Sexuality and the Experience of Love."
9. *Philosophical Writings*, vol. 1, 360. (By "we," does Descartes mean "men"?)

10. In addition to Walsh, see several essays in Robert Sternberg and Michael Barnes, eds., *The Psychology of Love*, 75, 90, 94, 104; Alex Comfort, *Nature and Human Nature*, 30; and Helen Fisher, *Anatomy of Love*, ch. 3.
11. Søren Kierkegaard, *Fear and Trembling*, 91.
12. In this translation of *Symposium* 210b (Suzy Groden's), I have replaced the third-person pronoun with the second-person pronoun and its congeners.
13. *Is Sex Necessary?* 62, 67.
14. *On Love*, 89. See Irving Singer, *The Nature of Love*, vol. 2, 323, for a similar thesis in Jean-Jacques Rousseau.
15. Phyllis Schlafly, *The Power of the Positive Woman*, 17.
16. See Joseph Diorio, "Sex, Love, and Justice."
17. "Adultery in deed or in desire is always wrong" (Germain Grisez, *Living a Christian Life*, 643).
18. The literature on multiple sexual relations, in and out of marriage, is enormous (everyone, it seems, has an opinion on the matter). Among the philosophers who have written on the topic are Mike Martin, *Everyday Morality*, 2nd ed., 230-44; Laurie Shrage, *Moral Dilemmas of Feminism*, 2-3, 37-41; Richard Taylor, *Having Love Affairs*; Richard Wasserstrom, "Is Adultery Immoral?"; Predrag Cicovacki, "On Love and Fidelity in Marriage"; and (on Cicovacki) Kathleen Higgins, "How Do I Love Thee? Let's Redefine a Term."
19. M. Scott Peck, *The Road Less Traveled*, 91. Despite his flights into metaphor in describing a union view of sexual activity, Rollo May at least notes that the *we* that is formed by two persons engaging in sex is temporary (*Love and Will*, 75):

    The two persons... participate in a relationship that, for the moment, is not made up of two isolated, individual experiences, but a genuine union. A sharing takes place which is a new *Gestalt*, a new being, a new field of magnetic force.

20. *Love and Responsibility*, 237.
21. See Geoffrey Gorer, "On Falling in Love," and countless others. For discussion and references, see Dorothy Tennov, *Love and Limerance*, 142-6.
22. *Summa Theologiae*, 2a2ae, q. 154, a. 2.
23. *The Nature of Love*, vol. 3, *The Modern World*, 6. Singer sounds like Judge William in Kierkegaard's *Either/Or* ("Aesthetic Va-

lidity of Marriage," in vol. 2) and *Stages on Life's Way* ("Various Observations About Marriage in Reply to Objections").

24. *The Modern World*, 378. Some would say "and good riddance" (recall Victoria Woodhull's complaint about a man's insatiable lechery for his wife; Chapter Four, note 18).

25. Ibid., 386, 439.

26. Ibid., 381.

27. Ibid., 382.

28. *Sexual Desire*, 244.

29. Ibid., 314.

30. Ibid., 244.

31. *Lectures on Ethics*, 168. Although Kant meant this remark to explain the absence of incestuous sexuality among siblings, the principle remains the same.

32. *Sexual Desire*, 244.

33. See Jean Duncombe and Dennis Marsden, "Whose Orgasm Is This Anyway?" 220-38, especially the section "Sexual Experimentation, Pornography and Masturbation," 229-31.

34. See Dolf Zillman, *Connections Between Sex and Aggression*, 198; he worries that an attempt to overcome the boredom of sexual activity leads to sadomasochism, because "pain is extremely resistant to habituation."

35. "When Harry and Sally Read the *Nicomachean Ethics*," 185, 187.

36. Ibid., 192.

37. Mary Lyndon Shanley, "Marital Slavery and Friendship: John Stuart Mill's *The Subjection of Women*," 241. See John's dedication to Harriet in *On Liberty* and, on their relationship, Phyllis Rose, *Parallel Lives* (95-140); and Gertrude Himmelfarb, *Marriage and Morals Among the Victorians* (10-11) and *On Liberty and Liberalism* (passim).

38. "Sexual Paradigms," 60-1.

39. "Love and Lust," 53.

40. "Can Sex Express Love?"

41. See Janice Moulton, "Sexual Behavior," 68-9, and Alan Goldman, "Plain Sex," 78-80; both in A. Soble, ed., *Philosophy of Sex*, 2nd ed.

42. *A More Perfect Union*, 50.

43. See, for example, Kalman Applbaum, "Marriage with the Proper Stranger: Arranged Marriage in Metropolitan Japan."

44. See Erich Fromm, *The Art of Loving*, 2-3. But do we utilize this freedom "authentically"?
45. You know this tune (composed by Jimmy van Heusen). It's the theme song of the television program about Al, Peg, Kelly, and Bud Bundy, "Married With Children." (My favorite Kellyism: "That's the squaw that stroked the camel's sack.")
46. Over a century ago, Victoria Woodhull pompously declared ("The Principles of Social Freedom," 17):

    [M]arriage consists of a union resulting from love.... It is certain by this Higher Law, that marriages of convenience... are adulterous.

47. On different philosophies of marriage, see Dorothy Tennov, *Love and Limerance*, 182-3, 293 n. 42; K. Anthony Appiah, "The Marrying Kind."
48. "Fighting For Same Sex Marriage" and "Gay Marriage: A Civil Right."
49. See Frederick Elliston, "Gay Marriage"; Andrew Sullivan, *Virtually Normal*; Richard Mohr, *A More Perfect Union*; and Gabriel Rotello, "To Have and To Hold: The Case for Gay Marriage."
50. Thurber and White, *Is Sex Necessary?* 96, 98.

CHAPTER EIGHT: GENDER

1. "Abortion and the Sexual Agenda," 238.
2. *Connections Between Sex and Aggression*, 193.
3. *The Nature and Evolution of Female Sexuality*, 108-14, 134-40. Sheila Jeffreys interprets Sherfey as describing "women as mindless, uncontrollable sexual animals" (*Anticlimax*, 229). Jeffreys is a lesbian feminist, not a conservative Christian.
4. *What's Love Got To Do With It?* 22, 220. Both men and women, on her view, are pulled between being monogamous and having multiple lovers (151).
5. *Connections Between Sex and Aggression*, 193.
6. *What's Love Got To Do With It?*, 120.
7. M. Morris, "Telling Tails Explain the Discrepancy in Sexual Partner Reports."
8. Laumann et al., *The Social Organization of Sexuality*, 184.
9. Ibid., 185.
10. See Dorothy Einon, "Are Men More Promiscuous Than Women?"

11. But if the men and women are not answering this question truthfully, why think that they answer any survey question truthfully?
This explanation thus brings into doubt the reliability of surveys about sexual behavior. For discussion, see R. C. Lewontin,
"Sex, Lies, and Social Science."

12. *Social Organization*, 176. See also the mass-market version of
Social Organization, Robert Michel et al.,*Sex in America*, 253-
4.

13. Small, *What's Love Got To Do With It?*, 120.

14. Other complications exist. Does the survey definition require
(or did the subjects read it as requiring) that*both* persons in the
event be "really turned on"? If so, then the men might not count
their sexual activity with prostitutes for this additional reason,
if—which is common—the prostitute performed only fellatio.
There is another reason men might not count events with prostitutes: the survey definition of sexual activity requires that the
event be "mutually voluntary." Some men might not think that
the prostitute participates voluntarily; other men might not think
that the event is "mutual."

   We have been assuming that if, in a given sexual event, the
woman is not "really turned on," the man knows this. But, in
general, do men know this when it is true? If they do, and if they
think the definition requires both persons to be aroused, there
should be no discrepancy between men's and women's reports
to begin with; none of the events in which the woman was not
"really turned on" would be counted by either the men or the
women as sexual activity. On the other hand, if a man does not
think his partner is not aroused, he will count the event as sexual,
as long as he is aroused; but the woman will not count this same
event as sexual because she knows that at least one person, herself, is not aroused (she can rely on his erection to determine
whether he is aroused). Then there should be a discrepancy in
their reports, a discrepancy that reflects a real difference in their
nonmoral evaluations of sexual activity, not a difference in the
number of sexual partners they have had.

15. See the movie "Goodbye, Columbus," or read Philip Roth's
novella *Goodbye, Columbus*.

16. So my students say in class.

17. Homosexual couples seem to have the same problems as het-

erosexual couples: "preserving the sexual spark within relationships over extended years" is difficult for them as well (Christine Gudorf, *Body, Sex, and Pleasure*, 148). Gudorf worries that homosexual relationships are erotically doomed *because* they are egalitarian within a culture that has "eroticized dominance."

18. Thus Callahan reverses *My Fair Lady*'s "Why can't a woman be more like a man?"

19. "Abortion and the Sexual Agenda," 238.

20. Ibid., 237. See also Dolf Zillman, *Connections Between Sex and Aggression*, 196.

21. Michel et al., *Sex in America*, 156. I once read in an Ann Landers column that men, on the average, think about sex once every ten minutes (not counting dreams).

22. Evelyn Fox Keller opines that "almost certainly, human nature is such that tension between autonomy and intimacy, separation and connection, aggression and love, is unresolvable" (*Reflections on Gender and Science*, 112-13).

23. See Lillian Rubin, *Intimate Strangers*, 65-97, or the selection reprinted in A. Soble, ed., *Eros, Agape, and Philia*, 12-28.

24. *Embattled Eros*, 128.

25. On the relative rarity of female sexual perversion, see Dorothy Tennov, *Love and Limerance*, 221, 299 n. 21; Paul Gebhardt, "Fetishism and Sadomasochism," 161.

26. *Connections Between Sex and Aggression*, 182.

27. *Sex, Art, and American Culture*, 65.

28. *Female Perversions*, 14.

29. Ibid., 199.

30. Ibid., 200.

31. "Why Homosexuality Is Abnormal," 277.

32. *Sex, Art, and American Culture*, 24-5.

33. Donald Symons, *The Evolution of Human Sexuality*, 292-305.

34. Ibid., 292.

35. See Keith Thomas, "The Double Standard."

36. See Kenneth Dover, *Greek Homosexuality*, 171-84, for Sappho's life and work.

37. "To Anactoria in Lydia," in *The Poems of Sappho*, 7.

38. *The Dialectic of Sex*, 149.

39. "The One-Caring," 324.

40. See Carol Gilligan's studies in the psychology of moral devel-

opment, *In a Different Voice*, and the sympathetic summary in David Cooper, *Value Pluralism and Ethical Choice*, ch. 6, "Gender Differences in Ethics," 91-107. For criticisms of a distinctively female ethics of care, see Katha Pollitt, "Marooned on Gilligan's Island," *Reasonable Creatures*, 42-62; Colin McGinn, "Mothers and Moralists"; and Carol Tavris, *The Mismeasure of Woman*.

41. See Barbara Andolsen, "Agape in Feminist Ethics"; and Valerie Saiving, "The Human Situation: A Feminine View."

42. Fromm, *The Art of Loving*, 33-7.

43. Nancy Chodorow, *The Reproduction of Mothering*. According to Chodorow, men and women must spend equal amounts of time parenting ("mothering") their children, if many of the gender differences mentioned in this chapter are to disappear.

44. David Buss, *The Evolution of Desire*, 60-3. This difference also seems to hold between gay men and lesbian women. See also Buss, "Sex Differences in Human Mate Preferences," which includes Buss's original research report, twenty-seven commentaries, and Buss's replies.

45. Symons, *The Evolution of Human Sexuality*, 253-85.

46. Buss, who defends the biological, evolutionary explanation, and his critics cover the ground in "Sex Differences in Human Mate Preferences." See also Symons, *The Evolution of Human Sexuality*, and Helen Fisher, *Anatomy of Love*.

47. Mary Wollstonecraft, *Vindication of the Rights of Women*, 53.

48. See Naomi Wolf, *The Beauty Myth*, 25ff., and Sandra Bartky, *Femininity and Domination*, 39-42.

49. William Graziano et al., "Social Influence, Sex Differences, and Judgments of Beauty," 530.

50. Kim Wallen, in Buss, "Sex Differences in Human Mate Preferences," 37. Buss replies that "women who make *more* money tend to value monetary and professional status of mates *more* than those who make less money" (41). Further, according to Buss, the importance of physical attractiveness as a selection criterion has been increasing in the U. S. since 1930, but the gap between the sexes has remained constant (*The Evolution of Desire*, 58).

51. See John Stuart Mill, *The Subjection of Women*.

FURTHER READING

For students who would like to pursue the matters discussed in this book both comprehensively and in depth, the following books are recommended.

Baker, Robert, and Frederick Elliston, eds. *Philosophy and Sex*, 1st edn. (Buffalo: Prometheus, 1975); 2nd edn. (1984).

Boswell, John. *Christianity, Social Tolerance, and Homosexuality* (Chicago: University of Chicago Press, 1980).

Buss, David M. *The Evolution of Desire* (New York: Basic Books, 1994).

Dworkin, Andrea. *Intercourse* (New York: Free Press, 1987).

Fromm, Erich. *The Art of Loving* (New York: Harper Perennial Library, 1974).

Hamer, Dean, and Peter Copeland. *The Science of Desire* (New York: Simon and Schuster, 1994).

Hunter, J. F. M. *Thinking About Sex and Love* (New York: St. Martin's, 1980).

Jung, Patricia, and Ralph Smith. *Heterosexism: An Ethical Challenge* (Albany, N.Y.: State University of New York Press, 1993).

LeVay, Simon. *The Sexual Brain* (Cambridge, Mass.: M.I.T. Press, 1993).

Lamb, Roger, ed. *Love Analyzed* (Boulder, Colo: Westview, 1997).

Lewis, C. S. *The Four Loves* (New York: Harcourt, Brace, Jovanovich, 1960).

MacKinnon, Catharine A. *Feminism Unmodified* (Cambridge, Mass.: Harvard University Press, 1987).

Noonan, John T. *Contraception: A History of Its Treatment by the Catholic Theologians and Canonists*, enlarged ed. (Cambridge, Mass.: Harvard University Press, 1986).

Outka, Gene. *Agape: An Ethical Analysis* (New Haven, Conn.: Yale University Press, 1972).

Posner, Richard A. *Sex and Reason* (Cambridge, Mass.: Harvard University Press, 1992.

Rubin, Lillian. *Intimate Strangers* (New York: Harper and Row, 1983).

Ruse, Michael. *Homosexuality: A Philosophical Inquiry* (New York: Blackwell, 1988).

Russell, Bertrand. *Marriage and Morals* (London: George Allen and Unwin, 1929).

Scruton, Roger. *Sexual Desire: A Moral Philosophy of the Erotic* (New York: Free Press, 1986).

Soble, Alan. *Sexual Investigations* (New York: New York University Press, 1996).

_____ , ed. *Eros, Agape, and Philia* (New York: Paragon House, 1989).

_____ , ed. *Philosophy of Sex*, 1st ed. (Totowa, N.J.: Rowman and Littlefield, 1980); 2nd ed. (Savage, Md.: 1991); 3rd ed. (Lanham, Md.: 1997).

_____ , ed. *Sex, Love, and Friendship* (Amsterdam: Editions Rodopi, 1997).

Solomon, Robert C., and Higgins, Kathleen M., eds. *The Philosophy of (Erotic) Love* (Lawrence, Kan.: University Press of Kansas, 1991).

Stein, Edward, ed. *Forms of Desire* (New York: Routledge, 1992).

Stewart, Robert M., ed. *Philosophical Perspectives on Sex and Love* (New York: Oxford University Press, 1995).

Stoltenberg, John. *Refusing To Be a Man* (Portland, Ore.: Breitenbush Books, 1989).

Sullivan, Andrew. *Virtually Normal: An Argument About Homosexuality* (New York: Knopf, 1995).

Vannoy, Russell. *Sex Without Love: A Philosophical Exploration* (Buffalo, N.Y.: Prometheus, 1980).

Whiteley, C. H. and Winifred N. Whiteley. *Sex and Morals* (New York: Basic Books, 1967).

Wojtyla, Karol. *Love and Responsibility* (New York: Farrar, Straus, and Giroux, 1981).

BIBLIOGRAPHY

Alexander, W. M. "Sex and Philosophy in Augustine," *Augustinian Studies* 5 (1974): 197-208.

American Psychiatric Association. *Diagnostic and Statistical Manual of Mental Disorders*, 4th ed. (Washington, D.C.: American Psychiatric Association, 1994).

Andolsen, Barbara Hilkert. "Agape in Feminist Ethics," in C. Williams, ed., *On Love and Friendship* (Boston: Jones and Bartlett, 1995), 167-81.

Anscombe, G. E. M. "Contraception and Chastity," in M. Bayles, ed., *Ethics and Population* (Cambridge, Mass.: Schenkman, 1976), 134-53.

_____. "You Can Have Sex Without Children," in *Ethics, Religion and Politics* (Minneapolis: University of Minnesota Press, 1981), 82-96.

Appiah, K. Anthony. "The Marrying Kind," *New York Review of Books* (June 20, 1996), 48-54.

Applbaum, Kalman D. "Marriage With the Proper Stranger: Arranged Marriage in Metropolitan Japan," *Ethnology* 34:1 (1995): 37-51.

Aquinas, Thomas. *On the Truth of the Catholic Faith* [*Summa Contra Gentiles*, bk. 3, pt. 2], trans. V. Bourke (Garden City, N.Y.: Image Books, 1956).

_____. *Summa Theologiae* (Blackfriars, 1964-76).

Aristotle. *Nicomachean Ethics*, trans. T. Irwin (Indianapolis: Hackett, 1985).

Atkinson, Ronald. *Sexual Morality* (London: Hutchinson, 1965).

Atkinson, Ti-Grace. *Amazon Odyssey* (New York: Links, 1974).

Augustine. *Confessions* (New York: Penguin, 1961).

_____ . *On Marriage and Concupiscence*, in *Works*, vol. 12 (Edinburgh: T. & T. Clark, 1874).

Baber, H. E. "How Bad Is Rape?" *Hypatia* 2:2 (1987): 125-38; reprinted in A. Soble, ed., *Philosophy of Sex*, 2nd ed. (Savage, Md.: Rowman and Littlefield, 1991), 243-58.

Badhwar, Neera. "Friends As Ends in Themselves," *Philosophy and Phenomenological Research* 48:1 (1987):1-23; reprinted, revised, in A. Soble, ed., *Eros, Agape and Philia* (New York: Paragon House, 1989), 165-86; and, further revised, in A. Soble, ed., *Sex, Love, and Friendship* (Amsterdam: Editions Rodopi, 1997).

Baird, Robert M., and M. Katherine Baird, eds. *Homosexuality: Debating the Issues* (Amherst, N.Y.: Prometheus, 1995).

Baker, Robert, and Frederick Elliston, eds. *Philosophy and Sex*, 1st ed. (Buffalo, N.Y.: Prometheus, 1975); 2nd ed. (1984).

Barrowclough, Susan. Review of "Not a Love Story," *Screen* 23:5 (1982): 26-36.

Bartky, Sandra Lee. *Femininity and Domination* (New York: Routledge, 1990).

Baumrin, Bernard. "Sexual Immorality Delineated," in R. Baker and F. Elliston, eds., *Philosophy and Sex*, 2nd ed. (Buffalo, N.Y.: Prometheus, 1984), 300-11.

Beauvoir, Simone de. *The Second Sex* (New York: Bantam, 1961).

Belliotti, Raymond. "A Philosophical Analysis of Sexual Ethics," *Journal of Social Philosophy* 10:3 (1979): 8-11.

_____ . *Good Sex: Perspectives on Sexual Ethics* (Lawrence, Kan.: University Press of Kansas, 1993).

Bloom, Allan. *Love and Friendship* (New York: Simon and Schuster, 1993).

Blum, Larry. "Deceiving, Hurting and Using," in A. Montefiore, ed., *Philosophy and Personal Relations* (Montreal: McGill-

Queens University Press, 1976), 34-61.

Boorse, Christopher. "On the Distinction Between Disease and Illness," *Philosophy and Public Affairs* 5:1 (1975): 49-68.

Boswell, John. *Christianity, Social Tolerance, and Homosexuality* (Chicago: University of Chicago Press, 1980).

_____ . *Same-Sex Unions in Premodern Europe* (New York: Villard Books, 1994).

Bowers v. Hardwick, 106 S. Ct. 2841 (1986); 487 U.S. 186 (1986).

Brentlinger, John. "The Nature of Love," in Plato, *Symposium*, trans. S. Groden (Amherst, Mass.: University of Massachusetts Press, 1970), 113-29.

Brown, Robert. *Analyzing Love* (Cambridge, Eng.: Cambridge University Press, 1987).

Bullough, Vern L., and Bonnie Bullough. *Sexual Attitudes: Myths and Realities* (Amherst, N.Y.: Prometheus, 1995).

Burr, Chandler. "Homosexuality and Biology," *Atlantic Monthly* (March 1993), 47-65.

Buscaglia, Leo. *Love* (New York: Ballantine Books, 1982).

Buss, David M., et al., "Sex Differences in Human Mate Preferences: Evolutionary Hypotheses Tested in 37 Cultures," *Behavioral and Brain Sciences* 12 (1989): 1-49.

_____ . *The Evolution of Desire* (New York: Basic Books, 1994).

Byne, William. "The Biological Evidence Challenged," *Scientific American* (May 1994), 50-5.

Byne, William, and Bruce Parsons. "Human Sexual Orientation," *Archives of General Psychiatry* 50 (1993): 228-39.

Byrne, Donn E., and Sarah K. Murnen. "Maintaining Loving Relationships," in R. Sternberg and M. Barnes, eds., *The Psychology of Love* (New Haven, Conn.: Yale University Press, 1988), 293-310.

Califia, Pat. "A Thorny Issue Splits a Movement,"*Advocate* (October 30, 1980), 17-24, 45.

Callahan, Sidney. "Abortion and the Sexual Agenda," *Commonweal* (April 25, 1986), 232-8.

Card, Claudia. *Lesbian Choices* (New York: Columbia University Press, 1995).

Carol, Avedon. "Snuff: Believing the Worst," in A. Assiter and A. Carol, eds. *Bad Girls and Dirty Pictures* (London: Pluto Press, 1993), 126-30.

Chodorow, Nancy. *The Reproduction of Mothering* (Berkeley: University of California Press, 1978).

Christina, Greta. "Are We Having Sex Now Or What?" in D. Steinberg, ed., *The Erotic Impulse* (New York: Jeremy P. Tarcher/Perigee, 1992), 24-9; reprinted in A. Soble, ed., *Philosophy of Sex*, 3rd ed. (Lanham, Md.: Rowman and Littlefield).

Cicovacki, Predrag. "On Love and Fidelity in Marriage," *Journal of Social Philosophy* 24:3 (1993): 92-104.

"Code of Ethics for Prostitutes," *Coyote Howls* 5:1 (1978): 9.

Cohen, Carl. "Sex, Birth Control, and Human Life," in R. Baker and F. Elliston, eds., *Philosophy and Sex*, 2nd ed. (Buffalo, N.Y.: Prometheus, 1984), 185-99.

Coleman, Eli. "Bisexuality: Challenging Our Understanding of Human Sexuality and Sexual Orientation," in E. Shelp, ed., *Sexuality and Medicine*, vol. 1 (Dordrecht, Hol.: Reidel, 1987), 225-42.

Colker, Ruth. "Feminism, Sexuality, and Authenticity," in M. Fineman and N. Thomadsen, eds., *At the Boundaries of Law* (New York: Routledge, 1991), 135-47.

Comfort, Alex. *Nature and Human Nature* (London: Weidenfeld and Nicholson, 1966).

Concar, David. "Sisters Are Doing It for Themselves," *New Scientist* (August 17, 1996), 32-6.

Cooper, David. *Value Pluralism and Ethical Choice* (New York: St. Martin's Press, 1993).

Cooper, John M. "Aristotle on Friendship," in A. Rorty, ed., *Essays on Aristotle's Ethics* (Berkeley: University of California Press, 1980), 301-40.

Davidson, Arnold. "Sex and the Emergence of Sexuality," *Critical Inquiry* 14:1 (1987): 16-48; in E. Stein, ed., *Forms of Desire* (New York: Routledge, 1992), 89-132.

Davidson, Julia O'Connell. "Prostitution and the Contours of Control," in J. Weeks and J. Holland, eds., *Sexual Cultures* (New York: St. Martin's Press, 1996), 180-98.

Dean, Craig R. "Fighting For Same Sex Marriage," in A. Minas, ed., *Gender Basics* (Belmont, Cal.: Wadsworth, 1993), 275-7.

_____ . "Gay Marriage: A Civil Right," in T. Murphy, ed., *Gay Ethics: Controversies in Outing, Civil Rights, and Sexual Science* (Binghamton, N.Y.: Haworth, 1994), 111-15.

Descartes, René. *The Philosophical Writings of Descartes*, vol. 1 (Cambridge, Eng.: Cambridge University Press, 1985).

De Sousa, Ronald. "Self-Deceptive Emotions," *Journal of Philosophy* 75 (1978): 684-97.

Devlin, Patrick. *The Enforcement of Morals* (London: Oxford University Press, 1965).

Diorio, Joseph A. "Feminist-constructionist Theories of Sexuality and the Definition of Sex Education," *Educational Philosophy and Theory* 21:2 (1989): 23-31.

_____ . "Sex, Love, and Justice: A Problem in Moral Education," *Educational Theory* 31:3-4 (1982): 225-35; in A. Soble, ed., *Eros, Agape, and Philia* (New York: Paragon House, 1989), 273-88.

Dover, K. J. *Greek Homosexuality*, rev. ed. (Cambridge, Mass.: Harvard University Press, 1989).

Duncombe, Jean, and Dennis Marsden. "Whose Orgasm Is This Anyway? 'Sex Work' in Long-term Heterosexual Couple Relationships," in J. Weeks and J. Holland, eds., *Sexual Cultures* (New York: St. Martin's Press, 1996), 220-38.

Dworkin, Andrea. "Prostitution and Male Supremacy," http:// www.igc.apc.org/womensnet/dworkin/MichLawJournalI.html

_____ . *Intercourse* (New York: Free Press, 1987).

_____ . *Pornography: Men Possessing Women* (New York: Perigee, 1981).

_____ . *Right-wing Women* (New York: Perigee, 1983).

Edwards, Susan. *Female Sexuality and the Law* (Oxford, Eng.: Martin Robertson, 1981).

Ehman, Robert. "Adult-Child Sex," in R. Baker and F. Elliston, eds., *Philosophy and Sex*, 2nd ed. (Buffalo, N.Y.: Prometheus, 1984), 431-46.

_____ . "Personal Love," *The Personalist* 49 (1968) 116-41; in A. Soble, ed., *Eros, Agape, and Philia* (New York: Paragon House, 1989), 254-71.

Einon, Dorothy. "Are Men More Promiscuous Than Women?" *Ethology and Sociobiology* 15 (1994): 131-43.

Elliston, Frederick. "Gay Marriage," in R. Baker and F. Elliston, eds., *Philosophy and Sex*, 2nd ed. (Buffalo, N.Y.: Prometheus, 1984), 146-66.

Engelhardt, H. Tristram, Jr. "The Disease of Masturbation: Values and the Concept of Disease," *Bulletin of the History of Medicine* 48 (Summer, 1974): 234-48; in T. Beauchamp and L. Walters, eds., *Contemporary Issues in Bioethics* (Encino, Cal.: Dickenson, 1978), 109-13.

Engels, Friedrich. *The Origin of the Family, Private Property, and the State* (New York: International Publishers, 1972).

Ericsson, Lars O. "Charges Against Prostitution: An Attempt at a Philosophical Assessment," *Ethics* 90:3 (1980): 335-66.

Ernulf, Kurt E., Sune M. Innala, and Frederick L. Whitam. "Biological Explanation, Psychological Explanation, and Tolerance of Homosexuals: A Cross-National Analysis of Beliefs and Attitudes," *Psychological Reports* 65 (1989): 1003-10.

Estrich, Susan. *Real Rape* (Cambridge, Mass.: Harvard University Press, 1987).

Farley, Margaret A. "Sexual Ethics," in W. Reich, ed., *Encyclopedia of Bioethics*, vol. 4 (New York: Free Press, 1978), 1575-89.

Farr, Susan. "The Art of Discipline," in Samois, ed., *Coming to Power* (Palo Alto, Cal.: Up Press, 1981), 181-9.

Fausto-Sterling, Anne. "The Five Sexes," *The Sciences* (March/April 1993), 20-4.

———. "How Many Sexes Are There?" *New York Times* (March 12, 1993), A15 (op-ed).

Finnis, John M. "Law, Morality, and 'Sexual Orientation'," *Notre Dame Law Review* 69: 5 (1994): 1049-76.

Finnis, John, and Martha Nussbaum. "Is Homosexual Conduct Wrong? A Philosophical Exchange," *New Republic* (November 15, 1993), 12-13.

Firestone, Shulamith. *The Dialectic of Sex* (New York: Morrow, 1970).

Fisher, Helen. *Anatomy of Love* (New York: Fawcett Columbine, 1992).

Fisher, Mark. *Personal Love* (London: Duckworth, 1990).

Foucault, Michel. *The History of Sexuality*, vol. 1: *An Introduc-*

tion (New York: Vintage, 1976); vol. 2: *The Use of Pleasure* (New York: Pantheon, 1985); vol. 3: *The Care of the Self* (New York: Vintage, 1986).

Freud, Sigmund. *The Standard Edition of the Complete Psychological Works of Sigmund Freud*, ed. and trans. J. Strachey (London: Hogarth Press, 1953-74).

Fromm, Erich. *The Art of Loving* (New York: Harper Perennial Library, 1974).

Frye, Marilyn. "Critique" [of Ehman], in R. Baker and F. Elliston, eds., *Philosophy and Sex*, 2nd ed. (Buffalo, N.Y.: Prometheus, 1984), 447-55; revised version, "Not-Knowing About Sex and Power," in *Willful Virgin* (Freedom, Cal.: Crossing Press, 1992), 39-50.

Gallie, W. B. "Essentially Contested Concepts," *Proceeding of the Aristotelian Society*, New Series 56 (1956), 167-98.

Gardell, Mary Ann. "Sexual Ethics: Some Perspectives From the History of Philosophy," in E. Shelp, ed., *Sexuality and Medicine*, vol. 2 (Dordrecht, Hol.: Reidel, 1987), 3-15.

Gardella, Peter. *Innocent Ecstasy* (New York: Oxford University Press, 1985).

Gay, Peter. *The Bourgeois Experience*, vol. 1: *Education of the Senses* (Oxford, Eng.: Oxford University Press, 1984); vol. 2: *The Tender Passion* (1986).

Gaylin, Willard. *Rediscovering Love* (New York: Viking Penguin, 1986).

Gebhardt, Paul. "Fetishism and Sadomasochism," in M. Weinberg, ed., *Sex Research: Studies From the Kinsey Institute* (New York: Oxford University Press, 1976), 156-66.

Gilbert, Paul. *Human Relationships: A Philosophical Introduction* (Oxford, Eng.: Blackwell, 1991).

Giles, James. "A Theory of Love and Sexual Desire," *Journal for the Theory of Social Behavior* 24:4 (1994): 339-57.

Gilligan, Carol. *In a Different Voice* (Cambridge, Mass.: Harvard University Press, 1982).

Goldman, Alan. "Plain Sex," *Philosophy and Public Affairs* 6 (1977): 267-87; in A. Soble, ed., *Philosophy of Sex*, 2nd ed. (Savage, Md.: Rowman and Littlefield, 1991), 73-92.

Gorer, Geoffrey. "On Falling in Love," in *The Danger of Equality* (New York: Weybright and Talley, 1966), 126-32; in A. Soble, ed., *Eros, Agape, and Philia* (New York: Paragon House, 1989), 6-11.

Gosling, J. C. B. *Marriage and the Love of God* (New York: Sheed and Ward, 1965).

Gray, Robert. "Sex and Sexual Perversion," *Journal of Philosophy* 75:4 (1978): 189-99; in A. Soble, ed., *Philosophy of Sex*, 1st ed. (Totowa, N.J.: Rowman and Littlefield, 1980), 158-68.

Graziano, William G., Lauri A. Jensen-Campbell, Laura J. Shebilske, and Sharon R. Lundgren, "Social Influence, Sex Differences, and Judgments of Beauty: Putting the *Interpersonal* Back in Interpersonal Attraction," *Journal of Personality and Social Psychology* 65:3 (1993): 522-31.

Green, Karen. "Prostitution, Exploitation, and Taboo," *Philosophy* 64 (1989): 525-34.

Green, Ronald. "The Irrelevance of Theology for Sexual Ethics," in E. Shelp, ed., *Sexuality and Medicine*, vol. 2 (Dordrecht, Hol.: Reidel, 1987), 249-70.

Gregor, Thomas. "Sexuality and the Experience of Love," in P. Abramson and S. Pinkerton, eds., *Sexual Nature/Sexual Culture* (Chicago: University of Chicago Press, 1995), 330-50.

Gregory, Paul. "Eroticism and Love," *American Philosophical Quarterly* 25:4 (1988): 339-44.

Grisez, Germain. *The Way of the Lord Jesus*, vol. 2: *Living a Christian Life* (Quincy, Ill.: Franciscan Press, 1993).

Griswold v. Connecticut, 85 S. Ct. 1678 (1965).

Gudorf, Christine E. *Body, Sex, and Pleasure: Reconstructing Christian Sexual Ethics* (Cleveland, Ohio: Pilgrim Press, 1994).

Halperin, David M. *One Hundred Years of Homosexuality* (New York: Routledge, 1990).

_____. *Saint-Foucault: Towards a Gay Hagiography* (New York: Oxford University Press, 1995).

Halperin, David M., John J. Winkler, and Froma I. Zetlin, eds. *Before Sexuality: The Construction of Erotic Experience in the Ancient Greek World* (Princeton, N.J.: Princeton University Press, 1990).

Hamer, Dean, and Peter Copeland. *The Science of Desire* (New York: Simon and Schuster, 1994).

Hamlyn, D. "The Phenomena of Love and Hate," *Philosophy* 53 (1978): 5-20; in A. Soble, ed., *Eros, Agape, and Philia* (New York: Paragon House, 1989), 218-34.

Hannay, Alastair. *Kierkegaard* (London: Routledge and Kegan Paul, 1982).

Harding, Sandra. *Whose Science? Whose Knowledge?* (Ithaca, N.Y.: Cornell University Press, 1991).

Hart, H. L. A. *Law, Liberty, and Morality* (Stanford, Cal.: Stanford University Press, 1963).

Hartsock, Nancy C. M. *Money, Sex, and Power: Toward a Feminist Historical Materialism* (New York: Longman, 1983).

Hegel, G. W. F. "On Love," in *On Christianity: Early Theological Writings*, trans. T. Knox (New York: Harper and Bros., 1948), 302-8.

Hein, Hilda. "Sadomasochism and the Liberal Tradition," in R. Linden, D. Pagano, D. Russell, and S. Star, eds., *Against Sadomasochism: A Radical Feminist Analysis* (East Palo Alto, Cal.: Frog in the Well, 1982), 83-9.

Herdt, Gilbert H. *Guardians of the Flute* (New York: McGraw-Hill, 1981).

_____ , ed. *Third Sex. Third Gender: Beyond Sexual Dimorphism in Culture and History* (New York: Zone Books, 1994).

Herman, Barbara. "Could it Be Worth Thinking About Kant on Sex and Marriage?" in L. Antony and C. Witt, eds., *A Mind of One's Own* (Boulder, Colo.: Westview, 1993), 49-67.

Hesiod. *The Poems of Hesiod*, trans. R. Frazer (Norman, Okla.: University of Oklahoma Press, 1983).

Higgins, Kathleen Marie. "How Do I Love Thee? Let's Redefine a Term," *Journal of Social Philosophy* 24:3 (1993): 105-11.

Himmelfarb, Gertrude. *Marriage and Morals Among the Victorians* (New York: Knopf, 1986).

_____ . *On Liberty and Liberalism* (New York: Knopf, 1974).

Hirschfeld, Magnus. *Transvestites: The Erotic Drive To Cross-Dress* (Buffalo, N.Y.: Prometheus, 1991).

Hopkins, Patrick D. "Rethinking Sadomasochism: Feminism, Interpretation, and Simulation," *Hypatia* 9:1 (1994): 116-41.

Hunter, J. F. M. *Thinking About Sex and Love* (New York: St. Martin's, 1980).

Hunter, Nan D., and Sylvia A. Law. "Brief *Amici Curiae* of Feminist Anticensorship Task Force et al., in *American Booksellers Association v. Hudnut*," in P. Smith, ed., *Feminist Jurisprudence* (New York: Oxford University Press, 1993), 467-81.

Jacobsen, Rockney. "Arousal and the Ends of Desire," *Philosophy and Phenomenological Research* 53:3 (1993): 617-32.

Jaggar, Alison. "Prostitution," in A. Soble, ed., *Philosophy of Sex*, 2nd ed. (Savage, Md.: Rowman and Littlefield, 1991), 259-80.

Jarvie, I. C. *Thinking About Society: Theory and Practice* (Dordrecht, Hol.: Reidel, 1986).

Jay, Karla. "School for Scandal," *Women's Review of Books* 1:3 (1983): 9-10.

Jeffreys, Sheila. *Anticlimax: A Feminist Perspective on the Sexual Revolution* (New York: New York University Press, 1990).

John Paul II. "Evangelium Vitae," *Origins* 24:42 (April 6, 1995): 689-727.

Jung, Patricia, and Ralph Smith. *Heterosexism: An Ethical Challenge* (Albany, N.Y.: State University of New York Press, 1993).

Kant, Immanuel. *Groundwork of the Metaphysic of Morals*, trans. H. Paton (New York: Harper Torchbooks, 1964).

_____ . *Lectures on Ethics*, trans. L. Infield (New York: Harper and Row, 1963).

_____ . *The Metaphysical Principles of Virtue*, trans. J. Ellington (Indianapolis: Bobbs-Merrill, 1964).

Kaplan, Louise J. *Female Perversions: The Temptations of Emma Bovary* (New York: Anchor Books, 1991).

Katz, Jonathan Ned. *The Invention of Heterosexuality* (New York: Dutton, 1995).

Katzenstein, Mary Fainsod, and David D. Laitin. "Politics, Feminism, and the Ethics of Caring," in E. Kittay and D. Meyers, eds., *Women and Moral Theory* (Totowa, N.J.: Rowman and Littlefield, 1987), 261-81.

Kellenberger, J. *Relationship Morality* (University Park, Penn.: Pennsylvania State University Press, 1995).

Keller, Evelyn Fox. *Reflections on Gender and Science* (New Haven, Conn.: Yale University Press, 1985).

Kierkegaard, Søren. *Either/Or*, vol. 1, trans. D. Swenson and L. Swenson (Princeton, N.J.: Princeton University Press, 1959).

_____ . *Either/Or*, vol. 2, trans. W. Lowrie (Princeton, N.J.: Princeton University Press, 1971).

_____ . *Fear and Trembling. Repetition*, trans. H. Hong and E. Hong (Princeton, N.J.: Princeton University Press, 1983).

_____ . *Stages on Life's Way*, trans. W. Lowrie (Princeton, N.J.: Princeton University Press, 1945).

_____ . *Works of Love*, trans. H. Hong and E. Hong (New York: Harper and Row, 1962).

Kittay, Eva Feder. "Pornography and the Erotics of Domination,"in C. Gould, ed., *Beyond Domination* (Totowa, N.J.: Rowman and Allanheld, 1984), 145-74.

Koss, Mary P., and Kenneth E. Leonard. "Sexually Aggressive Men: Empirical Findings and Theoretical Implications," in N. Malamuth and E. Donnerstein, eds., *Pornography and Sexual Aggression* (Orlando, Fla.: Academic Press, 1984), 213-32.

Kraut, Robert. "Love *De Re*," *Midwest Studies in Philosophy* 10 (1986): 413-30.

Kuhn, Thomas. *The Copernican Revolution* (New York: Vintage, 1959).

_____ . *The Structure of Scientific Revolutions*, 2nd ed., enlarged (Chicago: University of Chicago Press, 1970).

Laqueur, Thomas. *Making Sex: Body and Gender From the Greeks to Freud* (Cambridge, Mass.: Harvard University Press, 1990).

Laumann, Edward O., John H. Gagnon, Robert T. Michael, and Stuart Michaels. *The Social Organization of Sexuality: Sexual Practices in the United States* (Chicago: University of Chicago Press, 1994).

Leiser, Burton. *Liberty, Justice, and Morals*, 3rd ed. (New York: Macmillan, 1986).

Lesser, A. H. "Love and Lust," *Journal of Value Inquiry* 14:1 (1980): 51-4.

Letwin, Shirley Robin. "Romantic Love and Christianity," *Philosophy* 52 (1977): 131-45.

LeVay, Simon. *The Sexual Brain* (Cambridge, Mass.: M.I.T. Press, 1993).

_____ . *Queer Science* (Cambridge, Mass.: M.I.T. Press, 1996).

LeVay, Simon, and Dean H. Hamer. "Evidence of a Biological Influence in Male Homosexuality," *Scientific American* (May 1994), 44-9.

Levin, Michael. "Why Homosexuality is Abnormal," *The Monist* 67:2 (1984): 251-83.

Lewis, C. S. *The Four Loves* (New York: Harcourt, Brace, Jovanovich, 1960).

Lewontin, R. C. "Sex, Lies, and Social Science," *New York Review of Books* (April 20, 1995), 24-9.

Linden, Robin Ruth, Darlene Pagano, Diana E. H. Russell, and Susan Leigh Star, eds., *Against Sadomasochism: A Radical Feminist Analysis* (East Palo Alto, Cal.: Frog in the Well, 1982).

Lynn, Barry W. "'Civil Rights' Ordinances and the Attorney General's Commission: New Developments in Pornography Regulation," *Harvard Civil Rights-Civil Liberties Law Review* 21:1 (1986): 27-125.

McGinn, Colin. "Mothers and Moralists," *New Republic* (October 3, 1994), 27-31.

MacKinnon, Catharine A. *Feminism Unmodified* (Cambridge, Mass.: Harvard University Press, 1987).

_____ . *Only Words* (Cambridge, Mass.: Harvard University Press, 1993).

_____ . *Toward a Feminist Theory of the State* (Cambridge, Mass.: Harvard University Press, 1989).

MacLagan, W. G. "Respect for Persons as a Moral Principle--I," *Philosophy* 35 (1960): 193-217.

McMurtry, John. "Monogamy: A Critique," *The Monist* 56:4 (1972): 587-99; in R. Baker and F. Elliston, eds., *Philosophy and Sex*, 2nd ed. (Buffalo, N.Y.: Prometheus, 1984), 107-18.

_____ . "Sex, Love, and Friendship," in A. Soble, ed., *Sex, Love, and Friendship* (Amsterdam: Editions Rodopi, 1997) pp. 169-83.

Mappes, Thomas A. "Sexual Morality and the Concept of Using Another Person," in T. Mappes and J. Zembaty, eds., *Social Ethics*, 4th ed. (New York: McGraw-Hill, 1992), 203-16.

Martin, Mike W. *Everyday Morality*, 2nd ed. (Belmont, Cal.: Wadsworth, 1995), 230-44.

Matthews v. Superior Court, 119 Cal. App. 3d 309; 173 Cal. Rptr. 820 (1981).

May, Rollo. *Love and Will* (New York: Norton, 1969).

Meilaender, Gilbert. "When Harry and Sally Read the *Nicomachean Ethics*: Friendship Between Men and Women," in L. Rouner, ed., *The Changing Face of Friendship* (Notre Dame, Ind.: University of Notre Dame Press, 1994), 183-96.

_____. *The Limits of Love: Some Theological Explorations* (University Park, Penn.: Pennsylvania State University Press, 1987).

Michel, Robert T., John H. Gagnon, Edward O. Laumann, and Gina Kolata. *Sex in America: A Definitive Survey* (Boston: Little, Brown and Co., 1994).

Mill, John Stuart. *On Liberty* (Indianapolis: Hackett, 1978).

_____. *The Subjection of Women* (Cambridge, Mass.: M.I.T. Press, 1970).

Millgram, Elijah. "Aristotle on Making Other Selves," *Canadian Journal of Philosophy* 17:2 (1987): 361-76.

Mohr, Richard D. *Gay Ideas* (Boston: Beacon Press, 1992).

_____. *Gays/Justice* (New York: Columbia University Press, 1988).

_____. *A More Perfect Union* (Boston: Beacon Press, 1994).

Montaigne, Michel de. "On Affectionate Relationships," in M. Screech, ed. and trans., *The Essays of Michel de Montaigne* (London: Penguin, 1991), 205-19.

Morgan, Douglas. *Love: Plato, the Bible, and Freud* (Englewood Cliffs, N.J.: Prentice-Hall, 1964).

Morgan, Robin. *Going Too Far* (New York: Random House, 1977).

Morris, M. "Telling Tails Explain the Discrepancy in Sexual Partner Reports," *Nature* 365 (September 30, 1993): 437-40.

Moulton, Janice. "Sexual Behavior: Another Position," *Journal of Philosophy* 73:16 (1976): 537-46; in A. Soble, ed., *Philosophy of Sex*, 2nd ed. (Savage, Md.: Rowman and Littlefield, 1991), 63-71.

Muehlenhard, Charlene L., Irene G. Powch, Joi L. Phelps, and Laura M. Givsi, "Definitions of Rape: Scientific and Political Implications," *Journal of Social Issues* 48:1 (1992): 23-44.

Muehlenhard, Charlene L., and Jennifer L. Schrag. "Nonviolent Sexual Coercion," in A. Parrot and L. Bechhofer, eds., *Acquaintance Rape: The Hidden Crime* (New York: John Wiley, 1991), 115-28.

Murphy, Jeffrie. "Some Ruminations on Women, Violence, and the Criminal Law," in Jules Coleman and Allen Buchanan, eds., *In Harm's Way: Essays in Honor of Joel Feinberg* (Cambridge, Eng.: Cambridge University Press, 1994), 209-230.

Murphy, Timothy F. "Homosex/Ethics," in T. Murphy, ed., *Gay Ethics: Controversies in Outing, Civil Rights, and Sexual Science* (Binghamton, N.Y.: Haworth, 1994), 9-25.

_____ . "Homosexuality and Nature: Happiness and the Law at Stake," *Journal of Applied Philosophy* 4:2 (1987): 195-204.

Thomas Nagel. "Personal Rights and Public Space," *Philosophy and Public Affairs* 24:2 (1995): 83-107.

_____ . "Sexual Perversion," *Journal of Philosophy* 66 (1969): 5-17; in A. Soble, *Philosophy of Sex*, 1st ed. (Totowa, N.J.: Rowman and Littlefield, 1980), 76-88. Revised version, T. Nagel, *Mortal Questions* (Cambridge, Eng.: Cambridge University Press, 1979), 39-52; in A. Soble, ed., *Philosophy of Sex*, 2nd ed. (Savage, Md.: Rowman and Littlefield, 1991), 39-51.

Neu, Jerome. "Freud and Perversion," in J. Neu, ed., *The Cambridge Companion to Freud* (Cambridge, Eng.: Cambridge University Press, 1991), 175-208.

_____ . "What Is Wrong with Incest?" *Inquiry* 19:1 (1976): 27-39.

Newton-Smith, W. "A Conceptual Investigation of Love," in A. Montefiore, ed., *Philosophy and Personal Relations*

(Montreal: McGill-Queens University Press, 1973), 113-36; in A. Soble, ed., *Eros, Agape, and Philia* (New York: Paragon House, 1989), 199-217.

Nicholson, Susan T. *Abortion and the Roman Catholic Church* (Knoxville, Tenn.: Religious Ethics, 1978).

Nimmons, David. "Sex and the Brain," *Discover* (March 1994), 64-71.

Noddings, Nel. "The One-Caring," in C. Williams, ed., *On Love and Friendship* (Boston: Jones and Bartlett, 1995), 318-31.

Noonan, John T. *Contraception: A History of Its Treatment by the Catholic Theologians and Canonists*, enlarged ed. (Cambridge, Mass.: Harvard University Press, 1986).

Nozick, Robert. *Anarchy, State, and Utopia* (New York: Basic Books, 1974).

_____ . "Sexuality" and "Love's Bond," in *The Examined Life* (New York: Simon and Schuster, 1989), 61-7 and 68-86.

Nussbaum, Martha. "Platonic Love and Colorado Law: The Relevance of Ancient Greek Norms to Modern Sexual Controversies," *Virginia Law Review* 80:7 (1994): 1515-1651.

_____ . *The Fragility of Goodness* (Cambridge, Eng.: Cambridge University Press, 1986).

Nygren, Anders. *Agape and Eros* (Chicago: University of Chicago Press, 1982).

Ortega y Gasset, José. *On Love* (New York: Meridian, 1957).

Outka, Gene. "Love," in L. Becker and C. Becker, eds., *Encyclopedia of Ethics* (New York: Garland Press, 1992), 742-51.

_____ . *Agape: An Ethical Analysis* (New Haven, Conn.: Yale University Press, 1972).

Overall, Christine. "Heterosexuality and Feminist Theory," *Canadian Journal of Philosophy* 20:1 (1990): 1-18.

Padgug, Robert. "Sexual Matters: On Conceptualizing Sexuality in History," in E. Stein, ed., *Forms of Desire* (New York: Routledge, 1992), 43-67.

Paglia, Camille. *Sex, Art, and American Culture* (New York: Vintage Books, 1992).

Parrot, Andrea, and Laurie Bechhofer, eds. *Acquaintance Rape: The Hidden Crime* (New York: John Wiley, 1991).

Pateman, Carole. "Defending Prostitution: Charges Against Ericsson," *Ethics* 93 (1983): 561-5.

_____. "Sex and Power," *Ethics* 100:2 (1990): 398-407.

_____. *The Sexual Contract* (Stanford, Cal.: Stanford University Press, 1988).

Paul VI. "Humanae Vitae," *Catholic Mind* 66 (September, 1968): 35-48; in R. Baker and F. Elliston, eds., *Philosophy and Sex*, 2nd ed. (Buffalo, N.Y.: Prometheus, 1984), 167-83.

Peck, M. Scott. *The Road Less Traveled* (New York: Simon and Schuster, 1978).

Pierce, Christine. "Natural Law Language and Women," in J. English, ed., *Sex Equality* (Englewood Cliffs, N.J.: Prentice-Hall, 1977), 131-42.

Pineau, Lois. "Date Rape: A Feminist Analysis," *Law and Philosophy* 8 (1989): 217-43.

Pius XI. "On Christian Marriage," *Catholic Mind* 29:2 (1931): 21-64.

Plato. *Euthyphro* and *Phaedrus*, in E. Hamilton and H. Cairns, eds., *Plato: The Collected Dialogues* (Princeton, N.J.: Princeton University Press, 1963).

_____. *Symposium*, trans. S. Groden (Amherst, Mass.: University of Massachusetts Press, 1970); trans. W. Hamilton (London: Penguin, 1951).

Pollitt, Katha. *Reasonable Creatures* (New York: Knopf, 1994).

Posner, Richard A. *Sex and Reason* (Cambridge, Mass.: Harvard University Press, 1992.

Prager, Dennis. "Homosexuality, the Bible, and Us--A Jewish Perspective," *The Public Interest*, no. 112 (Summer, 1993): 60-83.

Price, A. W. *Love and Friendship in Plato and Aristotle* (Oxford, Eng.: Clarendon Press, 1989).

Primoratz, Igor. "What's Wrong With Prostitution?" *Philosophy* 68:264 (April 1993): 159-82.

Rice, Lee, and Steven Barbone. "Hatching Your Genes Before They're Counted," in A. Soble, ed., *Sex, Love, and Friendship* (Amsterdam: Editions Rodopi, 1997), pp. 89-98.

Rich, Adrienne. "Compulsory Heterosexuality and Lesbian Existence," in *Blood, Bread and Poetry* (New York: Norton, 1986), 23-75.

Roe v. Wade, 93 S. Ct. 705 (1973).

Rorty, Amelie. "The Historicity of Psychological Attitudes: Love is Not Love Which Alters Not When It Alteration Finds," *Midwest Studies in Philosophy* 10 (1986): 399-412.

Rose, Hilary. "Gay Brains, Gay Genes, and Feminist Science Theory, in J. Weeks and J. Holland, eds., *Sexual Cultures* (New York: St. Martin's Press, 1996), 53-72.

Rose, Phyllis. *Parallel Lives* (New York: Knopf, 1984).

Rosen, Deborah, and John Christman, "Toward a New Model of Sexuality," in A. Soble, ed., *Sex, Love, and Friendship* (Amsterdam: Editions Rodopi, 1997), pp. 199-213.

Rosen, Stanley. *Plato's Symposium*, 2nd ed. (New Haven, Conn.: Yale University Press, 1987).

Rossi, Alice. "Eros and Caritas: A Biopsychological Approach to Human Sexuality and Reproduction," in A. Rossi, ed., *Sexuality Across the Life Course* (Chicago: University of Chicago Press, 1994), 3-36.

Rotello, Gabriel. "To Have and To Hold: The Case for Gay Marriage," *Nation* (June 24, 1996), 11, 13, 15-16, 18.

Rubin, Gayle. "Misguided, Dangerous, and Wrong: An Analysis of Anti-pornography Politics," in A. Assiter and A. Carol, eds., *Bad Girls and Dirty Pictures* (London: Pluto Press, 1993), 18-40.

Rubin, Lillian. *Intimate Strangers* (New York: Harper and Row, 1983).

_____ . *Worlds of Pain* (New York: Basic Books, 1976).

Ruddick, Sara. "Better Sex," in R. Baker and F. Elliston, eds., *Philosophy and Sex*, 2nd ed. (Buffalo, N.Y.: Prometheus, 1984), 280-99.

Rudinow, Joel. "Manipulation," *Ethics* 88:4 (1978): 338-47.

Ruse, Michael. "Are There Gay Genes? Sociobiology and Homosexuality," *Journal of Homosexuality* 6:4 (1981): 5-34; reprinted in A. Soble, ed., *Sex, Love, and Friendship* (Amsterdam: Editions Rodopi, 1997), pp. 61-86.

_____ . *Homosexuality: A Philosophical Inquiry* (New York: Blackwell, 1988).

Russell, Bertrand. *Marriage and Morals* (London: George Allen and Unwin, 1929).

Russell, Diana E. H. "Pornography and Rape: A Causal Model,"*Political Psychology* 9:1 (1988): 41-73; revised version in D. E. H. Russell, ed.,*Making Violence Sexy: Feminist Views on Pornography* (New York: Teachers College Press, 1993), 120-50.

_____ . "Pornography and Violence: What Does the New Research Say?" in L. Lederer, ed., *Take Back the Night* (New

York: William Morrow, 1980), 218-38.

Saiving, Valerie. "The Human Situation: A Feminine View," in C. Christ and J. Plaskow, eds., *Womanspirit Rising: A Feminist Reader in Religion* (San Francisco, Cal.: Harper and Row, 1979), 25-42.

Samois, ed. *Coming to Power*, 1st ed. (Palo Alto, Cal.: Up Press, 1981); 2nd ed. (Boston: Alyson Publications, 1982).

Sanday, Peggy Reeves. *A Woman Scorned: Acquaintance Rape on Trial* (New York: Doubleday, 1996).

Sappho. *The Poems of Sappho*, trans. S. Groden (Indianapolis: Bobbs-Merrill, 1966).

Sartre, Jean-Paul. *Being and Nothingness*, trans. H. Barnes (New York: Philosophical Library, 1956).

Schlafly, Phyllis. *The Power of the Positive Woman* (New Rochelle, N.Y.: Arlington House, 1977).

Schopenhauer, Arthur. *The World as Will and Representation*, vol. 2, trans. E. Payne (Indian Hills, Colo.: Falcon's Wing Press, 1958).

Schroeder, Jeanne L. "Feminism Historicized: Medieval Misogynist Stereotypes in Contemporary Feminist Jurisprudence," *Iowa Law Review* 75 (1990): 1135-1217.

Schulhofer, Stephen J. "The Gender Question in Criminal Law," in J. Murphy, ed., *Punishment and Rehabilitation*, 3rd ed. (Belmont, Cal.: Wadsworth, 1995), 274-311.

Scruton, Roger. *Sexual Desire: A Moral Philosophy of the Erotic* (New York: Free Press, 1986).

Seidman, Steven. *Embattled Eros* (New York: Routledge, 1992).

Shaffer, Jerome A. "Sexual Desire," *Journal of Philosophy* 75:4 (1978): 175-89; in A. Soble, ed., *Sex, Love, and Friendship* (Amsterdam: Editions Rodopi, 1997), pp. 1-12.

Shakespeare, William. *Sonnets* (New York: New American Library, 1964).

Shanley, Mary Lyndon. "Marital Slavery and Friendship: John Stuart Mill's *The Subjection of Women,*" *Political Theory* 9:2 (1981): 229-47.

Shelp, Earl E., ed. *Sexuality and Medicine,* vol. 1: *Conceptual Roots*; vol. 2: *Ethical Viewpoints in Transition* (Dordrecht, Hol.: Reidel, 1987).

Sherfey, Mary Jane. *The Nature and Evolution of Female Sexuality* (New York: Vintage, 1973).

Shrage, Laurie. "Is Sexual Desire Raced? The Social Meaning of Interracial Prostitution," *Journal of Social Philosophy* 23:1 (1992): 42-51.

_____. "Should Feminists Oppose Prostitution?" *Ethics* 99:2 (1989): 347-61.

_____. *Moral Dilemmas of Feminism* (New York: Routledge, 1994).

Simmons, Paul. "Theological Approaches to Sexuality," in E. Shelp, ed., *Sexuality and Medicine,* vol. 2 (Dordrecht, Hol.: Reidel, 1987), 199-217.

Singer, Irving. *The Nature of Love,* vol. 1: *Plato to Luther,* 2nd ed. (Chicago: University of Chicago Press, 1984); vol. 2: *Courtlyand Romantic* (1984); vol. 3: *The Modern World* (1987).

Small, Meredith F. *What's Love Got To Do With It? The Evolution of Human Mating* (New York: Anchor Books, 1995).

Soble, Alan. *Sexual Investigations* (New York: New York University Press, 1996).

_____. *The Structure of Love* (New Haven, Conn.: Yale University Press, 1990).

_____ , ed. *Eros, Agape, and Philia* (New York: Paragon House, 1989).

_____ , ed. *Philosophy of Sex*, 1st ed. (Totowa, N.J.: Rowman and Littlefield, 1980); 2nd ed. (Savage, Md.: 1991); 3rd ed. (Lanham, Md.: 1997).

_____ , ed. *Sex, Love, and Friendship* (Amsterdam: Editions Rodopi, 1997).

Solomon, Robert. "Sex and Perversion," in R. Baker and F. Elliston, eds., *Philosophy and Sex*, 1st ed. (Buffalo, N.Y.: Prometheus, 1975), 268-87.

_____ . "Sexual Paradigms," *Journal of Philosophy* 71 (1974): 336-45; in A. Soble, ed., *Philosophy of Sex*, 2nd ed. (Savage, Md.: Rowman and Littlefield, 1991), 53-62.

Solomon, Robert C., and Higgins, Kathleen M., eds. *The Philosophy of (Erotic) Love* (Lawrence, Kan.: University Press of Kansas, 1991).

Spanier, Bonnie. "Biological Determinism and Homosexuality," *NWSA Journal* 7:1 (1995): 54-71.

Speers, W. "Newsmakers," *Philadelphia Inquirer* (August 10, 1995), F2.

Sprinkle, Annie. "Beyond Bisexual," in A. Jaggar, ed., *Living With Contradictions* (Boulder, Colo.: Westview, 1994), 510-12.

Stafford, J. Martin. "On Distinguishing Between Love and Lust," *Journal of Value Inquiry* 11:4 (1977): 292-303.

Stan, Adele M., ed. *Debating Sexual Correctness* (New York: Delta, 1995).

Stanley v. Georgia, 89 S. Ct. 1243 (1969).

Stein, Edward. "The Relevance of Scientific Research About Sexual Orientation to Lesbian and Gay Rights," *Journal of*

Homosexuality 27:3-4 (1994): 269-308.

_____ , ed. *Forms of Desire* (New York: Routledge, 1992).

Stephens, James Fitzjames. *Liberty, Equality, Fraternity* (London: Smith, Elgard and Co., 1873).

Sternberg, Robert J., and Michael L. Barnes, eds. *The Psychology of Love* (New Haven, Conn.: Yale University Press, 1988).

Stewart, Robert M. "Moral Criticism and the Social Meaning of Prostitution," in R. Stewart, ed., *Philosophical Perspectives on Sex and Love* (New York: Oxford University Press, 1995), 81-3.

_____ , ed. *Philosophical Perspectives on Sex and Love* (New York: Oxford University Press, 1995).

Stoltenberg, John. *Refusing To Be a Man* (Portland, Ore.: Breitenbush Books, 1989).

Strossen, Nadine. *Defending Pornography* (New York: Scribner, 1995).

Sullivan, Andrew. *Virtually Normal: An Argument About Homosexuality* (New York: Knopf, 1995).

Suppe, Frederick. "Curing Homosexuality," in R. Baker and F. Elliston, eds., *Philosophy and Sex* (Buffalo, N.Y.: Prometheus, 1984), 391-420.

_____ . "The Diagnostic and Statistical Manual of the American Psychiatric Association," in E. Shelp, ed., *Sexuality and Medicine*, vol. 2 (Dordrecht: Reidel, 1987), 111-35.

_____ . "Explaining Homosexuality: Philosophical Issues, and Who Cares Anyhow?" in T. Murphy, ed., *Gay Ethics: Controversies in Outing, Civil Rights, and Sexual Science* (Binghamton, N.Y.: Haworth, 1994), 223-68.

Symons, Donald. *The Evolution of Human Sexuality* (New York:

Oxford University Press, 1979).

"Symposium on Pornography. Appendix." *New England Law Review* 20:4 (1984-85): 759-77.

Taylor, Gabrielle. "Love," *Proceedings of the Aristotelian Society* 76 (1976): 147-64.

Taylor, Richard. *Having Love Affairs* (Buffalo, N.Y.: Prometheus, 1982).

Tavris, Carol. *The Mismeasure of Woman* (New York: Simon and Schuster, 1992).

Tennov, Dorothy. *Love and Limerance* (New York: Stein and Day, 1980).

Thomas, Keith. "The Double Standard," *Journal of the History of Ideas* 20:2 (1959): 195-216.

Thurber, James, and E. B. White. *Is Sex Necessary?* (New York: Harper and Brothers, 1929).

Tillich, Paul. *Love, Power, and Justice* (New York: Oxford University Press, 1960).

Turley, Donna. "The Feminist Debate on Pornography: An Unorthodox Interpretation," *Socialist Review* 16:3-4 (1986): 81-96.

Vacek, Edward. "A Christian Homosexuality?" *Commonweal* (December 5, 1980), 681-4.

_____. *Love, Human and Divine: The Heart of Christian Ethics* (Washington, D.C.: Georgetown University Press, 1994).

Vannoy, Russell. "Can Sex Express Love?" in A. Soble, ed.,*Sex, Love, and Friendship* (Amsterdam: Editions Rodopi, 1997), pp. 247-57.

_____. "Philosophy and Sex," in V. Bullough and B. Bullough, eds., *Human Sexuality: An Encyclopedia* (New York: Garland, 1994), 442-9.

_____. *Sex Without Love: A Philosophical Exploration* (Buffalo, N.Y.: Prometheus, 1980).

Vera, Diane. "Temporary Consensual 'Slave Contract'," in P. Califia, ed., *The Lesbian S/M Safety Manual* (Boston: Alyson Publications, 1988), 75-6.

Vlastos, Gregory. "The Individual as an Object of Love in Plato," in *Platonic Studies* (Princeton, N.J.: Princeton University Press, 1973), 3-34; in A. Soble, ed., *Eros, Agape, and Philia* (New York: Paragon House, 1989), 96-124.

Walsh, Anthony. "Love and Sex," in V. Bullough and B. Bullough, eds., *Human Sexuality: An Encyclopedia* (New York: Garland, 1994), 369-73.

Wasserstrom, Richard. "Is Adultery Immoral?" in R. Baker and F. Elliston, eds., *Philosophy and Sex*, 2nd ed. (Buffalo, N.Y.: Prometheus, 1984), 93-106.

_____, ed. *Morality and the Law* (Belmont, Cal.: Wadsworth, 1971).

Watt, E. D. "Professor Cohen's Encyclical," *Ethics* 80:3 (1970): 218-21.

Weeks, Jeffrey. *Sexuality and Its Discontents* (London: Routledge and Kegan Paul, 1985).

Weinberg, Thomas S., ed. *S&M: Studies in Dominance & Submission* (Amherst, N.Y.: Prometheus, 1995).

Wertheimer, Alan. "Consent and Sexual Relations," *Legal Theory* 2 (1996): 89-112.

West, Robin. "The Harms of Consensual Sex," *American Philosophical Association Newsletters* 94:2 (1995): 52-5.

Whiteley, C. H. and Winifred N. Whiteley. *Sex and Morals* (New York: Basic Books, 1967).

Willis, Ellen. *Beginning To See the Light* (New York: Knopf,

1981).

Wilson, George B. "Christian Conjugal Morality and Contraception," in Francis X. Quinn, ed., *Population Ethics* (Washington, D.C.: Corpus Books, 1968), 98-108.

Wojtyla, Karol. *Love and Responsibility* (New York: Farrar, Straus, and Giroux, 1981).

Wolf, Naomi. *The Beauty Myth* (New York: Anchor Books, 1992).

Wollstonecraft, Mary. *A Vindication of the Rights of Women* (Buffalo, N.Y.: Prometheus, 1989).

Woodhull, Victoria C. "The Principles of Social Freedom" and "Tried As By Fire," in M. Stern, ed., *The Victoria Woodhull Reader* (Weston, Mass.: M & S Press, 1974).

Yeats, William Butler. *The Collected Poems of W. B. Yeats*, ed. R. Finneran (New York: Macmillan, 1989).

Zillman, Dolf. *Connections Between Sex and Aggression* (Hillsdale, N.J.: Erlbaum, 1984).

Zillman, Dolf, and Jennings Bryant. "Pornography, Sexual Callousness, and the Trivialization of Rape," *Journal of Communication* 32:4 (1982): 10-21.

INDEX